A COMMUNITY OF ONE

SUNY Series, The Margins of Literature
Mihai I. Spariosu, editor

A COMMUNITY OF ONE

MASCULINE AUTOBIOGRAPHY AND AUTONOMY IN NINETEENTH-CENTURY BRITAIN

Martin A. Danahay

State University of New York Press

Cover photo of *Charles Reade in His Study* appears by courtesy of the National Portrait Gallery, London

Published by
State University of New York Press, Albany

© 1993   State University of New York

Printed in the United States of America

For information, address State University of New York
Press, State University Plaza, Albany, NY 12246

Production by Dana Foote
Marketing by Theresa A. Swierzowski

Library of Congress Cataloging-in-Publication Data

Danahay, Martin A.
      A community of one :   masculine autobiography and autonomy in
nineteenth-century Britain / Martin A. Danahay.
            p.   cm. — (SUNY series, the margins of literature)
      Includes bibliographical references and index.
      ISBN 0–7914–1511–2 (alk. paper). — ISBN 0–7914–1512–0 (pbk. :
alk. paper)
      1. English prose literature — 19th century — History and criticism.
      2. English prose literature — Men authors — History and criticism.
      3. Men — Great Britain — History — 19th century — Historiography.
      4. Men authors, English — Biography — History and criticism.
      5. Masculinity (Psychology) in literature. 6. Autobiography — Men
authors.   I. Title. II. Series.
PR778.A9D34   1993
820.9'008—dc20
      [B]   92–38402
                                                                                      CIP

10 9 8 7 6 5 4 3 2 1

But man is a true narcissus:
he makes the whole world his mirror.
(Goethe 1971, 50)

CONTENTS

ACKNOWLEDGMENTS

If I were to follow the usual academic paradigms, one person would have to be cited throughout this text. Instead of such citations this solitary acknowledgment of Debbie's intellectual and emotional contributions to the following pages will have to stand as inadequate recognition of her help, both as an anthropologist and as my wife. I don't want to sound like John Stuart Mill praising Harriet Taylor; I wrote this book myself, but I have profited from her lovingly skeptical questions that made me reconsider my initial blithe assertions about autobiography.

I was fortunate in the early stages of my thinking on the subject of autobiography to come under the guidance of Eugene Goodheart. It was an honor to work with someone who exemplifies some of the best aspects of academic inquiry in both his person and his publications.

At Emory I have benefitted from a congenial and stimulating intellectual atmosphere. Jerry Beaty has been willing to share his wisdom both on the subject of the Victorians and of baseball. Our chair, Walter Reed, and the other members of the department in various ways have helped to make my existence more pleasant and finishing this book a less daunting task. I have also benefitted from intense and searching discussions with those who participated in my graduate seminars on autobiography and on Victorian representation. Shortly after arriving at Emory I telephoned a senior faculty member who I noticed shared my interest in autobiography, and thus inagurated what was for me an extremely fruitful exchange of ideas. Elizabeth Fox-Genovese's publications on autobiography, especially her introduction to *The Autobiography of Pierre Samuel Dupont de Nemours,* proved invaluable resources while I was writing my introduction.

As a graduate student I stumbled upon a ready-made community of scholars all passionately interested in autobiography who met every year at the MLA Convention. This was then a Discussion Group, and is now the MLA Lifewriting Division. Becky Hogan, Joe Hogan, Tim Adams, Tom Smith, Julia Watson, and Sidonie Smith have all been friends and critics in equally helpful ways. Becky Hogan especially deserves my unbounded thanks for her infectious laughter and enthusiam, and for her untiring editorship of *A/B: Auto/Biography Studies*.

Finally, I want to acknowledge an anonymous commentator who responded to a paper I gave at the conference on "The Subject of Autobiography" at the University of Southern Maine in 1989. A member of the audience told me after my presentation that my research complemented her own feminist study of women's autobiography. This was the most gratifying response I have ever received after presenting a paper. My book obviously owes a great deal to the collective enterprise of feminist scholarship, and I hope that it will indeed stand as a complementary analysis to feminist critiques of the subject.

INTRODUCTION

A ROOM OF HIS OWN: THE MASCULINE
SUBJECT OF BRITISH AUTOBIOGRAPHY

In the painting *Charles Reade in His Study* (attributed to W. C. Mercier), the author sits alone at a table in a domestic setting. This painting summarizes in its iconography both the ideal of nineteenth-century masculine autobiography and its contradictions. Reade is alone, implying that writing requires a serene withdrawal from everyday life on the part of the author. In the Victorian period, as today, it was assumed that every writer needed a study, a room of his own, to which to retire and write. Reade's study opens out onto a garden, linking the domestic interior to nature. In this case nature is represented by an extremely formal and arranged landscape, the Victorian garden. The study embodies the suburban ideal and represents Reade's study as a domestic and pastoral retreat from the cares of urban life.

Effaced in this account, however, is the labor that is necessary to maintain an interior such as that depicted in the painting. This is not labor that Reade himself would undertake. His vocation is writing, and the clothes he is wearing are obviously unsuitable for any occupation that would require strenuous work or contact with dirt. As Mary Jean Corbett has pointed out, in the Victorian period "masculine authorship requires women's domestic labor" (Corbett 1992, 63). The roles of domestic servants and of a housekeeper or wife are thus assumed as the prerequisite for this way of life but not represented as part of the canvas. Feminine labor is separated from the masculine work of writing depicted in the canvas. Reade's books are disorderly, heaped upon tables and chairs as mute testimony to creative, intellectual labor, while the rest of the house is neat and orderly.

The female presence is not completely repressed in this painting, however; sitting watching Reade at work is a domestic pet, a dog, while a cat sleeps in the lower left corner. Both of these animals symbolize domestic tranquility and introduce the female presence into the room

1

surreptitiously. Women and pets were linked in Victorian iconography,[1] and it is no accident that women identified strongly with the Antivivisection League and were its most fervent supporters.[2] Just as in Ford Madox Brown's painting *Work* the mongrel, working-class dog and the sleek upper-class introduce class conflict into an attempt to represent the social classes as a harmonious whole, so the domestic pets in this canvas surreptitiously introduce the domestic, feminine virtues associated with the Victorian home.

The masculine labor depicted in *Charles Reade in His Study*, because it is situated in the home and not the street or the factory, brings the gender roles upon which it depends into particularly sharp focus. The painting underscores the sexual division of labor that informs such texts as Mary Shelley's *Frankenstein* (Mellor 1988b, 221) and the "cult of domesticity" in Dorothy Wordsworth's journals and William Wordsworth's poetry (Heinzelman 1988). It is the argument of this book that nineteenth-century British autobiographies from Wordsworth's *The Prelude* on efface the presence of the female in the same way as feminine domestic labor is overtly erased in the painting of Reade. For instance, much recent feminist criticism has brought to light the ways in which William Wordsworth was dependent upon his sister Dorothy's journals for inspiration, and how Dorothy herself was economically dependent on William, offering her texts as a form of "payment" for her keep.[3] Masculine authorship was dependent upon female labor, both physical and emotional.

Apart from such obvious and direct dependence on female labor, masculine autobiographers used the feminine as a sort of "mirror" through which to represent themselves as subjects. Masculine authors from the Romantic and Victorian periods "portray women as subject in order to appropriate the feminine for male subjectivity" (Richardson 1988, 22). Jenijoy La Belle in *Herself Beheld: The Literature of the Looking Glass* has documented the many times women are represented in literature as looking at themselves in the mirror, but could find only a few examples of men looking in mirrors (La Belle 1988, 21). While women could be represented as looking at themselves in mirrors, men were not represented as showing a similar self-interest. Women were themselves mirrors for the masculine subject; J. Hillis Miller has characterized this exchange in the following terms: "I look in the mirror and see not my own image but that of my female counterpart who looks not at me but at herself " (Miller 1991, 340). Women are the object of the gaze, but men are the hidden subject. Masculinity is thus mediated through women as "mirror images" of male desire. Christina Rossetti underlined this point in her poem on her brother Dante Gabriel's paintings, "In an Artist's Studio":

> That mirror gave back all her loveliness.
> A queen in opal or ruby dress,
> A nameless girl in summer-greens
> A saint, an angel—every canvas means
> The same one meaning, neither more nor less (4–8)

The paintings in her brother's studio are a "mirror" both for the features of the woman and for the artist, who paints his model "not as she is, but as she fills his dream" (line 14). The attitude expressed in the poem is ambiguous, in that it could be read as a tribute to her brother's creative powers, but when one reads in the next line that he "feeds upon her face by day and night" more disturbing possibilities are raised. The woman in the painting as mirror for Rossetti's desires becomes what Griselda Pollock has termed "woman as sign," a sign whose referent is "masculine creative energy" (Pollock 1988, 95). The woman's face as object becomes a vehicle for masculine self-representation and acts as a metaphorical mirror for the masculine subject. As Wendy Lesser says, however, this is a mirror "in which the protrait one gets back is not the self one expects, but the one for which one searches" (Lesser 1991, 11).

This book is about the uses made of a feminized other by nineteenth-century British writers. This other is sometimes a woman, as in John Stuart Mill's *Autobiography*, or nature, as in John Ruskin's writings. Whatever form this feminized other takes, however, it always stands for the excluded principle of the social. The painting *Charles Reade in His Study* represents the male writer as a solitary figure. The social context of his work is replaced by the domestic setting, which itself is taken to be separate from other public forms of labor. Similarly, in the textual self-representations analyzed in this book, the male authors represent themselves as autonomous and implicitly repress the social context of their labor. Masculine authors represent themselves, in other words, as autonomous individuals.

Such representations of autonomy have been characterized by Pierre Bourdieu in *Distinction* as part of the bourgeois "denial of the social" (Bourdieu 1984, 11). Bourdieu uses this phrase in a general discussion of the fine arts, pointing out that it is a characteristic of what is viewed as "high" culture to stress the autonomy of the producer of art from the social context. It is precisely the opposite of autonomy, the insistence on the social conditions that inform the production of a text, that characterizes women's and working-class autobiographies in the nineteenth century.[4] The aesthetic governing working-class autobiography is in many ways diametrically opposed to what Bourdieu calls the "pure gaze," the detachment from the social that is the product of a life of relative leisure that many nineteenth-century male authors enjoyed (Bourdieu 1984, 4). Regenia Gagnier has pointed out how most working-class autobiographers write "for communicative ends" and exhibit a more functionalist attitude to representation than their upper-class peers; she argues that working-class "functionalist uses of literacy contrast markedly with the aesthetic of detached individualism represented by literature in general and the autobiographical canon in particular" (Gagnier 1989, 42). Writers of higher social status tend to represent themselves as "detached" or autonomous from social exigencies.

The most famous canonical Victorian figure to exhibit "detached individualism" in his construction of his subjectivity is Matthew Arnold. Despite his renunciation of poetry in favor of prose and social criticism, Arnold still ends up affirming the radical separation of his consciousness from the social. In his preface to the 1853 edition of his *Poems*, Arnold criticized poetry that exhibited the debilitating effects of the modern "dialogue of the mind with itself" (Arnold 1927, 591). He was criticizing his own poem "Empedocles on Etna," but clearly also meant to condemn any poetry that showed the effects of a "diseased" and exclusively introspective state of mind that has lost contact with "things as they really are" (195). Arnold was criticizing a form of writing with which we are now very familiar, that of the autobiographical subject examining the mysterious origins of his or her sense of identity, creating a mirror-like situation in which the writer engages in a "dialogue of the mind with itself" (591). Arnold both inherited and attempted to repress his Romantic autobiographical legacy in his poetry, particularly the influence of Wordsworth. In criticizing the autobiographical "dialogue of the mind with itself," Arnold is apparently repressing what he views as dangerously solipsistic tendencies in both his Romantic forebears and his own writing.

I say "apparently" because Arnold's self-repression in his preface actually helped construct the very subjectivity he is criticizing. Far from escaping the dialogue of the mind with itself, Matthew Arnold, in his poetry and prose, is actually centrally concerned with the construction of his own subjectivity, even as he overtly represses self-consciousness. Arnold's position demonstrates the contradictory motives that inform nineteenth-century British autobiography.

Furthermore, his phrase *dialogue of the mind with itself* provides a key for the analysis of the dynamics of Victorian subjectivity. Arnold seems to be arguing for what M. M. Bakhtin characterized as the "dialogic" imagination, an imagination that actively addresses its social milieu and reflects in its language the social conflicts of its day. Bakhtin contrasts the "polyglossia" and "semantic openendedness" of dialogic forms such as the novel with the impulse toward "monoglossia" in other genres, particularly highly conventional poetry (Bakhtin 1985, 284). While not subscribing to Bakhtin's implicit denigration of poetry in favor of prose, I find that his comments do help elucidate the process that is at work in Victorian autobiography.

In writing autobiography, Victorian male autobiographers aligned themselves with monologism rather than dialogism. Monologism in Bakhtin's terms is a form of solipsism (Bakhtin 1985, 318). Monologism is a denial of alterity, as the writing subject represses the role of the social in the construction of his or her subjectivity. Monologic texts therefore involve a repression of other voices, as the writer seeks mastery over the unsettling forces of the contingent. Monologism is a gendered trait of Victorian male autobiography, as authors such as Matthew Arnold and John Stuart Mill both include women within their texts and silence them at the same time. Such a process can be seen at work in such Arnold poems as "The Buried Life," but the most famous example is John Stuart Mill's use of Harriet Taylor. By conflating Taylor's words with his own, Mill effectively erases her as a separate consciousness. His strategy has spawned a long, and ultimately undecidable, debate over who "really" wrote his texts. The issue is a red herring. Mill's hyperbolic descriptions of Taylor reveal her as the overdetermined site of his own fantasies. His descriptions of her have more to do with his own desire to escape the "incubus" of determinism than with any qualities she may have actually possessed. Jonathan Loesberg (1986) has noted how Mill "by praising her beyond human recognition...frees himself from human influence," thus reading into her his own transcendence (46). In the context of monologism, Mill's *Autobiography* is entirely concerned with the unilateral construction of his own subjectivity, not Harriet Taylor's. He reduces her to an object of his consciousness.

Matthew Arnold's phrase *dialogue of the mind with itself* seems to involve the negation of a solipsistic and self-referential form of writing in favor of a more socially oriented mode. Like Thomas Carlyle, Arnold ostensibly advocates a form of "anti-self-consciousness" in which the writer represses subjectivity in favor of disinterestedness. However, as

John Kucich's recent analysis of Victorian fiction (Kucich 1987) has made clear, repression in Victorian texts, far from negating self-consciousness, actually helped produce a distinctive form of subjectivity. Kucich, following Michel Foucault's redefinition of repression in *The History of Sexuality*, sees repression in the Victorian novel as part of the technology of Victorian subjectivity. The same is true of the role of repression in Victorian autobiography, as I argue in chapters 4 and 5.

Arnold's views depend upon the premise of a dichotomy between the individual and the social, in which the possibility of the self's complete autonomy from the social is assumed. The separation of the individual from the social was one of the central tenets of nineteenth-century individualism, as it is today. Alan Sinfield argues that "the autonomous human subject" is a "given which is undetermined and unconstructed and hence a ground of meaning and coherence" in both nineteenth- and twentieth-century thought (Sinfield, 65–66). The assumption of the subject's autonomy sets up the conflict between the individual and the social. An alternative to this view is to be found in the works of Mikhail Bakhtin and Valentin Voloshinov. Voloshinov argued that a key confusion in philosophy occurred because of a misuse of the word *individual* which has two possible meanings; biological specimen or person. The category of the person is not in fact the opposite of the social.

> What most complicates our problem in delimiting psyche and ideology is the concept of 'individuality.' The 'social' is usually thought of in binary opposition with the 'individual,' and hence we have the notion that the psyche is individual while ideology is social. Notions of that sort are fundamentally false. (Quoted in Morson and Emerson 1990, 201–2)

This approach suggests that the opposition between the individual and the social that informs nineteenth-century British autobiography was itself a product of ideology. If one adopts a Bakhtinian perspective, it is not possible to see the individual and the social in isolation from one another, because they all participate in the heteroglossia of language. However, some texts exhibit what Bakhtin terms "monologism," that is, the effort to repress the unsettling forces of heteroglossia and reduce language to a single voice. Arnold's anxiety about the dialogue of the mind with itself, therefore, betrays his unease at the unsettling heteroglossia of language and his desire to control signification through monologism. He attempts to ground his texts in the self as a single, monologic voice.

I argue in the following sections that the primary characteristics of nineteenth-century male autobiography are an emphasis upon the ideal of autonomy and a corresponding nostalgia for the lost intimacy represented by community. Nineteenth-century autobiography, as the preeminent exemplar of an individualist ideology that privileged individual self-possession over the communal, records most graphically the masculine libidinal investment in notions of autonomy. Nineteenth-century masculine autobiographers inscribe themselves within their texts as autonomous subjects free from the constraints of any social context. They exhibit the "hermetic isolation" that Peter Middleton has ascribed to contemporary images of masculinity (Middleton 1992, 6).

For example, Mill and Gosse enact in the narrative of their autobiographies the construction of an autonomous subjectivity at the expense of the social. Both Mill and Gosse enact dialogues that are in fact disguised monologues. Mill's "mental crisis," for instance, takes place entirely within his own mind, with no reference to external social forces. The internal dynamics of his own self-questioning actually take the place of any imagined social context. Mill is completely alone, according to his account.

Mill's isolation becomes even more apparent if we compare his autobiography to women's and working-class autobiographies of the Victorian period. In Margaret Oliphant's *Autobiography*, for example, one is continuously made aware of the presence of other people, especially her family. Her attitude toward the constraints laid upon her by the demands of her family is clearly ambivalent; she oscillates between appreciation of their presence and a nagging sense that her professional career has been hindered by their demands. Whatever her feelings, however, she could not escape the demands of family life. It was not possible for her to construct her identity as an autonomous individual in the same way as Mill.

> I had no table even to myself, much less a room to work in, but sat at the corner of the family table with my writing-book, with everything going on as if I had been making a shirt instead of writing a book...and I took my share in the conversation, going on all the same with my story. (Oliphant 1988, 23–24)

Oliphant gives an image here of writing as a social activity. This image presents a stark contrast with *Charles Reade in His Study*, where writing is a completely solitary activity. When Oliphant does retire from the communal table and find a solitary space in which to write, she is racked by guilt at being so antisocial (24). Oliphant, unlike Mill or Gosse,

clearly feels she does not have the right to claim the "human being's privilege to fashion his inner life for himself" but must always define herself in
relation to others.

The contrast here in terms of gender can also be shown in class
terms. The autobiography of George Mockford, an ordinary working
man, contains the narrative of a "crisis" similar to Mill's. Mockford's was
an overtly religious crisis and at first glance has little in common with
Mill's experience. However, Mill's reference to the similarity of his crisis
to the Methodist "conviction of sin" suggests that he in fact was undergoing an intellectual version of the common Victorian crisis of faith in
God. Both men were in fact undergoing a Victorian "rite of passage" in
their crises that cut across class lines. Mockford, like Mill, is deeply
depressed by the idea of determinism, feeling in periods of dejection that

> the doctrine of what is called Philosophical Necessity
> weighed on my existence like an incubus. I felt as if I was sci-
> entifically proved to be the helpless slave of antecedent cir-
> cumstances; as if my character and that of all others had been
> formed for us by agencies beyond our control, and was wholly
> out of our power. (Mockford 1984, 118–19)

As a reaction against his fear of determinism, which bespeaks his
fear of death, Mill seizes on the opposing "doctrine of free will."
Although he couches the debate here in terms of science and philosophy,
his "doctrines" have an obvious counterpart in the theological contro-
versy over predestination and free will. Mill's "debate" in his *Autobiography* is represented as occurring entirely within his own consciousness.
Unlike Mill, however, Mockford makes explicit the role other people play
in his crisis:

> I began to discover the doctrine of predestination and elec-
> tion as revealed in the scriptures, but O the enmity I felt
> against it, and God on account of it! Where was the justice of
> God in it? I asked, as the doom of all was fixed, and that noth-
> ing man could do or would or could turn the mind of
> God....For months this deep distress continued, and my
> teacher, the clergyman, and other church people who visited
> me, pointed out how wrongly I was acting in trying to look,
> as they said, into those secrets that belonged to God. (76–77)

Mockford becomes gravely ill as a result of his spiritual crisis. However, unlike Mill's mental crisis, Mockford's takes place in a recognizable community, and he reports conversations with other people and the effects others have on him. He eventually comes to terms with his crisis thanks to the Dissenters, a group his parents had taught him to despise. Where Mill converts to the doctrine of free will, Mockford finds salvation in a religious community. Mockford's narrative, therefore, stresses interdependence, where Mill's stresses autonomy. Mill represents his crisis as one of completely isolated consciousness, reinforcing the myth of the autobiographical self as autonomous from the social. Mill denies community, where Mockford and other working-class autobiographers place themselves within a community.

As men, both Mockford and Mill were able to draw upon the form of spiritual autobiography, with its model of progress and redemption, and present themselves as spiritual "success stories." As Linda Peterson has pointed out, this model became increasingly unavailable to women as they became inscribed within the Victorian ideology of the feminine as "selfless and self-effacing" (Peterson 1986, 213). Women did not "compose retrospective accounts of spiritual or psychological progress" (212). This is evident in Oliphant's autobiography, as she feels compelled to apologize that it "is not likely that such family details would be of interest to the public" (Oliphant 1988, 122). Oliphant represents herself in her domestic role as mother, rather than as the protagonist in a narrative of spiritual progress.

It is precisely the kind of "family details" for which Oliphant apologizes that are missing from Mill's autobiography. The masculine subject in Victorian autobiography emphasizes the autonomy of self at the expense of family and community. The apparent dialectic in Victorian masculine autobiography between the inwardness of the autonomous individual and the social is a false one, in that the apparent opposition it presents between the autonomous self and wider social responsibilities disguises a privileging of self over other. Victorian male autobiographers adopt the monologic rather than the dialogic mode. The use of repression in these texts supposedly turns the interest of the author outward rather than inward, toward the social and public rather than the private. However, what occurs in fact is an intensification of the individual's sense of inwardness at the expense of the outer world.

The "autobiographical fictions" of Arnold, Mill, and Gosse corroborate the model of masculine autobiography proposed by Shari Benstock in *The Private Self* (1988):

What is reinforced...is the *moi*, the ego; what is pushed
aside is the split in the subject...that language effects and cannot deny. Man enforces a "unity and identity across time" by
"reconstituting" the ego as a bulwark against disintegration;
that is, man denies the very effects of having internalized the
alienating world order. (15)

Benstock here is criticizing Georges Gusdorf's definition of autobiography in "Conditions and Limits of Autobiography" (Gusdorf 1980),
but her critique applies equally well to Victorian masculine texts. Benstock
is describing in Lacanian terms what I have referred to above as "monologism," the repression of the social in the construction of subjectivity. Victorian male autobiographers construct a unitary and autonomous subjectivity as a way of denying both the split in the subject and the determining
role of the social in their formation.

This split in the masculine subject finds its expression in the literary
convention of the "double." The nineteenth-century motif of the double
in fiction has been analyzed by Misa Miyoshi, Karl Miller, and most
recently John Herdman. Herdman argues that "the experience of self-
division...is almost an inseparable condition of consciousness" (Herdman
1990, 1). Similarly, in his seminal definition of autobiography in his article "Conditions and Limits of Autobiography," Georges Gusdorf has said
of the experience of writing about oneself that "the image is another
'myself,' a double of my being but more fragile and vulnerable, invested
with a sacred character that makes it at once fascinating and frightening"
(Gusdorf 1980, 32). Both critics connect the experience of the double
with the split in the writing subject. Gusdorf captures succinctly here the
simultaneous fascination and fear produced by the experience of doubleness in writing autobiography in calling it both "fascinating" and "frightening." However, both Gusdorf and Herdman view the theme of the
double as a universal, ahistorical product of consciousness. I would argue
that this theme in fiction, as in autobiography, is more a product of a particular conception of the subject, one caught between irreconcilable
dichotomies expressed in terms of the division between inner and outer,
private and public, and the individual and the social. Autobiography and
fiction, in representing men encountering their doubles, record the profound aporias of nineteenth-century individualism. Masculine split subjects in pursuing a double are pursuing aspects of their own identity that
they both fear and desire. Lesser in her study of men representing women
refers to "divided selves" in this context (Lesser 1991, 10). They repress

the knowledge of this "split" subjectivity and represent themselves as unitary, autonomous subjects who encounter their doubles as unrecognized aspects of themselves. In *Dr. Jekyll and Mr. Hyde,* for instance, Dr. Jekyll refers to Hyde as "he" because he cannot bring himself to recognize his double as a repressed aspect of his self and say "I."[5]

The history of autobiography is therefore bound up with the history of individualism in the nineteenth century. The genre that came to be called "autobiography" in the late eighteenth and early nineteenth centuries depends upon a set of assumptions that are coterminous with the ideals of individualism. In the following sections, therefore, I situate the term *autobiography* within the historical context of the development in nineteenth-century Britain of a fully articulated individualist ideology. Autobiography as "self-life-writing" is bound up with the elevation of the ideal of autonomy as "self-naming" in the nineteenth century.

AUTONOMY AND COMMUNITY IN NINETEENTH-CENTURY BRITISH AUTOBIOGRAPHY

The creation of the word *autobiography* in the Romantic period signaled the birth of a new literary form.[6] The addition of this word to the English language in the 1790s was a momentous occasion in intellectual history, indicating one of those shifts in outlook that are often sensed but seldom adequately described. In this study I define this distinctive form of subjectivity that led to the creation of the term *autobiography* in terms of the dialectic between autonomy and community. Autobiography formalized the existence of the nineteenth-century subject, a subject who inhabited the liminal space between the competing dualisms of the individual and the social. The nineteenth-century autobiographical subject was the product of a false dialectic between the inward sphere of the autonomous individual and the social claims of community. Autobiography records the destruction of communal ideals by the ideology of nineteenth-century individualism that was initially articulated in the Romantic period. I will argue that the literature of the Victorian period represents a post-Romantic attempt to come to terms with the social costs of the subjectivity that was inaugurated in the 1790s.

In arguing that this new form called "autobiography" was created to embody a new and distinctive subject, I am not implying that previous ages did not have the category of the individual.[7] Other historical periods and cultures did and still do have a category of the individual, but it is one that differs from the nineteenth-century subject in profound ways. In chapter 1 I locate this difference in historical terms through the ideal of imitation, an ideal that was thrown into question by the Romantic ideology of originality. In late eighteenth- and early nineteenth-century Britain the ideal of the unique, original, and autonomous subject became particularly important. The emergence of the word *autobiography* in 1797 marks the rise of an individualist ideology that locates all phenomena within the determining category of the autonomous individual. As Michael Sprinker points out, "Prior to the eighteenth century, works that are today labelled as autobiographies were known as confessions, memoirs, journaux intime"; the emergence of the word *autobiography* is connected to the emergence of "the concept of the author as sovereign subject over a discourse" (Sprinker 1980, 325). Autobiography is therefore preeminently the creation of nineteenth-century individualism and the category of the "sovereign subject." I use the term *individualism* here in the sense proposed by Alan Macfarlane in *The Origins of English Individualism* (1979):

> It is the view that society is constituted of autonomous, equal, units, namely separate individuals, and that such individuals are more important, ultimately, than any larger constituent group. It is reflected in the concept of individual private property, in the political and legal liberty of the individual, in the idea of the individual's direct communication with God. (5)

As can be seen, a nexus of political, social, and legal terms are linked by the word *individualism*. For instance, I argue in chapter 1 that autobiography as a form was created in tandem with the laws of individual ownership that underlie the law of copyright. Individualism in the early nineteenth century redefined the political, legal, and ethical categories inherited from the eighteenth century in terms of "autonomous units" that were defined as separate from the social.

Before the nineteenth century the law of copyright established by the Statute of Anne in 1710 was "a publisher's right...which functioned in the interest of the publisher with no concern for the author" (Patterson 1968, 12). With the redefinition of literature in terms of individual control of the text, the ability of an individual author to claim sole ownership of his or her text was created. As texts became identified with individual authors, the term *autobiography* entered the English language to codify the existence of texts that stood in one-to-one relationship with their authors. In autobiography the ideal of an absolute identification between author and text is given its most forceful expression. Unlike in a novel, in an autobiography the title of the text and the name of the author are assumed to be absolutely equivalent. That this is in practice not possible led to much anxiety for the authors in this study.

When I refer to "autobiography" in this book, therefore, I have in mind not a particular genre but a way of imagining the relationship between text and author. Jacques Derrida in "The Law of Genre" (Derrida 1980) has argued against the use of the term *genre* as a way of limiting the cancerous proliferation of meaning. Designating a text under the rubric of a genre is a way of isolating that text from others and ensuring that it follows a prescriptive set of rules. However, this theory of genre does not fit the practice of literary production. In the late nineteenth century Edmund Gosse felt it necessary to distinguish his autobiography from "specious" fictional imitations of the genuine article, and the long critical debate over the autobiographical status of *David Copperfield* shows the difficulty of distinguishing the first-person novel from a "genuine" autobiographical narrative. In contemporary usage, such terms as *infotainment* and *docudrama* show the uncomfortable slippage between supposedly factual genres such as the news or documentaries and other fictional forms. Regarding the nineteenth-century context, both Alan Liu and Mary Jacobus have analyzed *The Prelude*'s problematic status when considered under the rubric of "genre." Liu has referred to *The Prelude*'s "inmixing of genres" (Liu 1989, 361), while Jacobus (1984) has used *The Prelude* to question the possibility of establishing a theoretical justification for a genre (47). Jacobus asks:

> Is genre-theory, then, no more than a 'figure of reading or understanding'?—a means of stabilizing the errant text by putting a face on it, and so reading into it a specular image of our own acts of understanding? In this light theories of genre become inseparable from theories of the subject, and hence inseparable from theories of writing. (55)

Jacobus is quoting de Man's definition of autobiography as a "figure of reading or understanding" that occurs in all texts (de Man 1979, 921). I accept both de Man's and Jacobus's position here, with qualifications that I outline in the opening pages of chapter 1. Autobiography is a "figure of reading" that can be found in any text after the end of the eighteenth century. As Wordsworth himself said, the distinguishing mark of narrative poems is "that the Narrator himself is the source from which everything primarily flows" (Wordsworth 1974, 3:27) The writing subject becomes in the case of autobiography both form and content for the narrative. Jacobus quotes Wordsworth's list of possible genres for a narrative poem: "the Epopoeia, the Historic, Poem, the Tale, the Romance, and…that dear production of our days, the Metrical Novel" (Jacobus 1984, 50). Within this system of classification *The Prelude* seems closest to the "metrical novel," a definition that involves us in the double impossibility of defining both "autobiography" and the novel, or of separating truth from "fiction." *The Prelude* does not obey "the law of genre," nor do other nineteenth-century autobiographies.

Autobiography is not, therefore a genre in the sense of a distinct form that can be marked off in pristine isolation from other forms of first-person narrative. William Spengemann's definition of autobiography is closer to my own than his title *The Forms of Autobiography* would suggest, since "form" seems a circumlocution for genre.[8] Like Spengemann I would define autobiography in terms of the way the author imagines the relationship between his or her self and an other. As Spengemann (1980) says, in autobiography, "whatever the explicit, sensible referent of any linguistic figure may be, its ultimate and principle referent is the otherwise ungraspable self" (121). Spengemann's definition, like Wordsworth's above, makes any text that attempts to construct an "otherwise ungraspable self" in the metaphorical mirror of the text an autobiography. The autonomous self is the ultimate and determining referent of the autobiographical text. To write an autobiography is quite literally an act of self-naming, or in other words of autonomy.

Autobiographies reduce the social horizon to the interplay of a self and an other. This dualism can occur in poetry, prose, fiction, or nonfiction. I therefore identify the texts in this study more as autobiographical than autobiographies, in that they betray a distinctive way of viewing the process of narrating a life that distinguishes them from their precursors, the confession, and the early twentieth century modernist rejection of the self. The texts I analyze in this book betray monologism at work, in that the writer tries to efface the unsettling effect of heteroglossia and represent the text as the product of a single, undetermined self. I do not include within my scope, therefore, autobiographical novels such as *David Copperfield* or a parodic, carnivalesque text such as Carlyle's *Sartor Resartus*. In both these cases the dialogic and carnivalesque qualities of the text distinguish them from such monologic works as John Stuart Mill's *Autobiography* or Matthew Arnold's lyric poetry. In the latter cases the authors both repress and attempt to subsume within their own voice the presence of others, especially women. Writing an autobiographical text becomes an assertion of power, particularly the power of the author over the social context of writing.

Autobiography is therefore a creation of individualism in the way it enshrines the autonomous self as its paradigm. I read both Mary Shelley's *Frankenstein* and Robert Louis Stevenson's *Dr. Jekyll and Mr. Hyde* as commentaries upon the social cost of this enshrinement of the autonomous self. In both cases the attempt by the male protagonist to create a self-sufficient, autonomous self leads to the destruction of social bonds. Both texts therefore are critiques of individualism and of autobiography as an individualist enterprise. Both texts suggest that the severing of the individual from the community leads to the destruction of the self. Nineteenth-century writers were well aware of the unsettling effect of the ideal of the autonomous self, and all register in differing ways the effects of what they saw as the tension between the competing claims of the individual and the social.

Steven Lukes describes the philosophical underpinnings of individualism in a brief study that provides a good overview of its basic components. Lukes defines "the basic ideas of individualism" as autonomy, privacy, and self-development. He describes

> the notion of *autonomy* or *self-direction*, according to which an individual's thought and action is [*sic*] his own, and not determined by agencies or causes outside his control. In particular, an individual is autonomous (at the social level) to the degree to which he subjects the pressures and norms with which he is confronted to conscious and critical evaluation, and forms intentions and reaches practical decisions as the result of independent and rational thought. (Lukes 1973, 52)

As Lukes's definition suggests, there is an implicit antagonism between the social and the individual in the ideal of autonomy. To be autonomous is to resist "pressures" or constraints originating in the social. While Lukes's definition is succinct, it does not advance analysis very far, because it accepts a number of crucial assumptions that this study undertakes to question. Lukes, like the nineteenth-century authors he quotes, assumes that it is possible to separate the individual and the social. This is a crucial assumption in nineteenth-century individualism, and one that this study questions.

Lukes uses the term *critical evaluation* but never makes explicit that
the touchstone of judgment here is the autonomous individual assumed as
an ahistorical and universal category. The individual resolves the practical
and moral questions toward which Lukes gestures by evaluating them in
terms of their impact on him- or herself alone. That is, all decisions are
evaluated in light of a presumed autonomous self that can be defined without reference to its social context. The process here is essentially circular, in
that the individual assumes that he or she is already autonomous and evalu-
ates his or her conduct accordingly. The autonomy of the individual is
therefore a given that informs the subject's terms from the outset. The
individual's autonomy from the social cannot even begin to be questioned
because it is embedded so firmly in the discourse as a motivating force.

However flawed, Lukes's definition is an apt summary of the tenets
of autobiography. To write an autobiography presupposes the existence
of the autonomous self, a self that can be located as an entity distinct
from a wider social context. Elizabeth Fox-Genovese in her introduction
to *The Autobiography of Pierre Samuel Du Pont* (1985) gives the most
convincing description of the shift in attitude caused by individualism to
which I am referring. Placing Du Pont's autobiography within the context of the rise of bourgeois individualism in France, she argues:

> Bourgeois individualism did not introduce the self into
> human experience, but it did register a changing perception
> of the self, its legitimacy, and its relation to the fundamental
> values of society. With the triumph of bourgeois individual-
> ism, the self—individual right—became the basic unit of social
> organization, the source of political legitimacy, and the self-
> conscious locus of first knowledge and ultimately, truth. (6)

As Fox-Genovese suggests, the individual is the basic unit of autobiography, and its prerequisite. The emergence of autobiography as a form is
therefore a sign of "the triumph of bourgeois individualism." As Du Pont
and Rousseau show, individualism as a philosophy developed more quickly
in France than in England. The French word *autobiographie* and the first
autobiography in French, Rousseau's *Confessions* in 1782, predate the use
of the term in English and the composition of Wordsworth's *Prelude* by fif-
teen years.[9] The same transformation took place in England as in France,
but occurred later. When it did occur, this transformation was deeply
marked from its inception by a conservative reaction against the French
Revolution in particular and social upheaval in general. Nineteenth-century

British autobiography was a conservative genre that viewed the autonomous individual as a potential source of anarchy and social revolution and therefore valorized a self-repressive subjectivity, as I argue in chapter 3.

Nineteenth-century British autobiography registers the inward turn of the self away from the social. In arguing that autobiography marks a general turn inward and away from the social, I parallel Raymond Williams's analysis of the changing representations of nature outlined in *The Country and the City.* Williams describes the way in which landscape in Romantic poetry was consistently severed from its political and social context, becoming a vehicle instead for purely self-referential meditation. This move is an understandable reaction to the profound changes wrought by the transformation of England from a primarily agricultural to an industrial economy, and the consequent social upheaval. While it is a reaction with which I sympathize, it is obvious from the terms I outline in this study that I also feel it carried with it extremely unfortunate consequences. Williams argues that in the eighteenth century the poetry of John Clare represented a radically new way of viewing the country. The troubling consequence of this new view of landscape was that it led to withdrawal into a kind of "'Eden' of the heart" and a severance of connection to the social. The end result of this process is "a lonely, resigned and contemplative love of men" that ultimately privileges the detached individual's experience over the social (Williams 1973, 140).

As Williams indicates, this inward turn is an ambiguous development in literature. This new approach to landscape, which is linked to the investment of language with a sense of the internal life of the writer, enabled Romantic authors to express solidarity with marginalized people, most notably the homeless vagrants dispossessed by the transformation of the countryside. However, as Williams suggests, it also led the writer to imagine him- or herself as profoundly isolated and separated from the broader social movements of the age. The ultimate message of autobiography is of the "essential isolation, alienation, loss of community" of the writing subject (246).

A similar point about the inward turn in the literary history of individualism is made by M. M. Bakhtin in *The Dialogic Imagination* when he links the emergence of the idea of "landscape" to the construction of a "new private sense of self" in literature in classical times. Bakhtin characterizes this shift in the following terms:

> A whole series of categories involving self-consciousness and the shaping of a life into a biography...began to lose their

public and state significance and passed over to the private
and personal plane. Even nature itself, drawn into this private
and drawing-room world, begins to change in an essential
way. "Landscape" is born, that is, nature conceived as horizon
(what a man sees) and as the environment (the background,
the setting) for a completely private, singular individual who
does not interact with it. (Bakhtin 1985, 143)

Nature, like other ethical, political, and legal categories, is redefined
in the nineteenth century in terms of the isolate individual. It is this redefinition of a "whole series of categories" in terms of inward experience
that enabled the creation of autobiography as a genre. As both Williams
and Bakhtin indicate in their remarks, the history of autobiography in the
nineteenth century is bound up with the urbanization and industrialization of the British landscape. By 1860 England had become an urban
society, with more than half of its inhabitants living in the cities or their
suburbs. The initial reaction against cities recorded in the Wordsworth's
The Prelude had been replaced by the image of the suburbs and an attitude toward the country that viewed it in terms more of leisure than of
agricultural production (Bermingham 1986, 157). The creation of the
suburbs represented the fusion in the Victorian period of the previously
antithetical notions of the city and of nature.

Ann Bermingham in analyzing the changing representations of
landscape in nineteenth-century art describes the suburbs in terms that
recall the representations of community in the texts I examine in this
book. Bermingham says of the new category, "suburb":

Its promise of a model community was based on an idealization of individualism and privacy. The suburb was a flight from
both the old suffocating hierarchy of the country village and
the new bureaucratic impersonality of the city. This rather paradoxical conception of community appeared precisely at the
time when England was emerging as a centralized industrial
nation. The suburb reflected the increasing tendency for Eng-
lishmen to separate their social lives into work and leisure and
their social geography into workplace and home. (Bermingham
1986, 168)

The "social geography" of the suburb thus mirrors the mental landscape of the second half of the nineteenth century. Writers construct for

themselves "paradoxical conceptions of community" that try to balance images of isolation, usually in communion with an idealized nature, against the stresses of urban life in which the writer experiences the self as part of a mass or crowd that can only be described in vague terms as "society." Nature itself in this transition becomes domesticated, becoming more the suburban garden represented in *Charles Reade in His Study* than an untamed wilderness.

This transition can be felt most strongly in John Ruskin. A child of the suburbs, Ruskin turns to nature as a way of preserving values he sees as threatened by industrialization and urbanization. His sense of nature is, however, much more attenuated than Wordsworth's, and there is a slightly hysterical edge to his admonitions about the loss of a "pure," Edenic nature in England, especially in such lectures as "The Storm-Cloud of the Nineteenth Century." Like Wordsworth, Ruskin used landscape as a way of talking about community, but his idea of the natural repudiated the basis of even his own experience. Like Wordsworth he finds himself reacting against the transformation of the landscape and idealizing a preindustrial rural community. Ruskin's ideal becomes a rural landscape, and a rural community, that no longer exists.

Appreciation of the landscape and autobiography thus follow parallel lines of development. In both forms an elegiac mood for lost values helps reinforce the inward turn of the writer away from the social transformations taking place in nineteenth-century British society, transformations being registered in the landscape itself. My use of the term *community* in this study highlights deliberately this nostalgic sense of lost values that haunts nineteenth-century British autobiography. Raymond Williams links this sense of loss to changes in the landscape, but in this study I view it in the context of the loss incurred by the authors' acceptance of the idea of the self's autonomy from the social context. Although they chose to write autobiographical texts, authors from Wordsworth on were increasingly aware that in doing so they tacitly excluded a wider social horizon. The exclusive concentration on the inner workings of a single mind came increasingly to seem dangerously like narcissism or solipsism, so that by the Victorian era writers such as Carlyle, Arnold, and Mill followed an explicit program of anti-self-consciousness; that is, they deliberately tried to repress the self in favor of what they saw as wider social claims on the individual. The force of their reaction betrays the extent to which *community* denoted a threatened ideal in the nineteenth century.

FROM COMMUNITY TO SOCIETY: FERDINAND TÖNNIES AND VICTORIAN SUBJECTIVITY

The loss of social connection suggested by the uses of the term *community* in the nineteenth century finds its most powerful expression in Ferdinand Tönnies' seminal work *Gemeinschaft und Gesellschaft.* Published in 1887, this sociological study embodies many of the ethical problems that beset nineteenth-century British autobiographers. Tönnies' ambivalent attitude toward individualism, and his desire to overcome what he perceives as its antisocial implications, parallels the attitude of nineteenth-century British autobiographers. Tönnies identifies the "community" as a preindividualist, precapitalist form of existence, and associates "society" with the modern phenomena of individualism, industrialization, and urbanization. He says, "community is old; society is new as a name as well as a phenomenon" (Tönnies 1963, 34). Tönnies exhibits a nostalgia for the "old" community over the "new" society, and sees the possibility of "reconstructing" community out of society, thereby overcoming the worst excesses of individualism. Tönnies wishes to reverse the "process of the formation of society and the destruction of community," halting the "development" from the older into the newer form:

> Through this development the "individualism" which is the prerequisite of society comes to its own. However, the possibility of overcoming this individualism and arriving at a reconstruction of community exists. (166)

Tönnies proposes that the development of nineteenth-century individualism can be thrown into reverse in a return to a more "communal" age. Tönnies' dream of a reconstruction of community also informs nineteenth-century British autobiography. Like many British authors, Tönnies seems to have an almost mystical faith in the possibility of resolving the contradictions he diagnoses as afflicting society. Tönnies associates community with a set of powerful nineteenth-century ideals that also find their expression in the autobiographies in this study. Tönnies' work encapsulates many of the issues that Suzanne Graver in her study of George Eliot's novels cites as troubling British authors the most in the Victorian period. She asserts that "Victorian social critics often described the loss of community and the need for its renewal to be one of the major problems of the age, and much of the century's fiction, poetry, drama, theology, history and philosophy reflects this sense of loss" (Graver 1984, 1). As Graver's comments indicate, the Victorian recourse to community reveals a deep sense of loss, a loss directly connected with the rise of individualism.

Tönnies' text is particularly helpful in defining the terms of the problem facing Victorian authors, because of the way in which he systematically lays out the opposing terms in the debate. As Graver indicates, this debate informs a broad range of Victorian works. The anxiety to which Graver alludes is particularly acute in autobiography. It is a theme that recurs in contemporary criticism of autobiography, for instance, when Georges Gusdorf opposes autobiography to a previous situation of community in which "the important unit is thus never the isolated being—or rather, isolation is impossible in such a scheme of total cohesiveness as this" (Gusdorf, 30). Autobiography is thus linked to the possibility of the individual's "isolation," and community is seen as an antidote to such anomie.

Tönnies distinguishes community and society through a series of opposed terms. According to Tönnies, in community individuals "remain essentially united in spite of all separating factors," while in society "they are essentially separated in spite of all uniting factors" (Tönnies 1963, 65). Community is linked to the private and intimate, while society is identified with the atomistic and alienated individual. Community therefore represents unity, society represents separateness, isolation, and competition. In linking community and unity, Tönnies is opposing an ideal image of the self to contemporary experience in ways that find an echo in Victorian literature. Matthew Arnold, for instance, depicts his subjectivity as profoundly self-divided and conflicted, and constructs idealized images of community and unity as ways of compensating for this experience. These are issues I explore in more detail in chapter 6. Through his description of the idealized community of "aliens," Arnold tries to escape the separation and isolation he depicts in his poetry.

Tönnies' use of the term *community* therefore recalls oppositions such as Matthew Arnold's between the idealized community of culture and the "anarchy" of unchecked individualism. Tönnies sounds distinctly like Arnold when he calls community a social order that "rests on harmony" (Tönnies 1963, 233). Both Tönnies and Arnold are writing in a vein inaugurated by Hegel in his opposition between society and the state as community (Gordon and White 1979, 37). According to Hegel, in society subjective freedom counted for everything, community for nothing. For Hegel the state as an "imagined community" served as an antidote to the excesses of individual autonomy in society, just as the state did for Arnold. In the theories of Hegel, Tönnies, and Arnold, an imaginary community is posited as the cure for the ills of contemporary society.

Not only does community represent unity in Tönnies' terms, it is also linked to the organic and thus to the various idealized representations of nature to be found in nineteenth-century texts. In this it follows the history of descriptions of nature as opposed to the city outlined by Williams in *The Country and the City*. Tönnies asserts that community "should be understood as a living organism, society as a mechanical aggregate and artifact" (Tönnies 1963, 35). Society is thus linked to the industrial and artificial, while community represents the "natural" and rural as opposed to the urban and artificial. This image of community is therefore based on a nostalgia for a rapidly disappearing rural existence embodied in the "neighborhood" of the "rural village" (43). As Fox-Genovese points out, the emergence of bourgeois individualism "occurred in tandem with momentous changes in the social organization of economic production" (Fox-Genovese 1985, 6–7), and it is in this area that autobiography registers most strongly this kind of transformation. British representations of the self from Wordsworth through to Arnold are mediated through idealized images of nature that the authors oppose to the "mechanical" development of modern industrial society.

Community is also linked through Tönnies' conceptions of the "natural will" and the "rational will" with the dichotomies of inner/outer and private/public that I argue in the following pages underlie autobiography. The natural will, as the basis for community, is associated with the home, family, women, and poetry. The identification between women and community is particularly strong. The "realm of life and work in the community is particularly befitting women" since "staying at home is natural for women" (Tönnies 1963, 162). Community is linked through women to the inward sphere, since "all the women's activity is more inward than outward" (163).

Tönnies here draws upon gender stereotypes that hold true for all the texts in this study. Accepting a gender-based division of labor, he relegates the feminine to the domestic sphere, associating the masculine rational will with the realm of power and conflict. In this he privileges masculine autonomy of the rational will over female dependence. The masculine becomes identified with power, conflict, and prestige, the feminine with the home, privacy, and a maternal protectiveness. These gender-based distinctions between private/public, male/female, and work/home have troubling consequences for Victorian writers. In effect, they ensure that Victorian writers experience themselves as split personalities, caught between opposing and irreconcilable categories. If the inward, private, and feminized aspect of the self is emphasized, then the writer loses touch with the truly masculine and outer. Writers find themselves nostalgic for values such as community and home, but also aware that such values are threatened by their own system of masculine values. While Tönnies and other writers may pay lip service to the ideals embodied in community, they actually disempower these ideals, as they did women, by confining them to a domestic sphere cut off from what they perceived as the public arena of power and economic competition.

Both Arnold and Tönnies idealize a domestic, private, and intimate sphere that is protected from the arena of the rational will. The activities associated with industrialization and commerce are "averse to the feminine mind and nature" (Tönnies 1963, 165), so that women are confined to the home by "nature" rather than by social convention. Because women are associated in Tönnies' schema with community rather than society, the communal is relegated to a privileged but disempowered position vis-à-vis the atomistic and individualist sphere of society. Since women are also linked to art and imagination, if the feminine is averse to society, so by implication are poets and other imaginative writers, autobiographers included. Tönnies' hypothesis is borne out by the way in which nineteenth-century authors, particularly poets, linked community to the feminine and then emphasized its separation from the world of society, trade, and commerce.[10] The kind of community they have in mind is no longer able to survive under the pressure of "trade's unfeeling train."[11] Nineteenth-century male autobiographers thus simultaneously idealize and subvert the image of community in their texts.

The characteristic British attitude to community is illustrated graphically in George Henry Lewes's *Comte's Philosophy of the Sciences*:

> So long as individual minds do not adhere together from a unanimous agreement upon a certain number of general ideas, capable of forming a common social doctrine, the state of the nations will of necessity remain essentially revolutionary, in spite of all the political palliatives that can be adopted; and will not permit the establishing of any but *provisional* institutions. (Lewes 1883, 14)

Lewes here implies that community defuses the potential for revolution, a potential created by an individualism that prevents people from "adhering" together and forming a cohesive group. Individualism is seen as a corrosive force that creates unpredictable autonomous units. The dark suspicion of British autobiography, given its most powerful expression in Robert Louis Stevenson's *Dr. Jekyll and Mr. Hyde*, is that the autonomous individual must be restrained and repressed lest he unleash the forces of anarchy and aggression. The idea of community is used in British autobiography as an antidote to the seductive but deadly spectacle of the absolutely free self. The attempt to repress the self in nineteenth-century British autobiography is thus a reaction against the perceived revolutionary potential of the autonomous individual.

I use the term *community*, then, to denote a powerfully nostalgic ideal in nineteenth-century British autobiography, an ideal that is used to limit and contain the revolutionary potential of the autonomous individual. When I use the term *community*, I do not have in mind any particular group of people based in history or geography; rather, I use it to denote a shifting and ambiguous object of desire, an image of human intimacy and connectedness that the authors oppose to their actual experiences of isolation and alienation. The image of community in these texts is preeminently a response to the troubling social changes the authors have experienced.

Maurice Blanchot's *The Unavowable Community* represents one of the most sustained attempts to give an account of the nuances of the term *community*. For Blanchot, *community* rather than referring to an identifiable social group denotes a lack, an absence, signaling the very impossibility of the thing to which it refers. He takes the word *community* to represent a "principle of insufficiency," referring to an "impossible communion" that forever eludes the human subject (Blanchot 1988, 11). Blanchot rings the changes upon the word *community*, moving through its ecclesiastical connotations in *communion,* through blood and kinship ties, through the "ideal community of literary communication" (a construction strikingly close to Tönnies' "community of the mind"), and, finally, the "community of lovers," the "unavowable community" founded upon love or friendship between two individuals (21).

Community therefore represents the site of nostalgia, an inaccessible ideal that is used primarily as a contrast to current social conditions, as in Arnold's vision of culture as community in *Culture and Anarchy*. A number of nineteenth-century autobiographers, particularly in the Victorian period, present themselves as reformers of society. This social agenda is weakened, however, by their appeal to values that deflect their attention from the present to some "golden age," whether historical or personal. This is the syndrome that Raymond Williams has labeled "retrospective radicalism," in which "a necessary social criticism is then directed to the safer world of the past: to a world of books and memories, in which the scholar can be professionally humane but in his own real world either insulated or indifferent" (Williams 1973, 36). This description is equally applicable to the function of the past in nineteenth-century British autobiography and the use of the term *community*.

I am not accusing the authors in this study of willfully obscuring the social context. Indeed, what makes the texts so interesting, from my point of view, is that the authors themselves were aware of the falsification and sought ways to overcome it. Their use of the idea of community betrays their desire to compensate for what they see as the pernicious effects of individualism. However, so deeply imbued is their outlook by individualist assumptions that they are unable to imagine their way out of the inner-versus-outer dichotomy.

No matter how much the autobiographer may wish to assert a sympathy for other social groups, such sympathy is inevitably based upon the self. Rather than create an imaginative connection with wider social processes, authors from Wordsworth on could express solidarity with others only on an individual basis. Raymond Williams has an apt phrase to characterize this process: *negative identification*. While a writer may be sensitive to the suffering of other social groups and try to identify their own fate with his own, such an identification is "inevitably negative in the end," since "the present is accurately and powerfully seen but its real relations, to past and future, are inaccessible, because the governing development is that of the writer himself" (Williams 1973, 78).

Translating this into the terms that I have been developing here, the attempt to represent the author's ideal of community is subverted by inwardness, through which the suffering of others is validated only in terms of the writer's self. As Steven Lukes accurately implied, the individual becomes the touchstone for all moral judgments. Thus Wordsworth's attempts to come to terms with the social upheavals taking place around him, particularly during his residence in London, are subverted by the way he translates everything he sees into an aspect of his own personal drama. Other people become either a formless crowd or "types" expressing externally his own internal condition.

Ideals of community in nineteenth-century autobiography do not overcome the isolation they were created to combat. They are in fact an index of how deeply imbued the outlook of the writer has become by an individualist ideology that converts all phenomena into aspects of the viewer's own psyche. I wish to suggest, then, in the next section that the dialectic I have outlined above is in fact radically skewed in favor of the individual, and that even as the authors I study profess a desire to overcome the individual in terms of community, they in fact privilege the individual and turn the ideal of community into a shibboleth.

INNER AND OUTER IN AUTOBIOGRAPHY

The dialectic in nineteenth-century British autobiography between the inwardness of the autonomous individual and the outer world of community is false in that the apparent opposition between the autonomous self and wider social responsibilities it presents disguises a privileging of self over other. The self in the Romantic and Victorian periods is apparently repressed in favor of the other, whether the other is conceived of as nature or the figure of a deceased friend or lover. The dramatization of this encounter in prose or verse supposedly turns the interest of the author outward rather than inward, toward the social and public rather than the private. However, I will argue in this next section that what occurs in fact is an intensification of the individual's sense of inwardness at the expense of the outer world. Nineteenth-century autobiography enacts a dialectic between the inner self and an outer world of public forms.

I use "dialectic" here in the sense defined by Stephen N. Dunning in *Kierkegaard's Dialectic of Inwardness*. The term refers to "the dialectic between two distinct poles of consciousness in every individual: inwardness, subjectivity, and selfhood are understood in contradistinction to externality, objectivity, and social relations" (Dunning 1985, 6). Dunning names here the opposed terms that underlie nineteenth-century autobiography. Kierkegaard shared a faith with Hegel that a resolution of these polarities in the "dialectic of inwardness" was possible within the "'necessary' unity in consciousness" (Dunning 1985, 7). The question whether such a mystical union of opposites is possible or not lies outside the limits of this study. Rather than discuss the possibility of discovering a higher (or perhaps a "deeper," to continue the metaphors of interiority) unity, I wish to suggest that in the texts discussed in this study this apparent dialectic was in fact illusory, in that the external or social side of the contrast had already been robbed of any force. In this dialectic, inwardness is the term privileged over social relations.

The debate played out between the inner and the outer is irreconcilable except at the level of faith. Once you accept the premise of an inner as opposed to an outer experience, only a magical fusion can reconcile the two. My position here is similar to Stephen Toulmin's in "The Inwardness of Mental Life" (1979). Toulmin argues that our ideas of inwardness are distorted by a confusion of interiority and inwardness. While he concedes an inevitable interiority to human experience, he argues that inwardness is a cultural construct, not a natural or self-evident category.

> The things that mark so many of our thoughts, wishes and feelings as inner or inward are not permanent, inescapable, lifelong characteristics. On the contrary, inwardness is in many respects an *acquired* feature of our experience, a *product*, in part, of cultural history but in part also of individual development. (5)

Rather than talk of inwardness as a universal and ahistorical experience, I view it in this study as a product of a distinctive nineteenth-century individualist ideology. "Inwardness," like autobiography, has been produced as an idea by a long process of cultural development. The problem with the idea of inwardness, like with the idea of the autonomous individual, is that it presupposes a radical separation of inner experience from outward reality.

> Once the *interiority* of all our mental activities is taken for granted, the problem of developing any adequate conception of the external world (question-begging phrase!) is like the problem facing a lifelong prisoner in solitary confinement who has no way of finding out what is going on in the world beyond the prison walls, aside from the sounds and pictures reaching him via a television set in his cell. (Toulmin 1979, 5)

Aside from the appearance of the television set, Toulmin's illustration of an isolated self recalls the alienation depicted in Arnold's "The Buried Life." The pristine realm of the inner mind into which the individual can retreat to escape the pressures of society can modulate very easily into images of incarceration. The creation of an inner realm for the self poses the type of dilemma Toulmin describes here, a dilemma that has plagued autobiographers from Wordsworth on. The importance of community in nineteenth-century thought signals an effort to escape the prison of the inner mind and establish contact with a wider social reality beyond its walls. This is an insoluble paradox once it is granted; the only way to avoid this dichotomy is to question the separation of inner and outer itself, as Bakhtin does when he discredits the very metaphor of an "internal territory" (Morson and Emerson 1990, 51).

The attempt to establish community in face of this estrangement from the social leads to an apparently other-directed impulse in nineteenth-century autobiography. Many autobiographers claim a certain degree of social utility in writing their autobiographies, as Thomas de Quincey did in justifying his publication of the *Confessions of an English Opium Eater* or as John Stuart Mill did in the opening pages of his autobiography. The presentation of self in autobiography is thus given an apparently social imperative. The autobiographer evades possible charges of egocentrism or even narcissism by repressing self-consciousness in favor of attention on to social utility. In actuality self-repression is used to create an intensified subjectivity that insulates the self from the contingent forces of the social.

The argument I am advancing here in terms of autobiography is similar to that found in John Kucich's study of Victorian fiction, *Repression in Victorian Fiction* (1985). Writing in the context of George Eliot's novels, Kucich maintains:

> We must ask in what sense the widespread Victorian ideals
> of moral selflessness and renunciation...are what they seem to
> be—that is attempts to escape solipsism—and in what sense
> this affirmation of repression is actually a deepening of
> inwardness and a rejection of fusional tendencies. (116)

This is a central question for both Kucich's study of Victorian fiction and my study of autobiography. I am suggesting in this book that the apparent attempts of British autobiographers to escape solipsism in fact had the opposite effect and reaffirmed the essential isolation of the author. The emphasis upon community as an antidote to isolation and alienation only served to confirm the pristine autonomy of the individual. It is this paradoxical effect of repression in nineteenth-century autobiography that informs my title, "A Community of One"; stated baldly, my title suggests that the authors in this study, when they tried to imagine community, actually only affirmed their essential individuality. They produced texts whose logical extreme is a community of one, a self-enclosed and self-sufficient subjectivity in which the subject can refer only to other images of himself.

I argue that the apparent repression of self in autobiography, like George Eliot's in the novel, is in fact an intensification of inwardness. Just as in Eliot's fictional characters there is a "countermovement of desire...that can be seen to divert them from any orientation to others at all, and to turn them irrevocably inward instead" (Kucich 1985, 117), so in autobiographies by Wordsworth, Mill, Ruskin, or Arnold an apparent move away from the self toward the other in fact disguises a profound intensification of inwardness. Their texts create self-sufficient communities of one that enact the separation of the self from the social.

This deepening of inwardness is a product of repression. I see repression as a tool that produces an intensified self-consciousness, rather than denying such self-consciousness. Rather than use the term *repression,* however, I adopt the Carlylean notion of anti-self-consciousness to distinguish the apparently self-denying gesture I describe in the following pages from the Freudian model of repression. Rather than accept the "modern stigmatization of forms of self-negation as enemies of truth" (Kucich 1985, 2), Kucich argues that repression should be seen as "the very means of producing nineteenth century subjectivity," a means for "imagining and articulating a vast internal territory that might be reverenced as the mysterious origin of selfhood" (12). Repression in the nineteenth century is, in other words, part of the technology of subjectivity.

Both Romantic and Victorian autobiographers try to repress the self through anti-self-consciousness in an attempt to overcome the narrowing of horizons they see as the consequence of solipsism. The paradoxical nature of this effort is captured in the term, however, since it is an attempt to use the self to overcome the self. Self-consciousness is not denied but reinforced by anti-self-consciousness. This sort of self-overcoming is a consequence of the contradictions within individualism that Hartman describes in his essay on the Romantic poet.

> [The Romantic poet's] art is linked to the autonomous and the individual; yet that same art, in the absence of an actively received myth, must bear the entire weight of having to transcend or ritually limit these tendencies. No wonder that the problem of the subjective, the eccentric, the individual grows particularly acute. Subjectivity—even solipsism—becomes the subject of poems which *qua* poetry seek to transmute it. (Hartman 1970, 53)

Romantic and Victorian autobiographers, whether writing poetry or prose, attempt to transcend the subjective while accepting the premises of individualism. They find themselves committed to subjectivity, and ultimately to the specter of solipsism, yet profoundly distrustful of the ultimate consequences of their potentially antisocial stance. The problem of subjectivity that Hartman refers to is how to reconcile this apparently paradoxical situation and move beyond the isolated self to the realm of the social. Hartman seems to feel that anti-self-consciousness is at least partially successful. My analysis questions just how far nineteenth-century texts managed to transcend or limit the solipsism inherent in an individualist approach to literature.

Gestures toward the social by means of the self-repression implicit in anti-self-consciousness do not do what they purport to do. John Stuart Mill's *Autobiography* is perhaps one of the most graphic nineteenth-century examples of this process at work. As I argue in chapter 6, Mill's apparent resolve to focus not on the self but on others in fact masks just such an intensification of self-consciousness. Despite his famous resolve, following his "mental crisis," that happiness could be achieved only by a repression of self, his autobiography in fact betrays a relentless definition of other people in terms of himself. Mill defines the individual purely in terms of a self-divided and self-repressive interiority. Through anti-self-consciousness Mill actually insulates himself from the social realm that his reformist politics try to address, so that what he sees as "anti-individualism" and a curbing of the worst excesses of the solipsistic self in fact produces a profoundly isolated and atomistic subjectivity.

A sign of this isolation of subjectivity, and the consequent disempowerment of the self, comes in a brief, bizarre footnote in *On Liberty*. After Mill had just written in the first edition of *On Liberty* that the repressive English laws restricting the freedom of the press were unlikely ever to be enforced, the state embarked on "the Government Press Prosecutions of 1858," which provoked the following response from Mill:

> That ill-judged interference with the liberty of public discussion has not, however, induced me to alter a single word in the text....For, in the first place, the prosecutions were not persisted in; and, in the second, they were never, properly speaking, political prosecutions. The offence charged was not that of criticizing institutions or the acts of rulers, but of circulating what was deemed an immoral doctrine, the lawfulness of tyrannicide. (Mill 1986, 25)

Mill's definition of the "political" is so narrow as to render the term meaningless. If to advocate tyrannicide within the context of a monarchy is not a political, indeed an implicitly revolutionary, act, the idea of the political here is extremely weak. However, the deeper issue here concerns Mill's ideal of individual liberty. Liberty for Mill is preeminently an *internal* condition, a freedom located in an essentially private and isolated realm. For Mill the "appropriate region of human liberty" is preeminently "the inward domain of consciousness" (Mill 1986, 71). By seeing liberty only in terms of the inwardness of the individual mind, he is unable to appreciate the obvious political repression taking place before him. This is a danger inherent in inwardness that needs to be underscored, lest in our reconsideration of the mechanics of Victorian repression we lose sight of its significant blind spots.

Mill's definition of liberty in terms of a heightened interiority aligns him closely with an apparent political opponent, Matthew Arnold. Mill as the champion of individual liberty could not on the surface appear more different from Arnold, the critic of "doing as one likes." However, the extreme divorce between an inner realm of the self and an outer world of politics also marks Arnold's thought, as I argue in chapter 6. Arnold, like Mill, apparently tries to repress subjectivity in favor of social criticism, a desire dramatized by his renunciation of poetry for prose. However, Arnold's attempt to go beyond what he perceived as the limitations of a modern sensibility marred by an excess of subjectivity fails on precisely the same ground as Mill's.

There is no way to resolve the dichotomy of the individual and the social as it is named in nineteenth-century autobiography. The dichotomy between an autonomous self and a wider society that determines that self and deprives it of its liberty admits of no solution. The only way out of this dichotomy is to refuse to enter into its terms, in the way suggested by the authors of *Changing the Subject* (Henriques et al. 1984). The authors of this work tackle head on the individual-society dichotomy that I see as enabling the production of nineteenth-century British autobiography. They present their book as a "critique of the individual-society dualism and its effect on psychological theory and practices" (1). In their "deconstruction" of the assumptions behind the individual-society dualism, they attempt to "see them as historically specific products, rather than timeless and incontrovertible given facts" (12). My present analysis is very close in spirit to this ambition, and I wish in this section to denaturalize one aspect of the individual-society dualism in nineteenth-century texts, the opposition between an inner and an outer world, the inner world being the domain of the self, the outer that of the social.

From its inception, the self in British autobiography occupied an ambiguous position between the poles of inner and outer. In "Tintern Abbey" Wordsworth describes the presence of self in the landscape in a way that graphically underscores the point I wish to make here. For Wordsworth, nature is ambiguously both a product of his own perception and a reality independent of his consciousness, a landscape animated by a nebulous force that could be God or his own mind. In chapter 1, I explore the consequences of Wordsworth's technique as he translates outer into inner experience, so that the poem becomes what Jerome McGann has termed "a picture...of the 'mind' in its act of generating itself within an external landscape" (McGann 1983, 87). The emphasis upon "mind" here, and throughout *The Prelude* as the description of the "growth of a poet's mind," suggests the later mind/world split in Victorian autobiography.

The kind of blurring of boundaries that I describe has been analyzed by Charles Rzepka in *The Self as Mind* (1986). Rzepka documents what he terms the "transformation of something outside the mind into something inside" (3). Rzepka analyzes many instances of what he calls "visionary solipsism" in Romantic poetry, moments that he describes in the following terms:

> Visionary solipsism refers simply to a state of mind where attention is focused so exclusively on the "sole self"...and its sphere of perception that objects of perception no longer appear as objects of bodily sight, whatever their degree of correspondence to the world which is assumed to exist outside the mind. (24)

In adding the idea of the visionary to that of solipsism, Rzepka turns the potential negative connotations into positive ones, and falls short of mounting a full-scale critique of the individualist premises of Romantic poetry. Rzepka contends that he does "not mean to imply anything pejorative or, necessarily, delusory" in his term *visionary solipsism* (24). His term suggests, however, that such moments should be read critically as instances of the radical separation of the perceiving subject from his or her social context. These moments in which "the self begins to evanesce and incorporate the world outside as part if its consciousness" (25) were for Romantic authors themselves points of great anxiety. This anxiety is underscored by Robert Langbaum in *The Mysteries of Identity* (1977) when he has asserts that "solipsism was the condition dreaded by the Romanticists—the danger incurred by individualism" (7). Solipsism and individualism are intimately connected phenomena.

Langbaum's move from his earlier uncritical descriptions of the way in which Romantic poets enjoy an "expanding discovery of the self through the discovery of its imprint on the external world" (26) to his acknowledgment of the fear of solipsism that was the dark counterpoint to such moments shows a gradual critical shift. Rzepka himself names this shift directly and aligns the *Self as Mind* with such studies:

> Only very recently have critics begun to pay attention to the cost of such voyages of self-discovery and to what is left out of the equation of self with perception: in the experiential process of self-realization they have found the germ of a suffocating self-enclosure, alienation, estrangement, and isolation. (Rzepka 1986, 12)

Like Rzepka, I would situate this study within a growing number of critical works that stress the "self-enclosure, alienation, estrangement, and isolation" attendant upon the nineteenth-century discovery of the inward realm. However, I feel Rzepka's study itself, as Rzepka's reluctance to call the term *visionary solipsism* "pejorative" attests, is still committed to a celebration of the individualist ideals behind Romantic autobiography. He misnames the problem when he calls attention to the Romantic equation of self with perception as the primary focus of his study. At stake here is the way in which the dividing of the world into an inner mind and an outer reality itself masks a solipsistic strategy that privileged the self over all other phenomena. Although the Romantics abjured solipsism, they nonetheless reinforced the emphasis upon the subjective through their opposition of inner and outer. They may have feared the "danger incurred by individualism," that of a profoundly isolating solipsism, but they could not escape it, encoded as it was in their premises.

Rzepka's study, although it opens up a field of questions about the "self as mind" that I wish to exploit, accepts the validity of such dualisms. An alternative approach to this question has been suggested by feminist criticism and has been articulated most forcefully by Shari Benstock in *The Private Self*. Drawing upon a Lacanian model of the development of the self, Benstock provides an account of it not only as divided and contradictory, but also as endowed with an intense desire for unity:

The developing child drives toward fusion and homogene-
ity in the construction of a "self" (the *moi* of Lacan's termi-
nology) against the effects of division and dissolution. The
unconscious is not the lower depths of the conscious...but
rather an inner seam, a space between 'inside' and 'outside'—
it is the space of difference, the gap that the drive toward
unity of self can never entirely close. It is also the space of
writing, which bears the marks and registers the alienating
effects of the false symmetry of the mirror stage. (Benstock
1988, 12)

This idea of a "seam" between inner and outer is an apt way of
describing the model I am presenting in this study of nineteenth-century
autobiography. Benstock's Lacanian analysis suggests a way of approaching autobiography that fuses the categories inner and outer. Benstock
stresses here that the self is a fragile fiction, created as a compensation for
the "division and dissolution" in the subject's desire to represent a unified and coherent identity. In chapter 2, I use the image of the liminal
subject, an idea similar to Benstock's "seam," to help elucidate the position of the writing subject in Coleridge's poetry and De Quincey's prose.
Rather than being located in either an inner or an outer realm, subjectivity in this account is constructed in the liminal space opened up by the
dualism of inner and outer. The self in this account is a tenuous, ghostly
presence located ambiguously between a completely private inner realm
and a public, social world.

The strength of this approach is the way in which it emphasizes that
the dichotomy between inner and outer opened up a space for the writing
of autobiography. The autobiographer inhabits a seam, in Benstock's ter-
minology, that is the space of writing. Wordsworth gestures in "Tintern
Abbey" toward this seam as a "something," an ambiguous presence
poised between the inner and outer realms. The self is an amorphous and
fluctuating fiction that effaces the "split" in the subject. It is for this reason that writers such as Coleridge, De Quincey, and Matthew Arnold
portray themselves as ghosts or phantoms, as I argue in chapter 2.

As Benstock says, conventionally "psychic health is measured in the
degree to which the 'self' is constructed in separateness, the boundaries
between the 'self' and the 'other' carefully circumscribed" (Benstock
1988, 15). For the authors I study, the fact that they experienced the self
as divided and contradictory was a cause for anxiety. This anxiety is registered in Ruskin's prose by his simultaneous resistance to the pathetic fal-

lacy and his portrayal of inner states of feeling in terms of outer landscape, as I argue in chapter 4.

The stricture that the realms of inner and outer be separate is codified most severely by Sigmund Freud. In *Civilization and Its Discontents* Freud insists on the radical divorce between the ego and an outer world in terms of "psychic health":

> Pathology has made us acquainted with a great number of cases in which the boundary lines between the ego and the external world become uncertain or in which they are actually drawn incorrectly. There are cases in which parts of a person's mental life...appear alien to him and as not belonging to his ego; there are other cases in which he ascribes to the external world things that clearly originate in his own ego and that ought to be acknowledged by it. Thus even the feeling of our own ego is subject to disturbances and the boundaries of the ego are not constant. (Freud 1961, 35)

Freud states that in such cases the individual "ought" to acknowledge the confusion of boundaries that is taking place, and that not to do so is morally reprehensible. While we are all subject to these "disturbances" in the boundaries of the ego, which leads one to wonder why such experiences should be possible in the first place, to experience such a confusion is the equivalent of a bodily sickness. Benstock's characterization of this as a question of "psychic health" is therefore accurate; the moral imperative to keep separate the two categories of inner and outer translates easily into a contrast between bodily sickness and health, and implies that the inability to separate the two is a failure of mental health. However, Freud also surreptitiously acknowledges that such failures of boundary are common and easily made, suggesting that the situation is not as clear cut as he might wish. The authors I study show differing degrees of awareness of just how difficult it was to maintain the ideal of the separation of inner and outer against the experience of the interpenetration of the two categories. Whether they were conscious of it or not, however, they all betray the unavoidable conflation of the inner and outer realms that they ostensibly wish to keep separate.

In my conclusion I examine the modernist rejection of nineteenth-century individualism, especially Virginia Woolf's rejection of a Victorian patriarchal social system. Like contemporary critics, Woolf was extremely critical of the egotism involved in the nineteenth-century masculine autobiographical project. However, the individualism that undergirded nine-teenth-century autobiography persists to this day, as critiques such as Elizabeth Fox-Genovese's *Feminism without Illusions* have shown. Even Woolf, who rejected the masculine self as the basis for the construction of the autobiographical subject, represents herself in individualist terms. In my conclusion I suggest that to move beyond the dichotomies of the individual and the social and the inner and the outer requires more than the reformulation of critical terms; it involves the reformulation of a host of legal and ethical categories that interpellate us in our everyday practices as individual authors and citizens.

NOTES

1. See for instance Sir Edwin Landseer's "A Highland Breakfast," Walter Deverell's "A Pet." For a critical treatment of the way in which male artists portray women as "so much animal flesh," see Carol Duncan, "Virility and Domination in Early Twentieth-Century Vanguard Painting."

2. See Coral Lansbury's *The Old Brown Dog* for an account of women and the antivivisection movement.

3. In a perceptive critique of the different agendas at work in William's poetry and Dorothy's journals, Susan J. Wolfson has argued that not only did Wordsworth depend on her journals, but that Dorothy represented herself as "a recorder for the community" in contrast to her brother's "self-inscribing projects" (Wolfson 1988, 140).

4. On working-class autobiographies, see Gagnier 1989. Peterson (1986) and Corbett (1992)also discuss women's autobiographies in these terms.

5. The most striking visual representation of this theme is Dante Gabriel Rossetti's "How They Met Themselves," which Herdman uses as the cover of his book (Herdman 1990).

6. The first citation under the word *autobiography* in the *Oxford English Dictionary* is dated 1797. *The Oxford English Dictionary*, 2nd ed. (Oxford: Clarendon Press, 1989).

7. In this I concur with the position outlined by Elizabeth Fox-Genovese in the introduction to *The Autobiography of Pierre Samuel Du Pont*. A similar approach informs the cross-cultural perspective of *The Category of the Person: Anthropology, Philosophy, History* (Carrithers and Collins 1986).

8. Like Spengemann I would reject the distinction between fact and fiction

in autobiography because "the fictional detail we can trace back to some documented event in the writer's life is not more autobiographical than one we cannot discover" (Spengemann 1980, 119).

9. I follow Philippe Lejeune in *Le Pacte Autobiographique* in dating the emergence of autobiography in France to the posthumous publication of the *Confessions* in 1782. See also my discussion of Rousseau in chapter 1.

10. See for instance Tennyson's "The Lady of Shallott" and "The Palace of Art."

11. Oliver Goldsmith's "The Deserted Village," quoted in Williams 1973, 79. As Williams points out, poetry is linked by Goldsmith and others after him to the loss of community, to which I would add the identification of both poetry and community with an ideal of the feminine.

CHAPTER ONE

AUTOBIOGRAPHY AND THE LOSS OF COMMUNITY: FROM AUGUSTINE'S *CONFESSIONS* TO WORDSWORTH'S *THE PRELUDE*

Paul de Man in an influential essay on autobiography asserted that "any book with a readable title-page is, to some extent, autobiographical" (de Man 1979, 922). This statement apparently precludes the definition of autobiography in historical terms. Indeed, de Man went on to assert that "autobiography, then, is not a genre or a mode but a figure of reading or understanding that occurs, to some degree, in all texts" (921). De Man qualified his assertions in both these formulations by his use of "to some extent" and "to some degree," phrases that introduced uncertainties into his argument that he never directly addressed. As I have indicated in the Introduction, I agree with the broad outline of de Man's position that autobiography cannot be defined as a "genre" but only as a "figure of reading or understanding," but I am troubled by his repression of the historical context. In this chapter I will tackle the question that de Man raises and dismisses as impossible to resolve: Are there in fact identifiable differences between first-person texts written before the late eigh-

teenth century, when the term *autobiography* itself was coined, and those
written after the Romantic period? I will argue that there are, and that
these differences can be expressed in terms of the loss of an image of a
community of readers in the autobiographical text.

Many critics feel that there is no reason to distinguish between first-
person texts in historical terms, and therefore label any first-person narrative an "autobiography." This was the case, for instance, with the
extended letter written in the sixteenth century by Thomas Whythorne,
which was published as *The Autobiography of Thomas Whythorne*. Such
usage allows critics to refer to Augustine's *Confessions* as the "first autobiography" and to confuse first-person narratives from antiquity with those
from the twentieth century. However, de Man's linking of the ideas of
autobiography and a title page in the quotations above provides an opening for the definition of the difference between these texts in historical
terms.

De Man's formulation, in bringing together autobiography and the
ideological codes embodied in a title page, links the category of autobiography to history. Even as he dismisses the possibility of defining autobiography, de Man implicitly raises the possibility of doing so by this reference. Title pages have a history. Like the idea of autobiography, the
idea of a title page relies upon a network of philosophical, legal, and social
sanctions that have been developed over the last two centuries.

The terrain to which I am referring in invoking legal sanctions in
this context was first mapped by Michel Foucault in "What Is an
Author?" Foucault's characterization of the "author function" underscores how autobiography as a genre is dependent upon the ideology of
individual authorship that defines texts in terms of personal property
(Foucault 1977, 124). The link between autobiography and copyright is
the desire for possession, the desire that de Man locates as one of the primary motives behind Rousseau's *Confessions*. The ideal of individual possession of a text as a commodity unites authorship and copyright. Foucault locates the emergence of the "author" in the context of the
articulation of laws of copyright, in a period that coincides with the emergence of the term *autobiography* in the late eighteenth century:

> Speeches and books were assigned real authors...only when
> the author became subject to punishment and to the extent
> his discourse was considered transgressive...it was at the
> moment when a system of ownership and strict copyright
> rules were established (toward the end of the eighteenth and

beginning of the nineteenth century) that the transgressive properties always intrinsic to the act of writing became the forceful imperative of literature. (Foucault 1977, 124–25)

As Foucault emphasizes, the author is an economic category. Foucault in his essay elaborates the ways in which the concept of the author has been used to define "a certain field of conceptual and or theoretical coherence" (120), a description that applies particularly to autobiography. The ideal of the "single" self proposed by Wordsworth in *The Prelude* performs the function of denoting an ideal of coherence and unity across time, as we shall see later in this chapter. Behind the ideal of the single self lies the desire to possess a space of pristine individuality that will belong to the author alone. Like the law governing the absolute possession of property, autobiography defines an inner landscape of experience that belongs to the author alone. Above all, however, the law of copyright serves to limit the cancerous proliferation of texts. Copyright codifies the autobiographical ideals of uniqueness and originality by defining the text as the property of a single, unique and identifiable individual. Copyright creates sanctions to be used against those who commit the impiety of confusing the boundaries between texts, or duplicating another's text as if it were their own.

The definition of the text as the property of a unique individual is alien to Augustine's *Confessions*. I choose Augustine's *Confessions* as my reference point because the text has become the *locus classicus* for many literary histories of the form when they wish to designate the origins of autobiography. William Spengemann's *The Forms of Autobiography*, for example, begins with Augustine's *Confessions*. Spengemann links Wordsworth's *The Prelude* to the "evolutionary line described by Augustinian autobiography" (Spengemann 1980, 72), suggesting a deep continuity between the texts. While it is possible to see superficial similarities between Augustine's and Wordsworth's texts in their uses of "historical self-recollection, philosophical self-exploration and poetic self-expression" (Spengemann, 32), the ideals that inform these strategies are so divergent as to make such comparisons meaningless.

Augustine's text is a self-duplicating machine intended to produce conversion in its reader and thereby reproduce more conversions and more texts. A vision of a community of texts, and of texts embodying conversion, is built into the narrative of the *Confessions*. In a subtle analysis of the mechanics of conversion in the *Confessions*, Geoffrey Galt Harpham has analyzed the book's "elaborately mimetic form" (Harpham

1986, 43). Harpham himself clearly sees Augustine's *Confessions* as a species of autobiography, but I wish to suggest that in its "elaborately mimetic form" Augustine's text differs significantly from autobiography. Augustine's experience is not only mimetic, it aims to create the reader in its own image. The aim of the text is self-duplication. Augustine's conversion is just one in a series of conversions that Augustine and his friends hear and read about in the course of his narrative. Augustine establishes his conversion as a form of imitation; having read about a conversion, he himself undergoes an identical experience.

As Harpham points out, Augustine's "ambition for his own text is that it take place in the chain of imitable texts, speaking to others as he had been spoken to" (43). The ideal of imitation is the distinguishing characteristic of the conversion narrative and of confessions generally. Augustine situates himself by his act in a line of imitations that stretches back to Christ's "Follow me," and through Christ to God. His experience is by definition communal. It is not distinguished by originality or uniqueness, two of the characteristics claimed for themselves by writers of autobiography. Rather, it takes its place in a constellation of other texts with which it is shown in dialogue. The imperative to distinguish his texts from others, the imperative behind the law of copyright, does not operate in Augustine's text.

Literary precedent for Augustine is thus a source of imitation, and indeed the most important source, since the Bible itself is the authorizing and originating text in this sequence. Augustine does not distinguish between texts and acts, treating textual and hearsay narratives of conversion as equal in authority. Augustine therefore fuses texts and life, whereas the possibility of confusion between textual self-representation and experience was a source of anxiety for the Romantics. He links his own life and other texts by explicating the Book of Genesis as an integral part of his confession, joining his own conversion to the narrative of the Bible. The two dovetail so neatly as to make parts of a single text in what Harpham, following Gadamer, calls "mutual reflexive substitution" (Harpham 1986, 45). Mutual reflexive substitution defines the ideal of imitation as it operates in Augustine's text. It conveys the possibility that conversion narratives are replicas of one another and can be substituted for one another. This idea is anathema to writers of autobiography.

For autobiographers such mutual reflexive substitution is impossible. There must inevitably be for writers of autobiography a surplus of individuality that would make such an equation impossible. This surplus value is the essence of individualism, the sign of the "something" that Wordsworth referred to in "Tintern Abbey" that must inevitably exceed the capabilities of language and the self-reproductive capacity of the text. This residual something is the ineffable self-consciousness of the autobiographer, the sign of an individualism that denies the possibility of mutual reflexive substitution between subjects who are viewed as autonomous individuals.

De Man himself, despite his contention that autobiography cannot be defined, suggests a way of differentiating autobiographical and preautobiographical texts. In another essay on autobiography, this one on Rousseau's *Confessions,* he uses the terms *substitution* and *displacement* to unlock the structure of desire in the text. He analyzes the different "levels of desire" embodied in Rousseau's confession of the crime of stealing a ribbon and allowing a female servant to whom he was attracted to take the blame for his misdeed (de Man 1977, 21–33). De Man sees in the incident multiple levels of substitution: "We have at least two levels of substitution (or displacement) taking place: the ribbon substitutes for a desire which is itself a desire for substitution" (de Man 1977, 32).

Rousseau, however, finds his desire for substitution blocked. He can never substitute himself for another because, as we shall see, he defines himself in terms of his difference from others. Symbols within the text, such as the ribbon, bespeak a subjectivity that displaces its own search for a confirmatory presence into objects of desire such as other people or the landscape. In his analysis of Rousseau's text, de Man names one of the fundamental differences between autobiography and confession. The idea of displacement distinguishes Wordsworth's *The Prelude* and Rousseau's *Confessions* from confessional narratives. While displacement is the operative method of their texts for Rousseau and Wordsworth, they must deny its operation because of the Romantic ideology of the uniqueness of the individual, especially the individual genius.

As de Man's analysis of the mechanics of displacement makes clear, the dream of possession behind Rousseau's text is impossible to fulfill. He stole the ribbon in order to possess both it and Marion, but his desire is never realized. The mechanics of desire at work here have been summarized by Jacques Lacan in his formulation of the "mirror stage" in the child's development. In his description of the mirror stage, Lacan embodies a prototypical autobiographical narrative, as the writing subject pursues a specular image of unity and self-possession that it can never achieve (Lacan 1977). The subject is constantly thwarted in its search for an unified image of itself by its awareness of the difference between the "I" and the image in the mirror. Confessions, on the other hand, operate in terms of imitation.

The category of imitation continued to be an important one for narratives up until the end of the eighteenth century. Linda H. Peterson has described the essential character of this form in *Victorian Autobiography: The Tradition of Self-Interpretation*. Peterson points out that writers of confessions would fit their own experiences into episodes from the Bible, so that Old Testament figures not only prefigured the coming of Christ but "were also applied to the lives of individual Christians" (Peterson 1986, 7). This method, which Peterson labels "hermeneutic self-interpretation," shows how fundamental the idea of imitation and its complementary idea of prefiguration were for the confession. Peterson, however, goes on from this to argue a continuity between this method of self-interpretation and autobiography. She follows Spengemann and other commentators in arguing for a continuity or "tradition" linking confessions and autobiographies.

As I have argued elsewhere (Danahay 1986) it is impossible to describe a "tradition" of autobiography. The word *antitradition* might better capture the spirit of autobiography, because the premise of texts written by Wordsworth, Rousseau, and later writers was that the authors were unique and that their life histories fit into no recognizable pattern. Rather than look for biblical prefigurations of their own condition, autobiographers reject out of hand the idea that they imitate previous models. As Peterson herself admits, the "hermeneutic" method fell out of favor when the writer of autobiography felt he or she "needed to produce a work fully original rather than obviously dependent or imitative of other autobiographies" (Peterson 1986, 16). This describes the ideal behind all the texts in this study, and shows how far the model of "hermeneutic self-interpretation" she proposes in her book had been rejected by writers of autobiography.

An index of how far the ideal of imitation had fallen into disrepute is to be found in Edmund Gosse's *Father and Son* (1982), when Gosse laments the degree to which even children were pushed to be "original." Gosse says that his intellectual activity as a child manifested itself in "direct imitation," a form of activity he views as healthy even if it contravenes the drive for originality.

> The rage for what is called "originality" is pushed to such a length these days that even children are not considered promising, unless they attempt things preposterous and unparalleled. From his earliest hour the ambitious person is told that to make a road where none has walked before...to

create new forms of thought and expression, are the only
recipes for genius; and in trying to escape on all sides from
every resemblance to his predecessors, he adopts at once an air
of eccentricity and pretentiousness. (117–18)

Gosse's strict religious upbringing gives him a greater appreciation
for the forms of imitation than many of his contemporaries have, but he is
aware that in this he is an anomaly. The motive behind most autobiography is precisely to define how the writer differs from his predecessors and
expresses a desire to "escape resemblance," as Gosse says. Jean-Jacques
Rousseau, for instance, in his preface to the *Confessions* explicitly rejects
the possibility of his life's being modeled on a previous text, and the possibility of the reader emulating his life:

> I have resolved on an enterprise which has no precedent,
> and which, once complete, will have no imitator....I am unlike
> any one I have ever met; I will venture to say that I am like no
> one in the whole world. (Rousseau 1959, 17)

Rousseau breaks the chain of imitation that marked Augustine's text.
He explicitly rejects imitation as the basis of his text, and furthermore dis-
rupts the possibility of his text reproducing itself. Rousseau claims that
nature "broke the mould" after producing him, so that Rousseau's reproduction in other texts is blocked. Rousseau here expresses the ideal of
copyright through his image of the unreproducible and unprecedented
text.

The attempt to imagine a narrative for the self that relies upon no
previous models sets autobiography apart from the confession. Jerome H.
Buckley in *The Turning Key* isolates the distinguishing characteristic of
Wordsworth's poetical project in *The Prelude* in the idea of its being
unprecedented. Buckley quotes Wordsworth's letter to Sir George Beau-
mont in which he boasted that it was "a thing unprecedented in literary
history that a man should talk so much about himself" (Buckley 1984, 1).
Wordsworth therefore claims that his text is a break with the past rather
than an imitation of previous examples. Like Jean-Jacques Rousseau
before him, Wordsworth bases his justification for writing and publishing
the text on his individuality, on the fact that there exists for his self no
precedent, and that nobody can imitate his life. Both Rousseau and
Wordsworth present themselves as unprecedented and unreproducible.

Where Augustine wrote a text intended to reproduce itself and proliferate, Wordsworth and Rousseau produce texts intended to preclude the possibility of imitation. They implicitly accept the idea codified in copyright that their texts are their unique property. For another to imitate them would be to transgress this boundary. Similarly, for them to imitate another would be a transgression. The definition of the writing subject's boundaries thus becomes an overriding concern of the text. As I argue in the next chapter, the definition of boundaries was an enterprise fraught with uncertainty for many Romantic writers. Wordsworth possessed a faith in the "singleness" of his self that few of his contemporaries could match.

The link with previous texts is disrupted for the autobiographer by the unprecedented writing subject. The existence of previous models becomes a threat in the way that Harold Bloom has described in *The Anxiety of Influence*. The individual is defined in terms of his "swerve" or deviance from other people, just as his text is defined by the degree to which it differs from all other texts. The self thus becomes an isolated entity, and the task of the autobiographer, as opposed to the writer of the confession, is to reassert some sense of community in the face of this rupture.

This, then, is the most important and fundamental distinction between confession and autobiography. Where a sense of community was built into the ideal of the confession, the autobiographer must discover, or perhaps create, his or her own social context. The motives behind autobiography are akin to those attributed to authors of the social novel by Philip Fisher in *Making Up Society*. The autobiographer and the novelist have both lost the community as a premise and must reconstruct or re-create it on the basis of individual experience. Like the social novel, autobiographies register "the change from the representation of individuals within a community to the descriptions of selves surrounded by collections of unrelated others" (Fisher 1981, 4). Autobiography is founded on the basis of the redefinition of community as society and the creation of a space for the autonomous individual.

The loss of community initiates what Charles Rzepka in *The Self as Mind* has characterized as "the quest for an intimate yet authoritative audience" that would help validate an "ideal, interiorized self-image that the poet fears the world will otherwise deny or deface" (Rzepka 1986, 27). Rzepka echoes Lacan here in locating the Romantic quest within the context of a search for an idealized and unobtainable self-image. What he is also describing here, although he does not make this explicit, is the loss of the assumed basis of a community of readers, and the corresponding need of the author to create the sense of intimacy and audience that the word connotes. As Rzepka's comments indicate, this search for an intimate audience is a disguised quest for an other that would confirm the author's sense of self. Community is employed in the service of the self.

The idea of the autobiographical text as a self-duplicating machine by the Romantic period had literally become horrific. Conversion in Augustine's *Confessions* reproduces itself in the world, each text causing the generation of other acts and texts in a proliferation of records of the act of conversion. This attitude toward self-reproduction differs strikingly from the attitude toward autobiography I describe in chapter 3 in relation to *Frankenstein*, in which an act of literary self-creation is represented as a horrifying abomination that must not be allowed to reproduce itself. Informed by a Romantic ideology of uniqueness and originality, and by a revulsion against the productive capabilities of industrialization, *Frankenstein* betrays both an "anxiety of influence" and an "anxiety of influencing" (Bloom, 1973). There is no such anxiety in Augustine's *Confessions*, but rather its opposite, the acceptance of influence and the desire to influence in turn.

For the writer of the confession the existence of death was made far less traumatic and final than for the autobiographer. God guaranteed the existence of some form of afterlife for the soul in the confession. For the autobiographer, there is no such guarantee. Burton Pike maintains in "Time in Autobiography" that "post-Renaissance emphasis on the primacy and uniqueness of the individual has made his personal death...a much more emphatic event than it was in God-oriented times" (Pike 1976, 328). For Wordsworth and Coleridge it becomes part of their poetic mission to imagine an existence for the self beyond death. The figures of deceased loved ones come to stand for the possibility of a life beyond the limit of death, and as a vicarious symbol for community.

Pike characterizes Romantic autobiography as a reaction to the shift in view from a religious to a secular ideology. He argues that "some new cultural force...something pseudodivine" was needed to relieve the individual of the burden of what he calls "temporal linearity" (330). A striking difference between Augustine's *Confessions* and the autobiographical texts discussed in this study is the loss of direct address to God. Where Augustine carries on a dialogue with God in his text, the divine becomes an amorphous and indistinct presence in autobiography. In order to rescue an attenuated form of the Christian promise of immortality, nineteenth-century authors had to invent some inner force strong enough to overcome death. The "new cultural force" that was created to combat intimations of mortality was the idea of an inward realm that escaped the contingent forces of the social and historical. As Pike suggests, Romantic authors sought to transcend both time and space:

> The Romantics suggested solutions [to the burden of temporal linearity] in two directions: on the one hand, to anchor eternity in the individual consciousness, as in Wordsworth's "spots of time" (itself a contradiction in terms), or on the other hand to attempt to transcend time and space altogether as categories of consciousness. (Pike 1976, 330)

Both these "solutions" to the problem of individual mortality appear in the nineteenth-century autobiographies in this study. The autobiographer solves the problem of death as the ultimate human boundary by escaping time altogether. This is a familiar move in Romantic poetry, and one that has been described well by previous critics. I wish to emphasize here the dark underside to these moments of transcendence in Wordsworth's poetry, those moments when he comes to a realization that thanks to his position he cannot address the social context in which he moves—in short, those moments when he registers the loss of community attendant upon transcending time and space.

There are moments in *The Prelude* where Wordsworth finds that his self does indeed have limits or boundaries. Whereas in solitary contemplation of nature he experiences his self as transcendent, when face to face with other people he becomes aware of the limits both of his knowledge of them and of his self-knowledge. An example of such a moment is the "spot of time" Wordsworth describes in book 12, when he sees a lone Cumberland girl walking through a desolate landscape. Jerome Buckley in *The Turning Key* makes a suggestive comment about this "spot of time." He contrasts it with Wordsworth's description of the French peasant girl leading a heifer, who symbolized for Wordsworth the hopes of the French Revolution. The Cumberland girl symbolizes the opposite of the experience of the French Revolution, a loss of the vision and sense of social purpose that Wordsworth describes in books 10 and 11. The sight of the Cumberland girl is, as Buckley says, "an image of 'visionary dreariness' in itself and of no political or social consequence" (Buckley 1984, 59). In the interim between these two moments Wordsworth has lost the desire to see things in political and social terms, casting them instead as purely personal symbols. The Cumberland girl therefore attests to Wordsworth's loss of faith in the ability of a large-scale social movement to create a more just society, and his retreat into a private vision that entails no "political or social consequence."

Jerome J. McGann has analyzed the "displacement" of the social into private and personal concerns in Romantic poetry in *The Romantic Ideology.* Analyzing Wordsworth's "The Ruined Cottage," McGann notes how an eighteenth-century commentator would have seen the poem's events "in social and economic terms, but Wordsworth is precisely interested in preventing—in actively countering—such a focus of concentration" (McGann 1983, 84). As McGann points out, this move is particularly noticeable in "Tintern Abbey," a poem in which the events of the French Revolution are subsumed under a meditation upon the landscape.

In "Tintern Abbey" and the "spots of time," Wordsworth embodies what Charles Rzepka has suggestively termed "visionary solipsism." In his analysis of visionary solipsism, Rzepka fills out in detail the broad outlines sketched by Raymond Williams and M. M. Bakhtin in their descriptions of the way in which nature came to be seen as the backdrop for the individuated consciousness. Romantic poetry records the "transformation of something outside the mind into something inside" (Rzepka 1986, 3). Rzepka's use of the opposition of inside and outside is problematic here, as it subscribes to one of the fundamental Romantic dichotomies, but his characterization of the dark side of this process raises important questions for this study:

> Feelings of emptiness and insubstantiality, and the corresponding derealization of the embodied self, both one's own and others'; this is the negative moment in the dialectic of visionary solipsism, the price that must be paid for identifying the self wholly with a mind that imaginatively appropriates the world as its own and transforms it so as to reflect the contours of its own inchoate being.(26)

Rzepka's description of visionary solipsism and McGann's description of the role of mind in "Tintern Abbey" show how this "imaginative appropriation" works. McGann points out how, in "Tintern Abbey," "what might have been a picture *in* the mind" is replaced with a "picture *of* the mind" (McGann 1983, 87). As both critics suggest, the landscape itself comes to speak indirectly of Wordsworth's autobiographical project. A meditation on the abbey becomes a meditation on the workings of the individual's mind in contemplation of its object. The landscape, the abbey, and his sister bespeak Wordsworth's own "inchoate being."

Developing McGann's and Rzepka's analyses further, I would underscore the social cost of Wordsworth's inward turn in "Tintern Abbey." Wordsworth excludes the social and historical context of his writing and makes all phenomena, his sister included, dependent upon his presence as the perceiving subject. The turn inward inherent in autobiography displaces the social and political content of poetry into a purely self-referential meditation. The cost of this move inward is a sense of radical alienation and isolation. Wordsworth escapes such feelings in "Tintern Abbey" by introducing his sister Dorothy as an "intimate and authoritative audience." Dorothy comes to stand for the community Wordsworth excluded in his solipsistic endeavor. Her presence helps rescue Wordsworth from the antisocial effects of visionary solipsism. She is identified with community and intimacy, just as the communal and the feminine were equated in Tönnies' *Gemeinschaft und Gesellschaft*. However, far from representing community here, Wordsworth is in fact representing himself as a community of one. It is Dorothy Wordsworth who is the recorder of the community in her journals; William Wordsworth uses the community, and his sister Dorothy, as screens onto which to project his own desires.

The dynamics of his self-representation are the same as those analyzed by Mary Jacobus in the context of the story of Vaudracour and Julia, where the narrative is "a way of constituting Wordsworth himself as an autobiographical subject" (Jacobus 1984, 52). The emphasis in "Tintern Abbey" is upon the identity between Wordsworth and all he sees, not upon difference; the result is that "gender establishes identity by means of a difference that is fully excised. What we end up with is not difference...but the same: man to man" (Jacobus 1984, 53). In microcosm in "Tintern Abbey," and on a larger scale in *The Prelude*, Wordsworth finds his identity as a masculine, autonomous self confirmed by nature and by the feminine. Both the landscape and Dorothy function as mirrors for his construction of himself as an autobiographical subject.

Wordsworth thus uses Dorothy, just as he uses landscape, to stand for ideals of community and human intimacy that he himself values but that are undercut by his allegiance to individualism and by social change. At another level, however, Wordsworth is aware that these are threatened values. Michael Friedman has pointed out that at the time Wordsworth was writing, "modern capitalism was eroding traditional affective relationships" and replacing them with relations defined by the marketplace (Friedman 1979, 11). Wordsworth's "strong need for an enclosing, supporting community" as represented by rural villages in the Lake District, or in his sister Dorothy, was a reaction against the kind of social transformation to which Friedman refers (1).

Wordsworth's representation of community is also bound up with his experiences during the French Revolution. Wordsworth here represents in his turn inward a reaction against the French Revolution that is typical of nineteenth-century British autobiographies. The social turmoil of the French Revolution engendered a profound mistrust of broad social movements and their consequent upheaval and made writers fearful of the attempt to imagine a more just order for society. Writers attempted an individual, instead of a collective, salvation through the writing of autobiography. This reaction to the French Revolution intensified the sense of isolation and estrangement already implicit in the idea of the unique individual, making it even more difficult for English autobiographers to represent political or social consequences in autobiography.

Wordsworth claimed that *The Prelude* was based upon himself alone. It is the idea of himself as an unprecedented, unique, and single self that provides both the subject and the justification for his autobiography, but it is also this idea that limits his work in damaging ways. Briefly stated, the ambition of representing himself as a unique, single individual makes it difficult for Wordsworth to assert a connection to any wider sense of human community. It is this limitation that underlies the "visionary dreariness" of the sight of the Cumberland girl. This is also a limitation implicit in the blind beggar episode, as we shall see later.

Wordsworth invokes the unity of his self, a self "single and of determined bounds" (7.640), at the beginning of *The Prelude* as a way of limiting a subject that threatens to stretch to infinity. He falls back upon the ideal of the autonomous and single self of the individual as a way of controlling the potential proliferation of subjects. In the same way Edmund Burke uses the individual as a fundamental principle in *A Philosophical Enquiry Concerning the Origin of Our Ideas of the Sublime and the Beautiful.* Having admitted that his enquiry runs the danger of becoming a limitless quest, Burke says that his own individuality will provide a boundary for the otherwise formless subject.

> The matter might be pursued much further; but it is not the extent of the subject which must prescribe our bounds, for what subject does not branch out to infinity? It is in the nature of our particular scheme, and the single point of view in which we consider it, which ought to put a stop to our researches. (Burke 1958, 27)

For Burke, like Wordsworth, the unity embodied in the "single point of view" makes for a work that is itself "of determined bounds" and thus much more manageable than a purely philosophical and abstract topic that threatens to "branch out to infinity." Burke names here the fear that underlies visionary solipsism, the fear that subjectivity will erase all boundaries and stretch out to infinity. Wordsworth and Burke invoke the idea enshrined in copyright, the ideal of the author as a property of determined boundaries, as an antidote to visionary solipsism. Burke and Wordsworth seek a commanding presence in nature that would legislate their boundaries for them.

Both Wordsworth and Burke demonstrate great interest in the sublime, and this is because, as Frances Ferguson argues, "the sublime object is particularly important in attaching one to consciousness of oneself because...it gets defined, most notably by Kant, as what cannot stand alone without a supplementary human consciousness" (Ferguson 1977, 8). Thus the sublime landscape comes indirectly to confirm the presence of the human consciousness that gives it life. The sublime is an individualist category in that it defines the viewer as a supplement or surplus that cannot be encompassed. The role of the sublime or of landscape in *The Prelude* is to confirm the presence of Wordsworth as an individual, speaking indirectly of his own self. Wordsworth's single, unique self is the implied basis for the unity of *The Prelude*, just as it was for Burke's philosophical work.

There is, however, an implicit contradiction here in Burke's simultaneous claim to be considering the sublime from a "particular" and "single" point of view, and his ability to make generalizations about "our" ideas on the sublime on that basis. The ideal of uniqueness imperils the interchangeability of experience implied in the collective "we." The communal or social is in fact threatened by the premises of this individualist argument. Wordsworth shares with Burke a faith in his ability to generalize about human experience based upon his own experience, but as in Burke's case we can see a latent contradiction in his terms in *The Prelude*:

> Points have we all of us within our souls
> Where all stand single; this I feel, and make
> Breathings for incommunicable powers;
> But is not each man a memory to himself? (3.185–88)

The collective "we all" contrasts oddly with the claim that everyone is "single" in sharing the attribute of uniqueness. It is not quite clear how we can reconcile the singular individual and the plural collective.

Wordsworth's own uneasiness on this point is marked by two things. Firstly, Wordsworth feels he cannot embody what he is saying in language. His subject here "in the main / Lies far hidden from the reach of words" and so represents a purely subjective reality that cannot be embodied in public language. Defined as a surplus or surfeit, his individuality cannot be represented in a public vocabulary. He is forced therefore to "make breathings," not being able to speak articulately about the subject. He also ends this meditation with a question, a sign of his own uncertainty. He does not answer his own question, and turns away from such speculation back to his own autobiography, saying, "A Traveller I am / Whose tale is only of himself" (3.194–95). His subject here threatens to lead him to areas of unbounded speculation, so he returns to the certainty of his own single self. In the final analysis, Wordsworth is here only sure of the singleness of his own self, not of other people's selves.

The final question in these lines is, however, an odd and disturbing one. The image of each man being a "memory to himself" turns the exercise of writing autobiography into a self-reflexive exercise. The question mark turns what in other contexts is an affirmation of faith into a moment of doubt. This line raises the spectral image of an isolation that is made explicit in other places in *The Prelude.*

In the final book of *The Prelude* Wordsworth links the idea of singleness with the faculty of imagination and explicitly expresses the isolation that such a view implies.

> Here must though be, O Man!
> Power to thyself; no helper hast thou here;
> Here keepest thou in singleness thy state:
> No other can divide with thee thy work:
> No secondary hand can intervene
> To fashion this ability; 'tis thine,
> The prime and vital principle is thine
> In the recesses of thy nature, far
> From any reach of outward fellowship
> Else is not thine at all. (14.209–18)

The reference here to "the recesses of thy nature" recalls the feeling that Wordsworth had of his subject lying "far hidden from the reach of words." The idea of singleness for Wordsworth connotes a laudable individuality that lies beyond the reach of language. This quotation, however, underlines that not only does each person's singleness make it impossible to convey subjective experience in language, it also cuts the individual off from other people, as one is "far / From the reach of outward fellowship." This phrase reworks the phrase *far hidden from the reach of words,* substituting the idea of "fellowship" or community for language.

Wordsworth's term for community, *fellowship,* invokes a range of connotations, from the religious associations of communion and holy orders to secular images of intimacy. Wordsworth invokes fellowship at the same time as he undermines its possibility in the face of singleness or individuality and suggests that his singleness makes fellowship an unobtainable ideal. He is experiencing the impossibility of representing community when one accepts the premise of the autonomous individual.

Wordsworth acknowledges in these lines how the ideal of the autonomous individual, who is "a power to himself" without reference to values of reciprocity or interdependence, threatens community. The celebration of isolate individualism can modulate very easily, as it did in the Victorian period, into laments for the alienation and isolation of the individual. Matthew Arnold's poetry, for instance, reworks such themes in ways that underscore their social cost. In later autobiographical writings, the double loss here of the presence of God and human fellowship is seen as cause for lament rather than celebration.

The idea that the individual has "recesses" into which he or she can retire from society is important for Wordsworth. The term indicates to what extent experiences of nature for Wordsworth are at base a retreat into secure recesses that ultimately turn experiences of nature into experiences of his self. Renato Poggioli has termed this Romantic form of pastoral "a new Narcissus" in which the "pastoral becomes the vehicle for solipsism" (Poggioli, 30). Despite his love of humanity, celebrated in book 8, one of his most frequent comments is how he left the noisy companionship of his peers to retire into the solitude of nature. For instance, Wordsworth says that when he was an undergraduate at Cambridge he often left the town to escape into solitude:

> Oft when the dazzling show no longer new
> Had ceased to dazzle, ofttimes did I quit
> My comrades, leave the crowd, buildings and groves
> And as I paced alone the level fields
> Far from those lovely sights and sounds sublime
> With which I had been conversant, the mind
> Drooped not; but there into herself returning,
> With prompt rebound seemed fresh as heretofore. (3.90–97)

Wordsworth's move away from "the crowd" is double here. He literally leaves the town of Cambridge, but this literal movement also stands for a more figurative retirement into his own mind. He returns in memory to the landscapes of his childhood, retiring into his own mind as an escape from the "dazzle" of urban life. The contrast between his solitude and the noise of the crowd, and the contrast between "the level fields" and the mountainous landscapes of the Lake District, help both reinforce Wordsworth's sense of his difference from his setting and reinforce his individuality.

Such passages as this help underscore how *The Prelude* is framed as an anti-urban retreat into an idealized memory of the landscape and corroborate Williams's account in *The Country and the City* of the inward turn of representations of nature. *The Prelude* begins as an escape from "the vast city" (1.7) and the "unnatural self" (1.21), casting the city as an antinatural, anti-individual force. Given England's increasing urbanization in the nineteenth century, such a frame places Wordsworth at odds with the major social developments of his time. Images of the landscape in *The Prelude* thus represent a deliberate turn away from England's rapid industrialization and urbanization, and make nature the site of nostalgia for a threatened sense of community or, in Wordsworth's terms, fellowship. Despite Jonathan Bate's recent attempt to rehabilitate Wordsworth for the ecological movement in *Romantic Ecology*, this is not a very promising basis for social criticism. Bate argues that Wordsworth's poetry embodies an anti-utilitarian vision of "human community" (Bate 1992, 29). Wordsworth's experience of nature, far from reinforcing community, seems more to emphasize his own singleness and isolation.

Wordsworth experiences the contrast between his singleness and the crowd as an affirmation of his self, as he does in the blind beggar episode in book 7. Just as his mind turned round "with the might of waters" in that episode, here he "returns into himself," experiencing his individuality in opposition to the "dazzle" of the crowd. Wordsworth's sense of himself, then, depends upon a contrast between his consciousness and its social setting. His individuality is asserted by a deliberate rejection of the social context and a rechanneling of his energies into internal meditation. Wordsworth here enacts the displacement of the social to which McGann has referred.

I wish here to examine the movement of thought in the blind beggar episode in some detail, as it will serve as a model for the larger pattern behind *The Prelude*, a model that pits Wordsworth's sense of himself as a single individual against the noise and dazzle of the crowd. Wordsworth

opens the episode with an explicit contrast between himself, the solitary
individual, and the crowd:

> How oft, amid those overflowing streets,
> Have I gone forward with the crowd, and said
> Unto myself, "The face of every one
> That passes by me is a mystery!"
> Thus have I looked, nor ceased to look, oppressed
> By thoughts of what and whither, when and how
> Until the shapes before my eyes became
> A second-sight procession, such as glides
> over still mountains, or appears in dreams;
> And once, far-travelled in such a mood, beyond
> The realm of common indication, lost
> Amid the moving pageant, I was smitten
> Abruptly, with the view (a sight not rare)
> Of a blind Beggar who, with upright face,
> Stood, propped against a wall, upon his chest
> Wearing a written paper, to explain
> His story, whence he came, and who he was.
> Caught by the spectacle my mind turned round
> As with the might of waters; an apt type
> This label seemed of the utmost we can know
> Both of ourselves and of the universe;
> And on the shape of that unmoving man,
> His steadfast face and sightless eyes, I gazed
> As if admonished from another world. (7.626–49)

Just as Wordsworth finds in the figure of the blind beggar an "apt
type" for the human condition, so for the purposes of this study the inter-
action between Wordsworth and his subject here will stand as a typical
moment in nineteenth-century autobiography. Wordsworth in this
episode reaches a limit that informs all the autobiographical narratives I
will analyze in this study, as he tries to come to terms with the presence of
a larger society but is forced to generalize about the human condition
instead in terms of individual figures with whom he can sympathize on a
personal level. We can see in Wordsworth's reactions to the mass of
humanity an implicit difficulty that will become crucial to Victorian autobiography. Stated bluntly, the problem is that Wordsworth, as a solitary
individual, can sympathize only with other individuals, not with large

groups of people, who must be dehumanized under terms such as *crowd* or *mass*.

It is the single figure of the beggar who attracts his attention in this episode, a figure who in his affliction is a more obvious candidate for sympathy than the crowd passing him by. Wordsworth experiences the crowd only as an "oppression" and sees the faces he meets as a "mystery" rather than as a "volume" telling its own story, as did the faces of his neighbors at home (5.67). The crowd loses its tangibility for Wordsworth, becoming a product of the imagination like a "second sight procession" seen in a dream. In this state of mind Wordsworth loses any sense of connection with the people he sees, being "beyond the reach" of the usual human pathos that engages his imagination.

In his description Wordsworth's actual movement through the London streets becomes a metaphor for how far he has "travelled" from the love of humanity that he celebrates in the next book, book 8. In this frame of mind he is "smitten" by the beggar like a physical blow, an abrupt admonition for his lack of humanity. However, as Wordsworth makes clear in the lines that precede this episode, the crowd is in some ways essential for his appreciation of the single figure of the beggar, acting as it does as a contrasting background.

> As the black storm upon the mountaintop
> Sets off the sunbeam in the valley, so
> That huge fermenting mass of humankind
> Serves as a solemn background, or relief,
> To single forms and objects, whence they draw,
> For feeling and contemplative regard,
> More inherent liveliness and power. (7.619–25)

The "single" figure of the beggar is in Wordsworth's account in a parasitic relationship with the crowd, drawing "liveliness and power" from the contrast between his individuality and the "fermenting mass." If it were not for the presence of the crowd, the beggar would not stand out so clearly. However, it is not the beggar in fact who is feeding off the contrast here, but Wordsworth, whose presence is all but excised by the anonymity of the phrase on how the "huge and fermenting mass" serves as a background "for feeling and contemplative regard." The presence of a viewer is introduced parenthetically and barely interrupts the flow of the verse, but it signals the all but invisible presence of Wordsworth as the third term in this relationship. It is Wordsworth himself, the only other single figure in this scene, who derives "liveliness and power" from the contrast between the beggar and the crowd. However, Wordsworth does not name himself as the beneficiary of this contrast, because he himself feels guilty about the use to which he is putting the crowd.

Wordsworth uses the words *smitten* and *admonished* to describe the effect of this scene upon him, words that suggest retribution for a guilty act. Wordsworth feels himself to have done violence to the humanity of the crowd, and experiences the sight of the beggar as a return upon himself of his own thoughtlessness. Wordsworth obviously feels uneasy with his lack of sympathy for the crowd that passes him by, and he is distressed that with their faces, unlike the faces he knows in his home district, he can connect no story. The beggar strikes him with particular force because, unlike the "mysterious" faces passing him by, he wears his autobiography upon his chest for all to see. However, the beggar does not here act as a bridge between Wordsworth and the crowd, but rather reminds him of "another world" quite apart from the London streets through which he is walking. Rather than make Wordsworth realize the humanity of the crowd, the sight of the beggar reinforces his sense of separation from the world of the city.

Wordsworth's primary experience in this episode is one of limitation. In this I agree with Paul Jay's analysis of this moment in *Being in the Text*. Jay points out that "Wordsworth inscribes his sense of the limits of his autobiographical project in the 'emblem' which is the Beggar's note" (Jay 1984, 90–91), so that the beggar becomes an external representation of an internal limitation. However, I would amend Jay's further comments, as he links the idea of limitation with his argument that Wordsworth in *The Prelude* is engaged in a process of limitless self-analysis. Jay says that the "limitations serve less to cut off the project than to interminably extend it" (64). I disagree fundamentally with this point. It is difficult to see how a limitation could serve to "interminably extend" an analysis. Rather, such a moment as this shows the outer limit of Wordsworth's self, and thus of his autobiography. It is my argument that Wordsworth at this moment experiences here as a limitation precisely the aspect of his subject that he elsewhere celebrates, that his "project" concerns only himself.

Far from seeing his self-analysis as limitless, Wordsworth invokes the unity and boundedness of his self as a way of defining his subject and setting limits on the scope of his project. Wordsworth chooses to write about himself because he feels therein lies a certain and definite subject that will allow him to hone his own poetic powers before moving on to bigger and better themes. Jay is of course right to argue that Wordsworth finds the process of writing such a poem more difficult than he expected, but he nonetheless persisted in seeing the subject of *The Prelude* as "single and of determined bounds."

In the blind beggar episode, however, these bounds are experienced as constricting limits. By choosing to write only about himself, Wordsworth has excluded a great deal of other possible subjects. For instance, Wordsworth describes how at one phase in his life he studied his own society and tried to "anatomise the frame of social life" (11.280). However, he does not pursue this topic, expressing instead regret that he cannot encompass this subject within the theme of *The Prelude*.

> Share with me, Friend! the wish
> That some dramatic tale, endued with shapes
> Livelier, and flinging out less guarded words
> Than suit the work we fashion, might set forth
> What then I learned, or think I learned,
> of truth. (11.282–86)

Although Wordsworth here bemoans the fact that he cannot include the results of his social studies in his present work, he refers to his activities at this point in his life as "misguided and misguiding." The wider social conditions of his time are seen by Wordsworth as inappropriate subject matter for *The Prelude*, and his research at this point as a distraction from the true path, his love of nature. Wordsworth here in *The Prelude* makes explicit the move that McGann has described as implicit in "Tintern Abbey": he eschews analysis of his social context for an exploration of his own states of consciousness. Wordsworth implies that his researches at this time might make a suitable topic for a work with larger scope, like the proposed philosophical work *The Excursion*, perhaps, but it is disturbing that Wordsworth was never able to write this poem. The writing of *The Prelude* turned out to be the work itself, a work within which a larger vision of Wordsworth's own society could not find a place. Wordsworth is here naming the limit of his own autobiographical project, a limitation that leads him to see his fellow countrymen only in terms of a "fermenting mass" and as a topic unsuitable for his purposes. He names here the loss of the social context as the price of his autobiographical project.

This is not the only point in the London sections of *The Prelude* where Wordsworth has an experience of the limits of his own ability to come to terms with subjects that exceed the scope of his poem. Another such moment occurs when for the first time he hears "the voice of woman utter blasphemy" (7.385). Just as in the blind beggar episode, Wordsworth experiences at this moment a sense of separation or isolation:

> I shuddered, for a barrier seemed at once
> Thrown in, that from humanity divorced
> Humanity, splitting the race of man
> In twain, yet leaving the same outward form. (7.388–91)

Wordsworth here faces a sense of internal contradiction that he represents in terms of a split in humanity itself. His own idealized image of woman cannot come to terms with the reality of a woman who blasphemes. As in the blind beggar episode, he represents the contrast in terms of two different worlds. The "barrier" that Wordsworth encounters here is the same boundary that he celebrates in book 1, the sense of himself as a single individual. Suddenly Wordsworth comes across an image that is not susceptible to the sympathetic identification that is the usual basis for his "love of humanity." He is suddenly faced with a symbol of the limits of his own self. Wordsworth's poem comes to an abrupt halt as he finds himself faced with a theme profoundly disruptive of the tenor of his autobiographical poem.

> Later years
> Brought to such a spectacle a milder sadness,
> Feelings of pure commiseration, grief
> For the individual and the overthrow
> Of her soul's beauty: farther I was then
> But seldom led, or wished to go; in truth
> The sorrow of the passion stopped me there. (7.393–99)

Wordsworth literally "stops" here and, taking a deep breath, resumes, "less moved," the "argument" of *The Prelude.* Just as in the blind beggar episode he has "travelled…beyond the realm of common indication" and must be brought back to his theme, so here he finds himself exceeding the scope of his subject. In this case, however, rather than have a single figure appear and remind him of his theme, his single self, Wordsworth stops himself and acknowledges that he has reached a limit. He cannot come to terms with the figure of the blaspheming woman and can only reconcile her existence by positing a radical dichotomy "splitting the race of man in twain." Wordsworth here experiences a limit to his benignly egotistical method of sympathetic identification, just as he does when looking at crowds. He comes perilously close to naming himself as a split subject, as his usual method of figuring women as idealized sites of community and unity breaks down. Wordsworth's definition of himself as single is threatened in this episode, and in his experiences in cities generally. His isolate individualism threatens to bifurcate into mutually exclusive halves. These are moments in *The Prelude* when his individualism comes under pressure from social forces beyond his control.

My account of Wordsworth's lack of sympathy for this woman or for the crowd contradicts his statement in book 8 that his love of nature led him to a love of man. However, if we look at what elements of humanity Wordsworth is actually celebrating in book 8, it becomes obvious that he is talking about the same kind of sympathy as that at work in the blind beggar episode. Wordsworth celebrates the sight of individual shepherds, shepherds moreover seen against the contrasting background of nature, set off by this background just as the blind beggar is set off against the crowds of London. The book opens with an implicit contrast between St. Bartholomew's fair in London and a small rural fair in Switzerland. The contrast between the huge mountains and the humans made "through utter weakness pitiably dear" (7.61) by the majestic background makes the Swiss fair more appealing to Wordsworth.

Similarly, Wordsworth is attracted to shepherds by the idea of the single figure dwarfed by natural forces or, as he puts it, "man suffering amid awful Powers and Forms" (7.165). This contrast makes the shepherd "a solitary object and sublime" (8.272). Wordsworth celebrates in book 8 the same subject as in book 7, "those individual sights / Of courage, or integrity, or truth" that "set off by foil / Appeared more touching" (7.599–600). What Wordsworth means by "love of humanity" in this book is not an appreciation of humans in society, but single, solitary individuals given pathos by the contrast between the powers around them and their own slender resources.

Wordsworth himself indicates that in his portrayal of the shepherds he is setting up an idealized image of human nature that has little to do with the mundane existence of most people. He is defensive about his image of the shepherd, challenging the unsympathetic reader to call it "a shadow, a delusion" (7.296). What he celebrates here, he indicates, is not the literal reality of shepherds, it is the "spirit" of man, what he called earlier "the human creature's absolute self" (7.123). However, this idealized image is damagingly distant from the kind of scene he sees in London, an image that is "purified, / Removed, and to a distance that

was fit" (8.305) and is "a sure safeguard and defense" against the pressures of "the ordinary world / In which we traffic."

Wordsworth's appreciation of the shepherd leads him to deprecate
"the deformities of crowded life" (7.688). He associates autonomy and
individualism with rural life, as opposed to the "blank confusion" (7.722)
of the city. As Raymond Williams indicates, nature functions here as a
compensation for and displacement of industrialization. Wordsworth is
by temperament repelled by crowds and cities, because he can find nothing with which to sympathize in them. When he talks of a "love of Man"
in book 8, then, he is talking about a very idealized image of people in
their individual, not their collective and urban, state. One reason why
Wordsworth finds shepherds so appealing is that they in their solitary and
withdrawn lives represent an indirect image of himself. He himself values
solitude and a close relationship with the natural landscape, and this is
precisely what shepherds represent for him. It is no wonder, then, that he
can sympathize with shepherds but not with the crowd. This does, however, place a damaging limitation on his ability to come to terms with life
in increasingly industrialized and crowded nineteenth-century England.

The effect of the blind beggar episode is not to provoke Wordsworth
to consider the dehumanizing effect of cities or industrialization upon people, and thus perhaps to reflect upon the reasons for their condition, but
rather to lead him to meditate upon the significance of such episodes as
compared with those that rise "full-formed" from nature. The scene as a
whole has the effect of turning Wordsworth back in upon himself, powerfully and in some ways violently reminding him of his own individuality. As
in "Tintern Abbey," the sight does not lead him to reflect upon the social
significance of what he sees; rather, it emphasizes his own act of imaginative appropriation. The sight of the beggar causes his mind to turn round
"as with the might of the waters," and in this overwhelming reaction the
crowd becomes lost in internal meditation. The effect of the single figure
of the beggar is in fact to reinforce the singleness of Wordsworth's own
self. It is for this reason that the beggar is described as an apt "type." The
beggar is typical in the sense that he represents all we can know of the universe, the inclusiveness of Wordsworth's "we" making the beggar an
Everyman, but he is also a symbol for Wordsworth of the limits of his own
self-knowledge. On this level the beggar has an obviously personal significance. The beggar and his autobiography stand for Wordsworth and his
own autobiographical project.

The movement in this episode from a contemplation of the crowd,
led by the sight of a single figure, to an internal meditation, is typical of

the general pattern behind all the significant "spots of time" described in *The Prelude*. The net effect of this movement is to confirm the existence of William Wordsworth, the single, sensitive, observer, but to do so in apparently selfless terms. Wordsworth links the crowd to landscape when introducing this episode by using the analogy of the black cloud and the sunbeam. Landscape is an apt analogy here because in his descriptions of the effect of landscape Wordsworth follows the same general pattern as he does in describing the contrast between the beggar and the crowd. His descriptions of landscape inevitably lead to introspective passages on the workings of his own mind. In these passages it is the idea of a contrast between a single shape and a mass that triggers the introspection.

All Wordsworth's epiphanic moments in *The Prelude* are built upon this kind of contrast between noise and crowds and quiet solitude. For instance, in the skating episode in book 1, Wordsworth relates how "not seldom from the uproar I retired / Into a silent bay" (1.447–48) and there would experience a tranquility and solitude that contrasted markedly with the "tumult" of his games with his friends. Wordsworth moves from a description of the noisy companionship of his friends to the silence of "solitary cliffs" and a tranquility that is like "a dreamless sleep." The solitude and tranquility of nature stand for Wordsworth's own self-sufficient isolation. Wordsworth repeatedly expresses a preference for the tranquility and solitude of a lone communion with nature to the company of his friends or the crowded streets of London:

> Hence life, and change, and beauty, solitude
> More active even than 'best society'—
> Society made sweet as solitude
> By silent and unobtrusive sympathies. (2.294–97)

There is an implicit confusion of terms in these lines that helps explain how Wordsworth could claim that a love of nature could lead to a love of man. The idea of a solitary communion with nature in these lines becomes confused with the idea of human society because Wordsworth sees nature as a semidivine and active agent in his life. The "silent and unobtrusive" sympathies of an "active" nature are in Wordsworth's mind analogous to the effects of "best society" and by an extension of this thought come to replace the very need for society itself. Nature's "silent and unobtrusive sympathies" are, after all, much preferable to the noisy company of real people. This conclusion is implicit in the opening lines of the poem, where Wordsworth talks of the "fellowship" with nature in solitude in contrast with the "noisy crew" of his friends (1.479). Where *fellowship* earlier referred to human intimacy, here it refers to a solitary appreciation of nature. The early books of *The Prelude,* rather than being reminiscences about his boyhood friends, are rather the story of "How Nature by extrinsic passion first / Peopled the mind with forms sublime or fair" (1.545–46). The use of "peopled" to describe the effect of nature on his mind is another indication of how human society is displaced in the poem by natural landscapes.

The landscape in Wordsworth's poetry functions as a compensation for the loss of community attendant upon his individualist ideology. Wordsworth's autobiography is "peopled" by landscapes that confirm his individuality and replace his contemporary social and historical context. His use of a term like *peopled* represents the vestige of the social context that cannot be completely erased. As Jerome McGann points out, while social concerns are displaced, they are not entirely erased; however, "their presence is maintained in such an oblique way that readers...have passed by them by almost without notice" (McGann 1983, 85–86). It remained for later generations, particularly the Victorians, to confront directly the social cost to literature of the loss of community recorded in *The Prelude.*

Wordsworth does himself at one point muse, "I was taught to feel, perhaps too much / The self-sufficing power of solitude" (2.76–77), but this moment of doubt is far outweighed by the number of times he expresses regret that "Full oft quiet and exalted thoughts / Of loneliness gave way to empty noise / And superficial pastimes" (3.207–9). For Wordsworth, his most memorable moments are when he experiences a unity with the natural landscape rather than with fellow human beings. As we shall see in the case of John Ruskin, this inability to come to terms with other people was felt as a damaging limitation. Ruskin was torn between the role of "prophet of nature," as Wordsworth and Coleridge had been before him, and the role of social critic. The two roles were in many ways antithetical, thanks to the sensibility he inherited from the Romantics.

It is the double limitation on the self that Wordsworth describes in the blind beggar episode that informs the rest of this study. Wordsworth links the limits of his own self-knowledge to his lack of knowledge of other people by describing the faces in the crowd as a "mystery" to him, and then turns this experience into a purely personal debate about his own memory. Wordsworth's attempt to understand the mystery of his fellow beings in the crowd is defeated, and so he turns to an inward meditation on the limits of self-knowledge. Here too, however, he finds that his knowledge is limited, so that the blind beggar's text can stand for an apt type "of the utmost we can know / Both of ourselves and of the universe." The autobiographer finds his knowledge limited in both directions, so that it becomes a problem how to assert any positive connection between the insubstantial self and any sense of a wider human community. It is this kind of defeat that was the most troubling aspect of the Romantic legacy for Victorian writers.

In the next two chapters I will examine Romantic representations of subjectivity that bespeak the cost of the Romantic autobiographical project. In chapter 2 I analyze the image of the Specter of Brocken as a symbol for the autobiographical text in Coleridge's poetry and De Quincey's prose. In chapter 3 I compare Mary and Percy Bysshe Shelley's attitudes to autobiography, particularly Mary Shelley's depiction of the cost of the autobiographical exclusion of the social.

CHAPTER TWO

THE LIMINAL SUBJECT OF ROMANTIC AUTOBIOGRAPHY

Metaphors of ghostliness in Romantic and Victorian autobiography express the liminal status of the writing subject. The Romantic subject is created by the dichotomy between an "inner" self and an "outer" world of material objects. Reflecting the Cartesian divorce of mind from the sensory world of the body, Romantic and Victorian authors represent themselves as ghostly presences in their texts, inhabiting neither this world nor an afterlife, but a limbo between the two. They inhabit a space poised ambiguously between the private and the public, unable to believe completely in the pristine autonomy of the self or to give complete credence to a material world devoid of spirit.

Metaphors of ghostliness betray the anxiety that accompanied the attempt to represent the self in the text. Shari Benstock suggests in *The Private Self* that autobiography "reveals the impossibility of its own dream: what begins on the presumption of self-knowledge ends in the creation of a fiction that covers over the premises of its construction" (Benstock 1988, 11). Benstock does not suggest a particular location or history for this suggestive characterization of autobiography. In this chapter I will examine the creation of a fiction "that covers over the premises of its construction" in the poetry of Coleridge and the prose of De Quincey. In particular the liminal state of the autobiographical subject betrays the impossibility of the self-knowledge upon which it is predicated. This liminal state is what Benstock has characterized as the "seam" of writing, a space that she describes in terms of a Lacanian version of the unconscious in which "the unconscious is thus not the lower depths of the conscious...but rather an inner seam, a space between 'inside' and 'outside'—it is the space of difference, the gap that the drive toward unity of self can never close" (12). Similarly, Dalia Judovitz, in the context of Descartes' autobiographical texts, has referred to "the absent or empty space of the one who represents" (Judovitz 1988, 37). Benstock's description suggests the liminal status of the autobiographical subject extremely well. The subject is neither inner nor outer, but located in a nether world between the two. The creation of the inner space of the autonomous individual, the Romantic concept of inwardness, initiated the "drive toward unity" described by Benstock, as writers sought to overcome the gap between inner and outer, a gap they could never close. While attempting to define the single or unitary self, autobiographers also revealed "gaps...between the individual and the social" (11). In the Victorian period, this sense of self-contradiction and estrangement from the social became more and more acute, leading to the claustrophobic images of incarceration and isolation in Matthew Arnold's poetry.

Metaphors of ghostliness in the Romantic and Victorian periods self-consciously locate the writing subject in this liminal space. The dichotomy of inner and outer is translated in many Romantic poems into a contrast between the natural and the supernatural, where the writing subject is a supernatural and ghostly presence in the natural world. What must be emphasized here is that, as I discuss in my account of repression in the chapters 5 and 6, this dichotomizing helped produce the autobiographical subject itself. The split between the natural and the supernatural mirrors the divorce of the individual from the social, with the consequent derealization of the subject.

The autobiographical poetry of Coleridge and the prose of De Quincey register most strongly the effects of isolation and alienation attendant upon this derealization of the subject. In her recent study of the collaboration between Coleridge and Wordsworth, Susan Eilenberg has called Coleridge "a self-doubting parasite, writing, as he lives, in the margins of other men's texts and other men's lives" (Eilenberg 1992, x). This judgment is unnecessarily caustic but captures well Coleridge and De Quincey's marginality and isolation, and their dependence upon other peoples' texts as authorizing fictions. Experiences of ghostliness and marginality constitute the most fundamental subject matter of their autobiographies. These autobiographers repress the knowledge of their texts' fictional grounds of existence, and express their anxiety over the status of the self through images of ghostliness. As Eilenberg says,

"Coleridge's words live a ghostly existence in exile from both stable subjects and stable objects, unsure of their relation to things in themselves and liable to semiotic subversion and invasion" (p. x). In other words, Coleridge, like De Quincey, inhabits a linguistic limbo between the derealized subject and a world of objects.

Autobiographical texts enact the quest for a fictional and idealized unity that Jacques Lacan describes in terms of the "mirror stage." The specter in the text is both a symbol for the writing subject and the status of the autobiographical text itself. Through metaphors of ghostliness, autobiographers reveal the impossibility of the dream of a communion with an idealized self-image. The phantom in the text stands for the displaced desire of the autobiographical subject, diverted from social toward purely individual gratification. The ghost represents what Arnold in the Victorian period described in terms of the unspeakable desire after the "buried life."

Autobiographical texts in the Romantic and Victorian periods thus play out a drama of identity and difference that generates the liminal writing subject. They enact a pursuit, like Frankenstein's pursuit of his monster, that can never be concluded except in the annihilation of the subjectivity that produced it. This subjectivity is above all marked by its origins in a text, which metaphors of ghostliness betray. The self is a fiction created in the writing of the text. As an ambiguous blending of the inner and private self and the public realm of language and publication, the ghost in the text becomes a symbol for the status of the autobiography in the world beyond the subject's consciousness. Where Wordsworth used nature to represent his subjectivity, the authors discussed in this chapter locate themselves in a much more overtly textualized universe. Even Wordsworth, however, occasionally betrayed the fictional origins of his autobiographical project. For instance, the status of the autobiography as text emerges in Wordsworth's description of the blind beggar episode.

Frances Ferguson in *Wordsworth: Language as Counter-Spirit* describes the blind beggar episode in terms of a blending of inner and outer when she asserts that "the Blind Beggar episode operates both as an insight into the alienness of external form, and as a testimony to the power of external form for creating the very possibility of internality" (Ferguson 1977, 145). Ferguson's comments here underscore the way in which *inner* and *outer* are mutually reinforcing terms. The designation of the beggar as outer creates the possibility of Wordsworth's inner space. Ferguson, however, equates terms that in Romantic and Victorian terms are seen as opposites. Romantic and Victorian authors maintain the distinction between interior and exterior as part of their ideology. They deploy a subjectivity that depends upon the distinction between the internal experience of the autonomous individual and the external phenomena of the social. The internal is for them associated with the private and intimate, the external with the public and anonymous.

Ferguson's comments help underline how these supposedly antithetical terms threaten to coalesce, and how their separation helps open up a space for the writing subject. The difference between inner and outer is both problematic and the premise upon which autobiography depends. As I argued in the Introduction to this book, the ideal of inwardness creates a fruitful dilemma for Romantic poets in opening up a gap between the individual and the social. Looking at the blind beggar, Wordsworth is powerfully reminded of his own individuality and finds confirmation for the existence of what I referred to in the previous chapter as his "single" self. The distinction between this inwardness and the social life of the communal world was an essential component in the generation of the autobiographical consciousness. This consciousness presented itself as single, unitary and rational. However, this unity was maintained by repressing the knowledge of the interdependence of its terms, a knowledge that nonetheless surfaced in oblique ways.

The blind beggar registers the profound disempowerment that lay behind this form of subjectivity. The blind beggar is an emblem of imperfection, in that he cannot read his own autobiography, just as he cannot, as Wordsworth cannot, "read" the faces of the people passing him. Blindness in this episode is linked to the reading of texts both by the presence of the narrative on the beggar's chest and by Wordsworth's earlier association of the faces of his neighbors in the Lake District with books. Single figures such as the beggar thus represent for Wordsworth the inadequacy of his own text. He betrays his anxiety here that he will not be able to decipher his own text, and that others will not be able to read his text either. The creation of his inner space has effectively cut him off from those around him.

Wordsworth through the blind beggar represents the precarious status of the subject of Romantic autobiography. Another striking symbol of this liminal subject is to be found in the Spectre of Brocken. The peculiar natural phenomenon from the Hartz mountains of Germany known as "the Brocken-Specter" was an apparition that appealed profoundly to many writers in the early nineteenth century. References to the specter, or phenomena like the specter, can be found in Hogg, Wordsworth, De Quincey, and Coleridge.

For these writers the natural phenomenon of the "Brocken-Specter," in which an enlarged image of the viewer was cast onto a mist bank by the level rays of the rising or setting sun, like a projector throwing a picture onto a screen, apparently serves to unite the internal and external representation of self. The specter is a replica of the perceiving self. The mist bank acts as a huge mirror to the viewer, suddenly confronting the unsuspecting wanderer with a huge facsimile of himself. This figure, like the blind beggar for Wordsworth, serves in the text as an emblem for a self that has at the same time both an inner and an outer origin. While all four writers find the specter an appealing image, they all four interpret the significance of this admonitory vision in different ways. I will in this chapter explore the significance of the Specter of Brocken as a figure of autobiography in the poetry of Samuel Taylor Coleridge and the prose of Thomas De Quincey.

The Specter of Brocken is a particularly compelling image for De Quincey and Coleridge, because it provides a striking external representation of their own subjective experiences. The Brocken-Specter in both Coleridge's "Constancy to an Ideal Object" and De Quincey's *Autobiographic Sketches* is a "figure" of autobiography in the sense used by Avrom Fleishman in *Figures of Autobiography*, a metaphor that "expands the self beyond its original confines" (Fleishman 1983, 33). As Fleishman says, the term *figure* has a "pleasant ambiguity" in that it refers to "individuals as well as verbal expressions" (50). The specter thus functions as a symbol within the text for the act of writing autobiography itself, and dramatizes the text's ambiguous relationship with the wider social world.

The verbal figure in the text is the shade or ghost of the individual writer who attempts to embody his or her self in the medium of language. The Specter of Brocken, as a ghostly presence standing for the writer in the text, also registers the subversive doubts that plague both Coleridge and De Quincey while they write about themselves. They may be able to represent the self in the text, yet both text and the self have an ephemeral status. There is in this self-doubt the germ of the radical uncertainty about the self that was to afflict Victorian poets so deeply and led so many writers to bemoan the divorce of the individual from the social.

The Specter of Brocken is thus not simply a figure *of* autobiography, but also a symbol *for* autobiography. The specter represents the autobiographical text as poised between the purely personal and the social. It therefore registers a historical moment in the definition of the autonomous self when autobiography could be seen as an at least potentially social form. The specter, thanks to the halo around its head, raises the ghostly possibility of a religious and communal quest that is theoretically equally accessible to all. The specter thus stands for the possibility of community as communion, as a spiritual union of believers that transcends the limits of the mortal. The specter represents a residual religious ideal that was gradually being effaced by secular individualism.

Thanks to its supernatural connotations, the specter introduces a theological element into the representation of the self. For Coleridge the specter represents a religious and transcendent ideal that can overcome even death. Like Wordsworth finds in nature, Coleridge finds in the specter a guarantee of the continuity of his own consciousness in this phenomenon. His attitude to the specter is similar to Wordsworth's faith in the natural landscape as a guarantor of the transcendence of his own individuality. For De Quincey, as we shall see, the specter stands more for the possibility of enacting one's own emotions through a surrogate figure or double. Like the blind beggar, the specter serves as an emblem of the autobiographical project for both writers, yet, unlike the beggar, this figure represents the power of external forms to "expand the self beyond its original confines" (Fleishman 1983, 33) rather than the limited possibilities of the text as an expression of the isolate single self. The specter dramatizes Coleridge's and De Quincey's diffuse sense of self that could expand to include other peoples' words as easily as their own.

In the autobiographies of Coleridge and De Quincey this transcendence takes a peculiar and idiosyncratic form. Both Coleridge and De Quincey are inveterate plagiarizers, and in both the *Biographia Literaria* and the *Autobiography* they borrow heavily from other sources. They show a willingness to transgress the legal imperative of copyright, which insists that authors respect the boundaries of their own and others' texts, and consistently blur the distinctions between their own words and those of others. Rather than condemn them for these plagiarisms, I argue in this chapter that we should understand these instances as symptoms of a residual faith in the communal nature of experience. Like Augustine in the *Confessions,* these authors duplicate the experience of others within their texts. They transgress the boundaries between texts as the unique property of autonomous individuals that were legislated in the form of copyright. They enact what Eilenberg has referred to as "the relationship between a poet and what he takes to be his second or other self" in which the poet "mistakes" his words for another's, or another's words for his (Eilenberg 1992, 215). The Specter of Brocken is just such a "second or other self" that dramatizes Coleridge's and De Quincey's "relationship of mistake" to other peoples' words.

Coleridge's poem "Constancy to an Ideal Object" takes the Specter of Brocken as its subject. The poem places the specter in the context of a pressing personal dilemma that is introduced in philosophical and general terms. The poem is a meditation, an internal debate on a philosophical issue that is supposed to act as a guide for others and thus serve some useful public purpose. Although the poem tackles a broad philosophical issue, it obviously does so in personal terms, and yet the first-person pronoun occurs relatively infrequently. To what, then, do we owe the sense that this is an autobiographical exercise? The personal tone of this poem, despite the avoidance of "I," can be accounted for in terms of its concluding image, the Specter of Brocken. In the context of this poem the specter is an indirectly autobiographical image, providing a solution to the personal dilemma that motivated the poem in the first place. Despite several excellent studies of the specter in the context of Coleridge's poetry, I do not feel that the significance of this image has yet been adequately accounted for.

Stephen Prickett in *Coleridge and Wordsworth: The Poetry of Growth* relates Coleridge's treatment of the specter to an expression of "an eerie ambiguity" in the subject's perception of the world, an ambiguity that is paralleled in the eeriness of this strange apparition (Prickett 1970, 23). As Prickett points out, Coleridge's philosophy allotted to the perceiving consciousness an active role in shaping the materials of perception, so that significance in the world both was located "out there" in the world and had an internal source. The boundaries between internal and external in this philosophy are confused and uncertain, resulting in the ambiguity in the poem about the specter's status.

This blurring of boundaries in Coleridge's poem parallels that found in Wordsworth's poetry. For instance, Wordsworth describes the external landscape in *The Prelude* as a "prospect," a vista already framed and arranged for human aesthetic appreciation. This external landscape becomes confused with his own consciousness of self:

Oft in these moments such a holy calm
Would overspread my soul, that bodily eyes
Were utterly forgotten, and what I saw
Appeared like something in myself, a dream
A prospect in the mind. (2.348–52)

The landscape can come to seem "something in myself" at moments such as this, rather than something "out there" in the world.

The external landscape becomes "a prospect in the mind," located ambiguously both within and without his consciousness. As in the blind beggar episode, the external world here becomes a token or emblem of the perceiving consciousness, and what starts off as a description of the world becomes a description of the mind. It is because the landscape is already "shaped" into a "prospect" by some unseen power that such an easy transition from "bodily" to figurative perception is possible.

A difference between Wordsworth and Coleridge can already be detected here, however. Where Wordsworth suggests a fundamental continuity between his self-consciousness and nature, Coleridge in his poem uses the terms *nature* and *thought* as distinct, even opposing, terms.

> Since all that beat about in Nature's range
> Or veer or vanish, why should'st thou remain
> The only constant in a world of change,
> O yearning Thought! that liv'st but in the brain? (1–4)

Coleridge is here emphasizing a disjunction that Wordsworth feels he can transcend. Coleridge suggests that the natural world is far less tangible and dependable than it appears in Wordsworth's account and that there is no such comfortable fit between mind and world as Wordsworth discovers in looking at a "prospect in the mind." Coleridge is more alienated in his experience of nature than Wordsworth, as his thwarted attempts to find a "home" in natural phenomenon for his "yearning thought" show. Coleridge is thus thrown back upon his own self-consciousness by a sense of the difference between world and self where Wordsworth finds a comfortable fit between his own mind and the enlarged consciousness of nature.

The subject of "Constancy to an Ideal Object" is, therefore, Coleridge's consciousness of himself, and of himself as distinct from the world of natural objects. He defines himself in opposition to nature, not in terms of nature. He is, he says, unable to find in the flux of inconstant nature an object that corresponds to his own internal condition. Wordsworth has a similar moment of disillusionment in *The Prelude* when he laments that he is unable to find an object that corresponds exactly to his self-consciousness:

> Oh! Why hath not the Mind
> Some element to stamp her image on
> In nature somewhat nearer to her own?

Why, gifted with such powers to send abroad
Her spirit, must it lodge in shrines so frail? (5.45–49)

Wordsworth, after maintaining that a divine Presence would outlast even the destruction of the landscape, is moved to express dismay at the impermanence of most vehicles for the human mind. His reference to nature here could conceivably extend the idea of "frail shrines" even to the landscape, but the explicit subject of his lament is in fact a human artifact, not the phenomena of nature. He is implicitly contrasting man-made and natural vehicles for the mind, specifically the ephemeral nature of books, to the landscape. For Wordsworth, as the blind beggar episode implies, texts are inadequate embodiments of the mind. It is only in certain sublime landscapes that Wordsworth can find a "type of Eternity."

This is an essential difference both between Wordsworth and Coleridge, and Wordsworth and De Quincey. Just as Coleridge defines transcendence in textual terms through the Specter of Brocken, De Quincey, as we shall see later, redefines Wordsworth's "wise passiveness" in the face of nature into a wise passiveness in terms of texts. Both Coleridge and De Quincey redefine the Wordsworthian vision of a transcendent nature into a vision of the power of the transcendent text. Coleridge even turns Wordsworth's animate nature into a "divine text," showing the power of the text as a transcendent metaphor in his thought.

Prickett in his study of "Constancy to an Ideal Object" identifies as the key term in the poem the idea of creativity, and characterizes the specter as a symbol of artistic creativity. He paraphrases the opening question of the poem as "What permanent value the artist's insight can have amid change and decay?" (Prickett 1970, 24). While it is undoubtedly true that creativity and imagination play an important role, and that the word *make* in the last line of the poem involves an idea of making in the sense of creating, a much more central term seems that announced in the title of the poem: constancy. The idea of creativity narrows the field of the potential audience to people with some creative gift, to artists as a special class, where the ambition of the poet seems to be to speak more broadly to a general audience, in keeping with the idea of a meditation as a guide for others. Coleridge chooses the "enamoured rustic" at the end of his poem as an example of someone "making what he pursues" to illustrate the universality of the situation he is describing here.

Jerome McGann has phrased the question behind the poem more broadly, placing it within the context of Coleridge's fear that "nothing seems dependable or secure around him" and that his pursuit of constancy may be "the ignorant pursuit of an illusion, even a potential disaster" (McGann 1983, 105). McGann's comments help underscore how Coleridge embodies in the specter a deep ontological crisis. He is threatened here by the knowledge that the unity and coherence of his identity may be an illusion, a fiction as ephemeral and insubstantial as the specter, or the text of his poem.

The initial vehicle for Coleridge's meditation is a much more readily accessible human capability than artistic creation, namely, love, and specifically the kind of love that persists even after its object is dead. The term *constancy* in the poem's title thus involves the idea of fidelity, of faith in some person or thing distinct from oneself even when that person has been literally disembodied and made into a phenomenon of memory, a "Thought." It is the persistent, perhaps naive, faith in the existence of something beyond the self, even when no longer physically verifiable, that is the central concern of the poem, and it is a faith that finds its embodiment in the ambiguous figure of the Specter of Brocken.

Coleridge asserts the continuity of something within him in face of the most profound form of change possible for the human individual: death. In this autobiographical poem, as in *The Prelude*, death becomes the most pressing problem for the poet of the self. Constancy is therefore contrasted not just with change, but with the most radical change that can overcome a human. In death the human form is made to "veer or vanish," like all other objects in nature, yet something somehow survives even this radical change. This survival of an ambiguous "something" points to the superiority of human thought or consciousness over nature. This something, as it is in Wordsworth's poetry, is the author's self.

The constancy or coherence Coleridge wishes to stress here resides in the perceiving or remembering self rather than in the object of thought, since this object has been rendered ideal and intangible by death. It is the unnamed subject of the poem, the "I," that provides the unity of thought in contrast to the flux of an inconstant world or the abrupt change in the state of the loved one. The poem is thus indirectly founded upon Coleridge's sense of his undefinable yet persistent sense of himself as an autonomous individual. His inability to rid himself of the memory of the woman is a guarantee of constancy, a guarantee of the coherence of his own self over time. In the contrast between the inner world of thought and the outer world of nature it is thought that exhibits the supreme virtue of constancy, even in the face of death.

Coleridge, unlike Wordsworth, is haunted by a sense of the inadequacy of anything in nature to do justice to the constancy of his thought.

Although nothing survives of the loved one's former physical presence but an intangible "Thought," this survival is seen by Coleridge as in itself a cause for hope. In some way this persistence of memory in the thought of the woman defies death, although perhaps not easily or directly. Coleridge tries to imagine himself past death into the future directly, but cannot:

> Fond Thought! not one of that shining swarm
> Will breathe on thee with life-enkindling breath,
> Till when, like strangers shelt'ring from a storm,
> Hope and Despair meet in the porch of Death!

Thought or memory is defeated by a direct attack on death, and made to seem foolish in such a stark contrast. The situation here is like that in John Clare's "Love Lives Beyond the Tomb," where a faith in the power of love to defeat death is seen as foolish, yet the poet still professes a belief in the "fond, the faithful, and the true." In both poems, the idea of faith or fidelity despite death is seen as the supreme virtue.

The optimism in Coleridge's poem, the persistent "yet" that rescues him from even this apparent defeat by death, comes from his very inability to answer the question he poses to his "Thought"—"And art thou nothing?"—or to decide between competing opposites like Hope and Despair or Thought and Nature. The true subject of the question "And art thou nothing?" is not the figure of the woman, but the status of his own sense of a coherent and unified self. In this poem Coleridge's self is neither "nothing" nor "everything," but some shadowy presence in between these two. The voice of the poem originates in the seam between these conflicting opposites.

Coleridge's sense of self is thus described in terms of ghostly presences, like the thought that "haunts" him. Edward Kessler in *Coleridge's Metaphors of Being* suggests that Coleridge used the vocabulary of phantoms and ghosts as "a metaphor to explore his ambiguous personal relationships with both external nature and language" (Kessler 1970, 135). Like Eilenberg, Kessler stresses Coleridge's subversive doubts about the referentiality of his language. While Coleridge's use of ghosts and phantoms does express his sense of the ambiguous blending of inner and outer in his experience, it also suggests an undermining uncertainty in his representation of self. Coleridge's self, and by extension his text, could be a "nothing," that is, a cipher without substance unable to assert any presence in the world. The specter thus also expresses Coleridge's doubts about his self as a ghostly presence in his text. This doubt, however, is overcome by the mystical and religious connotations of the specter as a pseudoreligious figure that can overcome death.

The specter thus serves as an image for the uncertain relation between Coleridge's self and the world, between inner experience and external reality, and as an image for the process of creation involved in writing an autobiographical text. Just as in meeting the specter Coleridge meets a phenomenon that is apparently both a product of his own consciousness and an objectively verifiable apparition, in writing his poem on the specter he enters into an activity that embodies his own experience, but in a medium that can speak to the experience of others. Unlike the "frail shrines" of an inconstant and fluctuating nature, the specter and the text are constant creations of the human mind that embody the transcendent possibilities of the text.

Coleridge's attitude to the potential of autobiography is deeply ambiguous. From one perspective this poem is a celebration of the "God within" and a granting to the individual of almost divine powers. On the other hand, the poem registers his deep misgivings about the ability of his intellect to embody itself in a world conceived of as inimical to its products. Coleridge's suggestion that the thought to which he tries to give expression might live "but in the brain" implies that he may never be able to create an adequate textual facsimile of the self that he intuitively feels exists by virtue of its constancy. As Kessler says, in this poem "the poet questions not only the self he has created, but, moreover, the work of art in which that self momentarily appears" (Kessler 1970, 135). The question "And art thou nothing?" questions simultaneously the status of Coleridge's self, his memory of the dead woman, the Specter of Brocken, and the ephemeral and insubstantial text in which he tries to embody this "nothing."

The relationship between the "enamoured rustic" and the specter can thus also be seen as an emblem for the relationship between the reader and Coleridge's autobiographical text. The reader half "makes" the presence of Coleridge the writer and half perceives a figure that is really there. In the final analysis, no matter how ghostly or insubstantial Coleridge believes the survival of his self in the text to be, he has faith in the endurance of some vestige of himself beyond his death. Just as the memory of the woman haunts him after she has died, so the reader will be haunted by the spectral presence of Coleridge in his poem. This reading of "Constancy to an Ideal Object" confirms Charles Rzepka's account of the Romantic quest for self-knowledge as "the search for a 'proper greeting of the Spirit' from another or others so as to realize an ideal, interior-ized self-image" (Rzepka 1986, 27). Coleridge represents through the "enamoured rustic" the hope that his ghostly presence in the poem will be confirmed and actualized by an appreciative audience. Of course, his choice of a rustic as the surrogate for the reader also undercuts his hope; only naive bumpkins would believe in the specter, or his poem.

The Specter of Brocken in Thomas De Quincey's account in his *Autobiographic Sketches* similarly shows a debate on the ability of texts to embody an autobiographical consciousness. As in Coleridge's poem, in De Quincey's prose account the specter serves as a metaphor for the effect of the text on the reader and a dramatization of the ephemeral sta-tus of his sense of self. The importance of texts for De Quincey's sense of identity is evident in his description of the Specter of Brocken. In De Quincey's account of the Brocken-Specter there is an ambiguity about the status of the narrative that corresponds to Coleridge's characteriza-tion of the "eerie ambiguity" of the specter's existence. De Quincey, like Coleridge, suggests that the specter is a product of the perceiving con-sciousness, in fact its "servant," but also intimates that it is an autonomous force, in that it "has been known to unmask a strength quite sufficient to alarm those who had been insulting him" (De Quincey 1854, 12). The ambiguity in De Quincey's account, however, comes not so much from the specter's apparently supernatural origins, as from the many qualifications with which De Quincey prefaces his own narrative about the specter:

> In this instance the echoes...might be interpreted as con-nected with a real ascent of Brocken, which was not the case. It was an ascent through all its circumstances executed in dreams, which, under advanced stages in the development of opium, repeat with marvellous accuracy the longest succession of phenomena derived either from reading or from actual experience. (51)

De Quincey's description of the specter here is presented as a narra-tive already at several removes from any kind of "real" experience. This is an "echo," a diminished repetition of a past experience, an echo that is also enclosed within a dream, and so outside the normal bounds of wak-ing existence, and one that furthermore is related at a distance of fifty years from the original experience. There is in addition the presence of opium, which potentially colors the whole experience with its own peculiar effects. De Quincey apparently suggests that his account of the specter is a pale imitation of an original experience, just as Wordsworth in the Winander boy episode presented his narrative as a diminished echo of his past. The use of *echo* here also suggests that the Specter of Brocken stands at the nexus of an interlocking series of memories for De Quincey. The specter is what John Barrell has termed an "involute" (Barrell 1991, 32), a recurrent symbol that links a network of interlocking memories for De Quincey.

The boundaries between fiction and reality, between dreams and waking, and between memory and imagination, are all undermined in De Quincey's introduction to his dream of the Specter of Brocken, just as they are throughout his autobiographical writings. Frequently in De Quincey's autobiographical texts what is presented as his own experience is in fact drawn directly from his own reading, as Albert Goldman has documented in *The Mine and the Mint*. The self that De Quincey presents in his autobiographies is a loosely organized fiction, a composite of his own experience, of his dreams, and of texts he has read.

Both Coleridge and De Quincey show a willingness to lay claim to the words and ideas of others as if they were their own, a tendency that has caused critics such as Norman Fruman great concern. In *Coleridge: The Damaged Archangel* Fruman documents the many times that Coleridge "attributes to himself ideas and experiences properly belonging to others" (Fruman 1971, 10) and takes a very dim view of Coleridge's borrowings. Fruman and Goldman, however, have very different attitudes to the plagiarisms they uncover. Fruman clearly feels ambivalent about the morality of Coleridge's method and attributes his actions to "a compulsive acquisition of reputation and power" deriving from "overmastering personal needs" (59). Goldman, on the other hand, feels that there is nothing wrong with De Quincey's plagiarisms, and that even the parts of his autobiography that are lifted from other sources are of interest to the critic.

While admitting that a "heavy reliance upon printed source material is characteristic of De Quincey's entire literary career" (Goldman 1965, 13), Goldman believes that this only adds to our appreciation of "his capacities as an imaginative writer" (9–10). Goldman characterizes De Quincey's method of appropriating and transforming other people's texts as *rifacimento,* the reworking or remaking of a textual source. As Goldman points out, De Quincey could "when the occasion offered...interpolate in the account of his life various matters...which, although forming no part of his actual experience, could be made to fit within the general framework" of his autobiography (30). Goldman argues that in appropriating other texts De Quincey betrays a consistent method, and that "the workings of De Quincey's imagination...always have a certain consistency, whether acting on the stuff of his experience, dreams, and fantasies or whether assimilating such literary materials as memoirs, books, newspaper reports, and personal documents" (82–83)..

On this issue I agree with Goldman. It seems to me that in both De Quincey's and Coleridge's autobiographical writings the plagiarisms form part of a coherent and methodical presentation of self. John Barrell has described De Quincey's characteristic process of self-composition as "this/that/the other," a process in which "what at first seems 'other' can be made over to the side of self" (Barrell 1991, 10) by De Quincey's constituting himself as the third term in the opposition between the self and the other. Barrell's description of De Quincey's method of self-construction parallels my account of the status of the Romantic liminal subject. De Quincey in his texts, like Coleridge, mediates between his textual self and the other, creating a fictional "I" that is a synthesis of his own experiences and what he has read. These examples of plagiarism represent an elastic self that led to a blurring of the boundaries between personal experience and that embodied in texts. De Quincey shows a willingness to expand his sense of self to include episodes that do not arise from his own experience, and thus to overleap the imperative, embodied in the law of copyright, not to use another's words as one's own. For both Coleridge and De Quincey other texts could serve as emblems for their own sense of self, as could the Specter of Brocken. They betray in their autobiographical texts the kind of ill-defined and unbounded self that I have described in the context of Coleridge's poetry.

In his autobiographical writings De Quincey casts himself as an outsider, set apart from the conventional morality of his day, a free spirit who can roam the streets of London and sympathize with streetwalkers because he, like them, is beyond the pale of the law. He is "marginal" to other people's lives, like Coleridge. De Quincey is one of the first English writers to construct for himself a public persona that is explicitly "pathological," a deliberate aberration from the norms of the audience for whom he is writing, and also one of the first writers to use a pathological condition as a justification for publishing his autobiography. It is De Quincey's aberrations that provide both his subject matter and his justification for publication.

It is not surprising, then, that De Quincey should ignore so completely the ideal of property that came to embodied in the law of copy-

right. He defines himself by the degree to which he transgresses such
legal boundaries. His plagiarisms are another aspect of the fictional persona that he created for himself in his autobiographical texts. In his texts
he is as willing to leap over legal boundaries in composition as when playing the persona of the outcast, beyond the pale of the law.

That De Quincey invested a great deal in the idea of his persona
being somehow outside or beyond the realm of normal identity is best
illustrated by an episode in *The Confessions of an English Opium Eater*. At
one point De Quincey must establish his legal identity in order to borrow
money. This is a particularly fraught moment for him, because from the
opening page of the book he defines himself as outside the conventional
bounds of the morality of his audience. This pose is struck in the first
page of the preface, where he tries at once to link his text to, and distinguish it from, other confessional narratives. He claims that "the greater
part of our confessions (that is, spontaneous and extra-judicial confessions) proceed from demireps, adventurers, and swindlers" and are thus
morally suspect. While claiming that his own confessions violate "that
delicate and honourable reserve" in the way that criminal texts do, he also
tries to put a conventional moral gloss on the exercise of revealing his
"moral ulcers and scars" by an appeal to the conventional justification of
utility, claiming that he publishes "in consideration of the service which I
may thereby render to the whole class of opium eaters" (De Quincey
1979, 29). The argument is that the reader will be improved by reading
the text, because he or she will learn what not to do, and thus be morally
strengthened.

In the moneylenders' office De Quincey is asked to establish his
legal identity. This threatens his pose as an "extra-judicial" figure and
constrains him to define himself as a single individual. De Quincey experiences at this moment of crisis a bifurcation of his self, as he tries to
accommodate these competing claims upon his personality.

> It was strange to me to find my own self *materialiter* con-
> sidered (so I expressed it, for I doted on logical accuracy of
> distinctions) accused, or at least suspected, of counterfeiting
> my own self *formaliter* considered. (55)

The necessity of defining his identity at this point brings De
Quincey to express the division of his self into two categories. He represents himself as a split subject. The scene is particularly difficult for him
because he is asked to define the boundaries of his self and in doing so

limit its range. The elasticity of the ego that enables De Quincey to appropriate a wide range of texts and experiences is threatened by a legal and moral imperative. He is being constrained to represent himself in conventional legal terms. Not only does he acknowledge two selves where he is expected to own to only one at this point, he also signals the fictionality of his persona by the word *counterfeit*. So invested is De Quincey in a fiction of himself as outside the law that when he is called upon to establish a conventional legal identity, he experiences it as a form of dissimulation. De Quincey experiences the constraint of a law that insists he define himself in terms of a single unitary self.

Counterfeit is in fact an extremely suggestive word for De Quincey to use at this moment. The word *counterfeit* refers to both the production of fraudulent imitations of real currency and, in its older sense, to the impersonation of fictional characters by actors, an important usage in Shakespeare's plays, for example. De Quincey feels at this point that he is impersonating himself, and is furthermore impersonating himself in order to make money. The metaphor of the production or coining of money also occurs in one of De Quincey's most interesting comments on the process of literary creation, a comment that informs the title of Goldman's *The Mine and the Mint*. De Quincey says that "the labourers of the Mine (as I am accustomed to call them), or those who dig up the metal of truth, are seldom fitted to be also labourers of the Mint—i.e. to work up the metal for current use" (Goldman 1965, 38). In this contrast De Quincey is implicitly casting himself as "the labourer of the mint," the one who takes the original "metal of truth" and reworks it into currency. In the moneylenders' office De Quincey's usual method of self-creation is restrained by the need to define himself within the bounds of the law. The episode in the moneylenders' office reveals a dark suspicion on De Quincey's part that in his texts he is producing counterfeit currency.

De Quincey's counterfeit persona is based equally in his own experiences and his readings of fictional texts, and is thus doubly counterfeited. Ironically, it is by means of written texts that De Quincey validates his identity at this point, producing letters from friends as proof that he is the person he claims to be. Clearly, with De Quincey's autobiography it is not accurate to claim that he was writing solely from his own experience, as other texts are vitally important to his sense of identity.

Karen M. Lever in her article "De Quincey as a Gothic Hero" argues that the word *fiction*, in regards to the idea of a "fictionalized self," is especially resonant in the context of De Quincey's autobiographies. She argues persuasively that De Quincey's persona is made up of

Byronic and Gothic characteristics that are played off against the persona
of "a pious philosopher plagued by ill health and unfortunate circumstances" (Lever 1979, 333). This is undoubtedly true. The persona De
Quincey constructs is in fact a creature of literary convention, based upon
De Quincey's reading of Byron and of Gothic romance. Furthermore, the
subject matter of his autobiographies is drawn from other texts, both fictional and nonfictional.

It is clear that for De Quincey the categories of fiction and fact are as
blurred as are the boundaries of his own ego, a blurring signaled by his
prefatory remarks to his description of the Specter of Brocken. Just as the
specter serves for De Quincey as a vicarious image of himself, he discovers
in other texts versions of himself and includes them in his own autobiography. Albert Goldman points out that the entire Irish Rebellion episode is
interpolated into the *Autobiographic Sketches* from the Reverend James
Gordon's *History of the Rebellion in Ireland in the Year 1798* (Goldman
1965, 265). As Goldman says, De Quincey's account of his experiences in
Ireland is "rather meagre" until he embarks rather suddenly on an account
of the Rebellion of 1798. Rather than condemn De Quincey for plagiarism at this point, we should ask why he interpolated this narrative into his
autobiography at this point. This narrative does not arise from his own
personal experience, because by the time De Quincey actually reached Ireland the Rebellion was long over, having occurred two years before his
visit. What seems to fascinate De Quincey most about the Irish Rebellion
is the possibility of the existence of a secret society, a shadowy and mysterious organization with no actual basis in reality. De Quincey's description
of this organization is positively lyrical. He describes "a network of organi-
zations...as delicate as lace...as strong as the harnesses of artillery of
horses" (265) that supposedly links all levels of Irish society. It is this
aspect of the history of the Irish Rebellion that most attracted de Quincey,
and it is the strong similarities between this account of the relations
between the conspirators and his own relation to the world that led him to
interpolate the Reverend Gordon's narrative into his autobiography.

In the *Confessions* De Quincey refers to the "nexus" that provides
the "unity of the entire confessions" (De Quincey 1979, 205), the system
of connections that beneath the level of the text provides coherence to an
apparently random sequence, and in the *Sketches,* uses the same word to
express more generally the connection between the individual and his
past, in claiming that "man is doubtless one by some subtle nexus, some
system of links, that we cannot perceive, extending from the new-born
infant to the superannuated dotard" (De Quincey 1854, 44). Just as the

individual here is given coherence by a subtle network of links that may not be immediately obvious, so the secret society provides a unity for otherwise apparently disconnected events. The narrative of the Irish Rebellion that De Quincey found in the Reverend Gordon's book corresponded to De Quincey's own sense of himself and thus found a place within his autobiography. De Quincey reads Irish society in terms of his own self, expressing what is for him the strongest sense of connection possible. The secret society is a clandestine network of connections beyond the pale of the law and thus presents an appealing analogy to the persona De Quincey creates for himself in the *Confessions*.

Any events associated with crime or deviance speak strongly to De Quincey and appeal to his sense of the fictional, in that "the romances which occur in real life are all too often connected with circumstances of criminality" (De Quincey 1854, 179). An aura of "criminality" around an event is bound to appeal to De Quincey, thanks to his pose as an "extrajudicial" writer of confessions. Furthermore, the clandestine nature of the secret society excites his imagination and allows him to embroider upon his source at will. There is in this quotation the characteristic fusion of the categories of "real life" and the fictional category of "romance" that informs the *Confessions* as well as his description of the Specter of Brocken. Although there is a suggestion of moral condemnation in the phrase *all too often,* De Quincey betrays an overwhelming interest in, and affinity with, experiences connected with outcasts from society and criminals.

Where nature for Wordsworth revealed the hidden presence of a ministering and guiding power, for De Quincey it is words, and in particular words in texts, that perform this function. De Quincey redefines Wordsworthian ideas, such as "wise passiveness" or "The child is father to the man," in ways that tell more about himself than about Wordsworth. In the *Confessions* of 1856 he shows a fascination with "rhabdomancy," or the divination "from dark sources" that "some magnetic sympathy" can conjure (De Quincey 1979, 82–83). This fascination in the *Autobiographic Sketches* is explicitly linked to texts in the chapter entitled "Infant Literature":

> These cases of infancy, reached at intervals by special revelations...have some analogy to those other cases, more directly supernatural in which...deep messages of admonition reached an individual through the sudden angular deflexions of words, uttered or written, that had not been originally addressed to himself. (De Quincey 1854, 122)

This passage comes up in the context of Wordsworth's lines about a wise passiveness in the face of external powers that impress a shape upon the writer's past. De Quincey here translates *whispers,* a potentially Wordsworthian word for influence, into *admonition,* which is definitely De Quincey's darker term, suggesting as it does malign subterranean influences. The subject of Wordsworth's lines has been changed by De Quincey from the effects of nature on the child to the effects of "infant literature." It is books, not nature, that provide the "oracular legislation" he refers to, and it is the written word that provides "echo augury" (De Quincey 1854, 123). Like the "reverberations" of dreams, texts are an autonomous external force that help provide unity to the life of the writer. The effects of the specter and of texts are thus fundamentally the same; they render back to the autobiographer an indirect image of the unity of the self.

It is in this effect of rendering back to the writer an external image of his inner life that the specter becomes a metaphor for the working of the text. De Quincey discusses the role of the specter in his narrative in his introduction to the short section he entitles "Dream Echoes Fifty Years Later," a section that ends chapter 1, "The Afflictions of Childhood." As we have seen, he begins by casting doubt upon the authenticity of his narrative, saying that it is not "connected with a real ascent of the Brocken." He then goes on to describe the effect of writing this narrative from a distance of fifty years, the effect of dreams, and the influence of the specter itself.

> That softening and spiritualizing haze which belongs at any rate to the action of dreams and to the transfigurings worked upon troubled reminiscences by retrospects as vast as those of fifty years, was in this instance greatly aided to my own feelings by the alliance with the ancient phantom of the forest-mountain of North Germany. The playfulness of the scene is the very evoker of the memories that lie hidden below. The half sportive illusory revealings of the symbolic tend to the same effect. One part of the effect from the symbolic is dependent upon the great catholic principle of *Idem in Alio.* The symbol restores the theme...gives back but changes; restores but idealizes. (51)

This is a very complex passage because it interweaves a series of reflections on the effect of time, dreams, the specter, and the specter as an example for all symbols, upon the memory of loss or affliction. Perhaps the most important element in De Quincey's description is his emphasis upon the way in which symbols evoke indirectly emotions "that lie hidden below." De Quincey's style is itself allusive and indirect here, so it is not immediately clear that what he is referring to is the death of his sister. As Barrell has pointed out, the specter stands for "the guilt of having failed to prevent the death of Elizabeth" (Barrell 1991, 27). The "Dream Echoes Fifty Years Later" section reworks and makes bearable the guilty memory of the period of his life he has just finished describing in "The Affliction of Childhood." The most important agent in this reworking is the "symbol" of the specter, who serves somehow as an independent "evoker" of De Quincey's memories.

The effect of the specter, dreams, echoes, memory, and symbols is to filter past experience through "a spiritualizing haze." When past experience is placed in the context of a dream, or represented through the specter, the same effect is produced as in "the transfigurings worked upon troubled remembrances by retrospects so vast as those of fifty years." The specter, like the fifty-year retrospect, "idealizes" the past and thus makes it into an aesthetically pleasing form. The idealizing effect distances memory from its original emotion and makes it possible for De Quincey to write a coherent narrative by making it appear as if it were indirectly connected with himself. The implication is that, if it were not for this effect, De Quincey would not be able to write at all. Thanks to this spiritualizing haze, however, the rough edges of experience are softened, the harsh outlines of memory are muted, and that period of his life can be seen in the context of a larger, coherent pattern.

De Quincey in the *Confessions* describes in terms very similar to those used here the effect upon him of listening to music. As in seeing the specter, he finds his life "restored and idealized" for him, laid out as if organized by some unseen power:

> It is sufficient to say that a chorus. &c. of elaborate harmony, displayed before me, as in a piece of arras work, the whole of my past life—not as if recalled by an act of memory, but as if present and incarnated in the music: no longer painful to dwell upon: but the detail of its incidents removed, or blended in some hazy abstraction; and its passions exalted, spiritualized, and sublimed. (De Quincey 1979, 79)

In this account it is the music that is active, the music that "displays before him" his life. As he stresses, to remember his past life requires no

conscious act of recall on his part. We have here a figure for the whole of
De Quincey's autobiographical project, in which the activity of memory
plays no part. Instead what is emphasized is the way in which objects in
the external world, such as the landscape or music, offer up to the autobiographer an image of his own life. This image is, however, "fictionalized," turned into an aesthetically pleasing and ordered narrative. The
function of music is to frame and render less painful the memory of past
experiences. The same is true of the text. The text for De Quincey is
equally a "frame" through which to view his past, this frame making
palatable what would otherwise be too painful to recall. The image of the
specter summarizes for De Quincey his attitude to the writing of autobiography as a process over which he exerts no control and that makes
"exalted, spiritualized and sublimed" his past life by putting it within a
fictional context. This is one reason why so many textual metaphors
inform De Quincey's own view of his life. Not only does he draw on
other texts, he also sees his own life as a text.

One of De Quincey's most striking uses of textual metaphors to
describe his life occurs in the *Autobiographic Sketches* when he steps back
at one point to summarize the course of his narrative:

> So then, one chapter in my life had finished...had run its
> circle, had rendered up its music to the final chord—might
> even seem, like ripe fruit from a tree, to have detached itself
> forever from all the rest of the arras that was shaping itself
> within the loom of my life. (58)

Here we have again the ideas of music and the arras linked, and
specifically linked to De Quincey's image of his life as a text. As in his
description of the effect of music, this account presents De Quincey as a
passive observer rather than an active participant. If his life is an arras,
then the weaver is remarkably absent. De Quincey apparently renounces
control over writing his life story, and far from him actively shaping its
form, it shapes itself and "detaches" itself from him like ripe fruit. This
denial of any shaping or controlling activity is further promoted by the
title of the text in which this quotation occurs; autobiographical
"sketches" are presumably composed of unfinished gestures toward a
final form, a series of fragments rather than a coherent whole.

A particularly striking aspect of this quotation is the overabundance
of metaphors. Although talking about "my life," he sees it in terms of
music, fruit, tapestry, and of course, most importantly, fiction, his past

falling into neat chapters as if part of a novel written by another author. His autobiography is seen insistently in terms of something else, something not directly connected with his own past. The effect of these metaphors is to turn his life into something complete, whole, and "sublimed." In this way he puts a distance between himself and his memories, so that he can maintain the pose of the detached, analytic philosopher. The importance of the idea of "chapters" in the *Autobiographical Sketches* also betrays the crucial role that fiction plays in this process. Not only does De Quincey construct for himself a persona that has obvious literary precedent, he also self-consciously views his own life in fictional terms, describing it in terms of chapters as if it were already a narrative in the shape of a novel. Fiction is essential to De Quincey, not just as a source for his Byronic persona, but also as a way of anesthetizing the story of his past "afflictions." Without this anesthetizing distance, De Quincey implies, it would not be possible to write.

> The very act of deliberately recording such a state of suffering necessarily presumes in the recorder a power of surveying his own case as a cool spectator. (253)

If De Quincey did not view his life as a text and classify it into chapters, the implication is, he would not be able to represent it at all. De Quincey acknowledges the fictive distance he puts between himself and his memories when he states, "I imagine myself writing at a distance of twenty—thirty—fifty years ahead of the present moment" (206). If he did not maintain this distance, he feels, he would be unable to contemplate his former painful condition.

The persona De Quincey constructs in his autobiographical texts is a fragile fiction that is embodied in the Specter of Brocken. The specter is a fictional double, a textual self-representation that synthesizes De Quincey's memories, experiences, and reading and gives them back to him in an idealized and spiritualized form. De Quincey counterfeits himself, producing a fictional double who is both his mirror image and different from himself. The specter symbolizes an ambiguous mixture of identity and difference; on the one hand it is a likeness of De Quincey himself, on the other it is not real, it is a fake or duplicate. De Quincey's attitude to textual self-representation is interestingly divided on this question, as his comments about the possibility of a double reveal:

> If I had a doppel-ganger who went about personating me, copying me, pirating me, philosopher as I am I might...be so

far carried away by jealousy as to attempt the crime of murder on his carcase; and no great matter as regards HIM. But it would be a sad thing for *me* to find myself hanged; and for what, I beseech you? for murdering a sham, that was either nobody at all, or oneself repeated once too often. (De Quincey 1889, 11:460–61)

This rather odd flight of fancy bespeaks De Quincey's doubts about reproducing himself in autobiographical form. The doppelganger, like the Specter of Brocken, mimics De Quincey's movements but provokes in De Quincey an act of violence that turns out to be self-directed, in that he is killing a version of himself. It as if De Quincey were worried that his textual double was taking over his life, and that he had reproduced himself "once too often," so that he is either "nobody at all" or a mere simulacra of himself based upon a fictional reconstruction of his past.

This, then, is the "alliance" between the specter and the writing of autobiography that De Quincey refers to in his prefatory remarks. The specter stands as a symbol of the effect of drawing upon the memory of past affliction and turning it into a written record, a process that turns De Quincey into an "echo" of himself. De Quincey is caught in his own involute, unable to distinguish between inner and outer, real and imaginary. The Specter of Brocken, like his imaginary double, acts out the grief that De Quincey himself cannot directly express but only represent through surrogates.

Immediately you see that the apparition of Brocken veils his head...as if he also had a human heart; as if he also, in childhood, having suffered an affliction that was ineffable, wished by these mute symbols to breathe a sigh towards heaven in memory of that transcendent woe, and by way of record, though many a year after, that it was indeed unutterable by words. (De Quincey 1854, 54)

De Quincey uses the specter to express an emotion that is "unutterable by words." Instead of depicting his grief directly he uses the mediation of the specter as a "mute symbol" to represent his "transcendent woe." The specter acts as a textual double for De Quincey, miming the grief that cannot be embodied in words. This double, however, can also be threatening. Reproducing himself in the other of the text can also be attended by horror, as the strange self-inflicted violence of the quotation above indicates. In another piece, De Quincey meditates upon the effect of discovering that one's double is an "alien nature" housed within one's own body:

> The dreamer finds housed within himself—occupying as it were, some separate chamber in his brain—holding perhaps from that station a secret and detestable commerce with his own heart—some horrid alien nature. What if it were his own nature repeated—still, if the duality were distinctly perceptible, even that—even this mere numerical double of his own consciousness—might be a curse too mighty to be sustained. (De Quincey 1889, 13:92n.)

De Quincey here prefigures the plots of *Frankenstein* and *Dr. Jekyll and Mr. Hyde*, especially when he goes on to speculate as to what might happen if this "horrid alien nature," which is also "his own nature repeated," were to fight with its host. The benign duality of self and other represented in the Specter of Brocken modulates here into nightmare and horror. De Quincey is registering the dark side of Romantic autobiography in these morbid fantasies. The self is double, not single. The individual is split and conceals a secret, illicit double that represents the antisocial and violent impulses that De Quincey would like to view as the other but that in fact are an aspect of the self.

At this point the Specter of Brocken takes on the hues of horror and expresses in more morbid fantasies the kind of anxieties that attended Coleridge's self-representations. The dark anxieties that inform De Quincey's fantasies about his double existence are explored even more explicitly in two Romantic texts that I examine in the next chapter. In Percy Shelley's "Alastor" and Mary Shelley's *Frankenstein* the antisocial aspects of Romantic autobiography are represented in a form of "anti-autobiography" that questions the propriety of autobiography itself.

CHAPTER THREE

ROMANTIC ANTI-AUTOBIOGRAPHY AND REPRESSION

In two Romantic texts the quest for a complementary self-image represented by the Specter of Brocken that I discussed in chapter 2 is represented as a fatal quest for a double of the autobiographical subject: In Percy Bysshe Shelley's "Alastor" and Mary Shelley's *Frankenstein,* the search for a mirror image of the subject, their central characters' pursuit of a doppelganger or double, ends in death. In portraying this death, these two authors explicitly criticize the ideal of the autonomous and antisocial self. In their "anti-autobiographies" they portray the inglorious and untranscendent ends of their protagonists and suggest the human and social cost of the Romantic ideal of the autonomous self.

Both of these texts criticize the way in which "psychic health is measured by the degree to which the 'self' is constructed as separateness, the boundaries between the self and other carefully circumscribed" (Benstock 1988, 15), as it was defined by Freud in the quotation from *Civilization and its Discontents* in my Introduction. Both texts criticize an excessive emphasis upon the autonomy of the self at the expense of the wider claims of community. They therefore question the definition of subjectivity in terms of its separateness or autonomy from the social. They see autobiography as an attempt to create a distinction between the self and a communal other, an attempt that in both narratives leads to death.

Harold Bloom argues in his essay "The Internalization of Quest Romance" in *Romanticism and Consciousness* that there is a narrowing of social horizons in Romantic thought as a consequence of the new emphasis upon the self. This emphasis "tends to narrow consciousness to an acute preoccupation with self" and is in this way destructive of what Bloom calls the "social self" (Bloom 1964, 6). This loss of a wider social horizon is one of the most troubling consequences of the individualist ideology that informs Romantic and Victorian texts. The individualist emphasis on the value of the individual devalues the individual's social context. To write exclusively about the self excludes the "social self," an exclusion of which writers such as Wordsworth were aware. Wordsworth in *The Prelude* knows that his concentration on self excludes a wider social theme, yet he believes that his text can still serve a useful social purpose thanks to the universality of human nature. Just as he drew strength and hope from a return to his past, he felt that his readers, following his example, could do the same.

For Percy Bysshe Shelley and Mary Shelley, however, the act of writing an autobiography had implications that deeply disturbed them, implications that they explored in "Alastor" and *Frankenstein*. For them, to write exclusively about the self was a failing that outweighed the benefits of individualism. They represent as fatal for their protagonists an overexclusive concentration on self. Since their texts are also informed by their own senses of self, as they indicate in the prefatory remarks to their narratives, to write only about the self is by extension a fatal move for them also. Like many of the Victorian authors I discuss in the next three chapters, Percy and Mary Shelley in the Romantic period criticize the writing of autobiography, yet also write autobiographically themselves. The peculiar complexity of both "Alastor" and *Frankenstein* derives from the ambivalent attitudes of their authors toward the act of writing autobiography. Neither of the texts I examine in this chapter is overtly autobiographical, yet both deal with the act of writing about the self. Both are informed by strategies of displacement, in which the true subject of the text is suggested in indirect terms.

In an extremely suggestive analysis of Mary Shelley's *Frankenstein*, Barbara Johnson reads the story, as I do in this chapter, as a commentary on the process of writing an autobiography. She suggests that

> what is at stake in Frankenstein's workshop of filthy creation is precisely the possibility of shaping a life in one's own image: Frankenstein's monster can thus be seen as a figure for autobiography as such...*Frankenstein* can be read as the story of autobiography as the attempt to neutralize the monstrosity of autobiography. Simultaneously a revelation and a coverup,

autobiography would appear to constitute itself as in some way a repression of autobiography. (Johnson 1982, 4)

Frankenstein's monster, like the Specter of Brocken in the previous chapter, is thus a figure of autobiography, recording divergent impulses in the autobiographical text. Like De Quincey's nightmare double, the image of the author in these texts returns upon its creator and annihilates them both. The figures in these texts represent a commentary upon the dangers of autobiography, while the writer is engaged in the process of representing his or her subjectivity through the double as a figure for autobiography itself. For example, the narrative of *Frankenstein* is itself made up of concentric rings of autobiographical narrative, in which, as Johnson points out, the narrators address others as "mirror images" of themselves (3). The text thus enacts the revelation of one person to another, yet also the attempt at a "coverup," or what I would term "repression," dramatized most forcefully in Victor Frankenstein's attempt to deny responsibility for his creation.

Johnson does not, however, dwell upon the source of the "monstrosity" of the act of creating an autobiographical text. The sources of the anxiety that informs this representation of the autobiographical writer as monstrous have yet to be accounted for in previous studies of *Frankenstein*. I am not suggesting that there is a single cause for the depiction of monstrosity in the text, only that not all the reasons for the monster's existence have been enumerated. As feminist analyses of the novel such as Gilbert and Gubar's *The Madwoman in the Attic* or Anne K. Mellor's *Mary Shelley* have pointed out, the monster's depiction and Mary Shelley's obvious sympathy for his liminal position arise from Shelley's status as a woman writer in a predominantly male autobiographical form. However, the monster also represents the possibility of revolution, as Lee Sterrenburg (1979) has argued. The monster was interpreted in the nineteenth century as expressing the widespread fear of social upheaval. These fears centered on the French Revolution in Europe and the possibility of the English working classes rebelling against the government.

The monster in *Frankenstein* represents not any particular revolution or movement, but rather the potential for social disruption unleashed by the ideal of the autonomous individual. The monster is the quintessential autonomous self: He has no family, no history, no culture to restrain him. His very alienation from any community is what makes him monstrous. The monster thus represents a revolutionary potential that the text must repress. This is what produces the simultaneous appre-

ciation and fear of autobiography that Barbara Johnson has noted. While
a potential reformer of society herself, Mary Shelley is horrified by the
possible consequences of a revolutionary Romanticism founded upon the
ideal of the autonomy of a self that is free to question all precedent. The
monster is an embodiment of Wordsworth's "unprecedented self," but
its very lack of antecedents makes it monstrous.

It is this fear of the social cost of autobiography that makes Mary
Shelley an apparent sympathizer with Wordsworth's reaction against rev-
olution. The rhetoric of revolution for her is just another way the male
writer expresses his desire to escape the responsibilities of the social.
Unlike Wordsworth or Percy Shelley, Mary Shelley sees autobiography
not as an antidote to revolution, but as bound up with its problems. As
Anne Mellor points out, Mary Shelley's text betrays a double critique of
Romanticism:

> No revolutionary herself, Mary Shelley clearly perceived the
> inherent danger in a Promethean, revolutionary ideology:
> commitment to an abstract good can justify an emotional
> detachment from present human relationships and family
> obligations…and an obsession with realizing a dream that too
> often masks an egotistical wish for personal power. (Mellor
> 1988a, 86)

The common element underlying Mellor's description is the way in
which a concentration on the individual detaches one from the social and
justifies a completely self-referential position. Mary Shelly thus embodies
contradictory impulses in the monster, at once sympathizing with his
position as a writer in a liminal position herself, yet criticizing through his
very detachment from the community his antisocial potential. The monster thus stands for Mary Shelley's attitude toward the autobiographical
project as a whole, and as a commentary on the act of writing autobiography itself. *Frankenstein* is thus an autobiographical anti-autobiography.

Victor Frankenstein is by contrast a much less divided commentator
on autobiography, representing a reprehensible egotism as he defines his
scientific quest in self-referential terms. Like Percy Shelley's Poet, he sees
the world exclusively in terms of self and, like the Poet, dies as a result of
his quest. Victor Frankenstein and Shelley's Poet represent the Romantic
autobiographical subject. In their attitudes to their narrators both
authors represent critiques of the act of writing autobiographically.

To write an autobiography is for both authors an attractive idea, yet it is one they feel they must resist because of the social costs involved. For instance, Victor Frankenstein's creation of the monster gradually cuts him off from his family and society, plunging him into solipsistic isolation. Reading his act of creation as a metaphor for writing an autobiography, Mary Shelley is suggesting that the autobiographical impulse is inimical to the social bonds represented by the family. Victor Frankenstein's quest finally narrows the social horizon to one of polar opposites, fire and ice, in which he and the monster are consumed.

These two authors therefore enact a form of anti-self-consciousness, trying to repress the self even while taking the self as their subject. In this they prefigure the dominant mode of Victorian autobiography, in which the autobiographer tries to limit or contain the significance of his self in terms of some higher power or moral impulse. While the self is their subject, these autobiographies try to deny or repress these solipsistic tendencies. As I argue in the next three chapters, on Victorian autobiography, this repression actually leads to an intensification of the solipsistic tendencies of the texts.

The ambivalent attitude to self-representation involved in the idea of anti-self-consciousness is shown most clearly in Percy Shelley's "Alastor" by the contradictions between Shelley's preface and his poem. The preface is apparently a dark admonition about the folly of an overly self-centered view of the world. The second paragraph in particular takes aim squarely at a group of "actual men" that Shelley has in mind even as he writes, men who should read his allegory in moral terms:

> The Poet's self-centered seclusion was avenged by the furies of an irresistible passion pursuing him to a speedy ruin. But that Power which strikes the luminaries of the world with sudden darkness and extinction, by awakening them to too exquisite a perception of its influences, dooms to a slow and poisonous decay those meaner spirits that dare to abjure its dominion. (Shelley 1978, 33)

Shelley suggests in these lines that to write solely about the self leads to fatal ruin. In discussing the Poet's fate, Shelley invokes the idea of the "avenging daimon" that Harold Bloom describes as the return of the excluded "social self," an irresistible fury that will revenge itself upon the solipsistic poet. Shelley, like Bloom, feels that a too narrow focus upon the self excludes a wider social horizon.

The message of the preface becomes less clear, however, from this point on, as Shelley introduces another term in his argument, those "morally dead" souls who are "duped by no generous error," as is the Poet. Shelley at first appears to be building up to a resounding condemnation of the Poet's "self-centered seclusion," but he then introduces a class of character even more reprehensible than the solipsistic Poet. The paragraph proceeds from this point on in a clearly ambivalent vein, as Shelley praises the Poet, but in terms that undercut this praise even as it is offered. He calls the Poet "generous" but in "error," says the Poet has a "thirst for knowledge" but is in search of knowledge whose value is "doubtful." Shelley is working at cross-purposes with himself here, proffering praise with one hand and blame with the other.

As William Veeder remarks in his study of "Alastor" in relation to *Frankenstein* in *Mary Shelley and Frankenstein,* the preface "reflects deep divisions within Shelley himself," divisions that are also to be found in Mary Shelley's text (Veeder 1986, 95). Whereas Veeder sees this division in terms of gender and sexuality, I read the conflict here as a product of Shelley's ambivalent attitude toward the self and introspection. In his preface Shelley is presenting an argument in favor of a social use of the imagination and of a poetry that addresses wider human sympathies. However, the poem he writes in fact celebrates introspection and the lure of solipsism. Shelley's poem and preface are both deeply sympathetic to the Poet, because the Poet embodies Shelley's idealistic and solipsistic, as opposed to his pragmatic and social, side. Working against the attraction of solipsism for Shelley is his intellectual conviction that poetry should fulfill a social role.

This ambivalence is further played out in the poem itself in the contrast between the Narrator and the Poet. As Earl R. Wasserman says in his study of Shelley's poetry, in "Alastor" these two voices dramatize a conflict between two kinds of poetry that Shelley is considering.

> The fictional Narrator contemplating the career of the Visionary is, in effect, the extroverted, utopian Shelley now turning his eyes inward to explore his interior life—and since both Narrator and Visionary are Poets, the Narrator also represents one kind of poetry contemplating another. (Wasserman 1971, 18)

In "Alastor," then, Shelley turns his eyes inward rather than outward, no matter what his preface may maintain about the social uses of the imagination. The poem, like Mary Shelley's *Frankenstein,* becomes a meditation upon the grounds of its own being. The poem itself turns into an introspective exercise, undercutting its social ambitions. It plays out the displacement of the social to which Jerome McGann has referred. As Wasserman also suggests, to become introspective in this way goes against the grain of Percy Shelley's utopian intellectual convictions. Just as the preface bespeaks a divided and ambivalent mind, so the poem itself plays out a comparison of two different kinds of poetry, two kinds of poetry that may be incompatible with one another.

However, this parallel does not resolve the difficulties of the preface, because the contrast between the Poet (or "Visionary," as Wasserman calls him) and the Narrator is not the same as the contrast between the Poet and the ill-defined "actual men" of the preface. The subjects of the attack in the preface appear nowhere in the poem itself. It is true that, as Wasserman points out, the Narrator is the "norm against which the Visionary's love can be defined and measured, just as the somewhat distracting Preface introduces an additional standard" (Wasserman 1971, 17), but as his words "distracting" and "additional" imply, the Narrator does not represent the kind of poetry that the preface would lead one to expect.

The Narrator represents a form of Wordsworthian contemplation of nature, in which the natural world fulfills the need for community. As Wasserman says, the Narrator, "far from being a troubled solitary tormented by unsatisfied dreams...conceives of himself as a serene and equal member of the human community" (16). I would say of the Narrator, to qualify Wasserman's description slightly, that the Narrator is in serene and equal communion with nature, while the Poet is not. The Narrator in this stands for a Wordsworthian poet in rapt contemplation of the landscape. The "human community," however, does not play a part in either the Narrator's or the Poet's scheme of things and is noticeably absent from the whole poem.

It is here that the dissonance between the preface and the poem is most clear. The preface makes gestures toward an ideal of human solidarity that is nowhere visible in the poem. "Alastor" is a criticism of solipsism, but in the final analysis the poem shows Shelley himself unable to break out of the solipsistic mode. His preface announces an ideal of community and human sympathy that his poetry is unable to represent; hence the feeling shared by many critics that the preface is a distraction. "Alastor" is thus a perfect example of the situation Geoffrey Hartman has described in "Romanticism and 'Anti-Self-Consciousness'" where "subjectivity—even solipsism—becomes the subject of poems which *qua* poetry seek to transmute it" (Hartman 1970, 53). "Alastor" shows the twistings and inner turnings of a consciousness that seeks an ideal beyond solipsism while simultaneously realizing that this quest is doomed.

Shelley's preface argues for the employment of the artist's imagination in the creation of a poetry that would reinscribe in the text the excluded social horizon, yet his program is undermined by his haunting sense of the inadequacy of any earthly embodiment for the self-created ideals of his Poet. He is caught between incompatible versions of the self, that of a transcendent self that seeks to pass beyond the mortal and finite, and that of a subjectivity that is firmly grounded in a social reality and aware of its limitations. This contrast emerges clearly in the preface.

> So long as it is possible for his desires to point towards objects thus infinite and unmeasured, he is joyous, and tranquil and self-possessed. But the period arrives when these objects cease to suffice. His mind is at length suddenly awakened and thirsts for intercourse with an intelligence similar to itself. (Shelley 1978, 666)

The Poet is represented here in the kind of epiphany that Wordsworth describes when a contemplation of nature gives back an infinite and timeless version of self. In Shelley's view, however, this situation of "self-possession" cannot suffice and must give way inevitably to a thirst for some social contact. Shelley assumes this as a given, saying that a "period arrives" and "his mind is awakened." These passive constructions imply a process beyond the Poet's control, as a sort of natural law of the universe. Like Mary Shelley, Percy Shelley assumes that "as an ecological system of interdependent organisms, nature requires submission of the individual ego to the welfare and the larger community" (Mellor 1988a, 125). In this, community and nature are joined and imagined in gendered terms as female. Nature stands for those communal values that are opposed to the individualistic, masculine, and aggressive attributes.

The Poet, however, like Victor Frankenstein, repudiates these values when he embarks on his quest. This quest is, however, for an intelligence "similar to himself," and it is in this formulation that we see Shelley undermining his terms once again. The Poet's thirst is not for intercourse with some other, a force completely alien to the self, but with some version of the self. Like Walton or Frankenstein, the Poet looks for a sympathetic mirror within which to create an image of himself.

This ambiguity in Shelley's formulation is left unresolved in Wasserman's analysis of "Alastor" by his use of the term *Other Self* to describe the Poet's and Shelley's ideal. This term brings together the ideas of self and other and allows their contradictions to resonate without his explaining them. It is this central ambiguity, the peculiar mixture of self and other in the Poet's ideal image, that causes Shelley the greatest difficulty and is the hallmark of the autobiographical sensibility I describe in this book. Like all the authors I deal with in this study, Shelley recognizes the role that self plays in all perception, yet he still tries to go beyond self and imagine an autonomous other. Shelley's preface implies that there is a clear choice between human sympathy and self-love, but his poem belies this pat formulation. The poem plays out the return of self even in the desire to escape or go beyond the self. As Wasserman says, it is in the mirror imagery in the poem that this drama between self and other is most clearly represented, "because the Visionary's thirst is for union with his own soul's ideal mirror image, the perfect subject standing as coveted object to the imperfect subject, a dialectic of the symbol of reflection is threaded through all his experiences" (Wasserman 1971, 29).

While I agree that the mirror image plays a role similar to that Wasserman describes here, I disagree with the interpretation he places upon the image when it occurs in the poem, particularly the instance of the "crystal calm" cove into which the Poet is drawn after the "pool of treacherous and tremendous calm." Wasserman distinguishes between these two natural mirrors, saying that the "mirrored image of the human self" in the second reflection is "unlike that of nature" in the first (31). I would argue, however, that these two moments are fundamentally the same and reflect an ambivalence that Wasserman has suggested in his formulation "Other Self" but not adequately explained. The difficulty here is how to read the image of Narcissus that occurs in this scene:

> A little space of green expanse, the cove
> Is closed by meeting banks, whose yellow flowers
> For ever gaze on their own drooping eyes,
> Reflected in the crystal calm. (405–8)

Wasserman says that in this image "nature can reveal the self-fulfillment possible to it, but not possible to man," and that the Visionary's rejection of the impulse to deck his hair with flowers is "a symbolic distinction of himself from this order of being" (30). The anthropomorphizing of the flowers, their possession of "eyes," suggests, however, that what is being represented here is a moment of self-communion like the later, more explicit moment when the Poet himself does what Narcissus is doing here, and gazes at his own reflection:

> Hither the Poet came. His eyes beheld
> Their own wan light through the reflected lines
> Of his thin hair, distinct in the dark depth
> Of that still fountain; as the human heart,
> Gazing in dreams over the gloomy grave,
> Sees its own treacherous likeness there. (469–74)

As in the description of Narcissus, the emphasis here is upon eyes and sight. In both instances the Poet sees an image of himself, an image that prefigures his own death. Just as the stasis in the pool is "treacherous," the Poet's own likeness is described as "treacherous" here. Both instances of mirroring portray a situation in which to rest content with an image of self is fatal. In this reading I disagree fundamentally with the note to the Norton edition of "Alastor," which glosses the image of the flowers as signifying that "within the limits of the natural world, the correspondent Other satisfies the needs of the Self for community" (Shelley 1979, 677). It is precisely because the Poet holds communion with his image "as if he and it / were all that was" that the idea of community is excluded, leading to fatal solipsistic isolation. The Poet's rapt contemplation of himself denies community in the fiction that all the individual needs is to inhabit some vast hall of mirrors in which he encounters idealized images of himself.

However, the poem operates in a world in which the self is potentially all there is, so that any meeting with nature or any other natural phenomenon is a meeting with an image of the self. It is for this reason that the mirror image is such a central and provocative one in the poem. A few lines after passing beyond the image of Narcissus, the Poet comes across a natural scene in which the boundaries between things begin to break down, and nature becomes a hall of mirrors. The trees above the stream blend into a mass of "meeting boughs and implicated leaves," while the subterranean caves can be heard "mocking" the moans of the rocks. As the Norton edition says, "mocking" has the double implication of both mimicking and ridiculing (Shelley 1979, 677). Just as the phenomena of nature imitate and mock one another, so nature both imitates and mocks the Poet. This is a ridicule ultimately directed back upon the perceiving subject by Shelley, as he recognizes the futility of an attempt to escape the imitation of self in poetry. It is for this reason that Wasserman's formulation of the term "Other Self" is so provocative, suggesting as it does that all phenomena in this poem are composed of both self and other, in ways most clearly signaled by the ambiguity of the mirror image.

This intermingling and interpenetration betrays the position of the writer in the seam of language, as did the Specter of Brocken in the previous chapter. The writer is situated in the liminal space between the self and the other. However, for Percy Shelley the two terms are in some ways incompatible, and he must insist on their separation. He is committed, even as he criticizes it, to the ideal of an autonomous self with a unique and pristine inner landscape of experience. The dream of autonomy informs the very premises of his poem.

The fact that the Norton editor of "Alastor" and I can come to such diametrically opposed readings of the same image is evidence for me that Shelley is portraying a deeply divided attitude toward the self, at once acknowledging the role self plays in perception yet also criticizing a situation in which the Poet sees nature in terms of self. Unlike Wordsworth, Shelley has no faith in the tactile sense's being able to rescue him from the "abyss of idealism," and his protagonist never succeeds in escaping from the confines of self. The Poet's death signals the protagonist's, and Shelley's, ultimate defeat. Shelley at the end of "Alastor" is left with the ambition to go beyond the self without the ability to imagine an other that would simultaneously be different from the self and fulfill the self's desires for communion with an image like itself. The other in Shelley's poem is simply a version of himself; as Alan Richardson says, "The 'Alastor' poet envisions and pursues a feminized self-projection" (Richardson 1988, 20), underlining the use of the feminine as a mirror for the masculine self in the poem. His Poet doesn't so much die as disappear off the human map in his ultimately unfulfillable quest. Despite his intentions, Shelley ends up affirming a "Romantic ideology that represented its poems as self-consuming artifacts within a never-ending dialectical process" (Mellor 1988a, 80), so that his Poet dies in the kind of isolation he tries to resist.

Mellor's characterization of a Romantic ideology in terms of a "never-ending dialectical process" illustrates the similarity between the subjectivity embodied in Percy Shelley's poem and Victorian autobiography. The apparent dialectic between opposites such as inner and outer in Romantic poetry both creates the liminal space or seam of autobiographical writing and intensifies the concentration upon the single self. Instead of promoting a social vision, anti-self-consciousness actually creates a never-ending dialectic of identification and difference between self and

"Other Self," a self-enclosed and self-consuming drama of desire and its frustration. Images of the other are redefined in terms of the self, creating a hall of mirrors.

The poem "Alastor," like Shelley's preface, subverts its own ambition. While Shelley may desire to portray an ideal of community, his poem ends up affirming only the ubiquity of the self. He creates a community of one. He, like Wordsworth, finds that to write about the self is to exclude the idea of community, although his ambition is to criticize a concentration upon the self and rescue some form of human solidarity from the threat of solipsism. Shelley's poem is linked to the autonomous and the individual and ultimately trapped by its individualist premises, even while criticizing such an ideology. The Poet's quest, like Victor Frankenstein's, leads him away from the social in pursuit of the dream of an unrealizable autonomy.

It is in the dissonance between the preface and the poem that Shelley's difficulty is most clearly dramatized. While Shelley may wish to write a form of poetry that celebrates human community and solidarity, poetry in the nineteenth century becomes increasingly associated with the personal and the subjective. Wordsworth's long autobiographical poem *The Prelude* is an anomaly in nineteenth-century British literary history in that it describes the self in poetry in the form of a long, continuous narrative. This is the method of prose autobiography, and all the great autobiographies of the latter half of the nineteenth century are prose narratives. Tennyson's *In Memoriam* is a long, autobiographical piece, but as Tennyson himself acknowledges, it is composed of "short Swallow flights of song" rather than one continuous narrative. Tennyson can write about himself only in short bursts of poetry, not in a single, coherent narrative.

When Shelley writes poetry, then, he inevitably takes as his subject his self rather than the community to which he refers in his preface. His difficulty here prefigures the difficulties experienced by John Ruskin and Matthew Arnold, who felt drawn to poetry yet also felt impelled to write social criticism. Both men renounced poetry in favor of prose as the medium through which to express their social concerns. Shelley in "Alastor" is working at cross-purposes with himself, in that he chooses to try to express social concerns through what was becoming defined as a preeminently subjective medium. Shelley at least felt he could try to use poetry as social criticism. By the time of Ruskin, Mill, and Arnold, the situation was perceived as an either / or choice between incompatible methods. As Mill indicates in his comments on Wordsworth in his autobiography, poetry was seen as having to do primarily with the subjective, the poet's feelings, while prose was the province of more objective and impersonal thought.

Prose autobiography, however, is open to the same kind of criticism as that leveled against poetry by Percy Shelley in his preface. Mary Shelley in *Frankenstein* dramatizes the consequences of a solipsistic and isolating outlook in much the same terms as Percy Shelley in "Alastor." Both *Frankenstein* and "Alastor" involve the search for a double. This double, like the Specter of Brocken, is both a duplicate of and different from the perceiving consciousness, a form of "Other Self" like that sought by the Poet in "Alastor." However, where the relationship between the Specter of Brocken and the viewer was a benign one, in which the specter served as an indirect emblem of the transcendence of the writer's own self, the relationship between creator and double in these two cautionary tales is destructive. Both *Frankenstein* and "Alastor" warn, through the figure of the double of the dangers of a solipsistic outlook in which the central character looks upon the world in terms of self.

To explain how she came to write *Frankenstein*, Mary Shelley gives us in her preface a short autobiography that concentrates mainly on the influence of her childhood experiences on her imagination. The implication of the preface is that to understand the tale one must understand the childhood experiences of the writer. Thus, the story of Victor Frankenstein is linked for Mary Shelley in some way to her sense of self and her connection to her past. She finds a deep analogy between writing an autobiographical narrative and Victor Frankenstein's creation of the nameless monster. Like Frankenstein's monster, her apparently original and unprecedented autobiographical text is in fact made up of bits and pieces of the past recombined into a new hideous and horrifying shape intimately yet obscurely linked with the personality of the author.

Although Mary Shelley claims she is "very averse to bringing myself forward in print" (Shelley 1965,vi), *Frankenstein* in fact reflects her own self, albeit in an oblique fashion. In creating this autobiographical text, she has, like her protagonist, been "the author of unutterable evils" (87) and engaged in a solipsistic and antisocial enterprise by turning inward to her own world of imagination, memory, and dreams. Just as Victor Frankenstein produces an "Other Self," a being at once connected with and yet distinct from himself, Mary Shelley produces a text that is apparently an imitation of herself but also has an existence independent from her as it goes out into the world as one of her "progeny." The plot of *Frankenstein* critiques writing autobiography through metaphors of birth and creation in which the text is turned into a kind of progeny.

The autobiographical connection between Mary Shelley and Victor Frankenstein is made clear if we consider the nature of his act of creation. *Frankenstein* is not a work of science fiction, in that, although it makes references to scientific knowledge, this is not its primary focus. Its center of interest is the effect of the creation of the monster, not the creation itself. The effect of the creation of the monster is to precipitate a series of pursuits in which it is unclear precisely who is pursuing whom. Geoffrey Hartman has suggested in "The Internalization of Quest Romance "that the journey in Romantic literature can be seen as "a sustained metaphor for the experience of the artist during creation" (Hartman 1970, 54). In this light, the center of interest in *Frankenstein* is the process of literary creation, not scientific discovery. In *Frankenstein* Mary Shelley represents a fundamentally different relationship between the artist and his or her autobiographical creation from that embodied in the Specter of Brocken. Where male Romantic autobiographers equated the quest and the conquest of the other (Ross 1988), Mary Shelley represents the attempt to create the other in the image of the self as a "usurpation of the feminine role of reproduction" (Mellor 1988b, 220).

At the end of the preface to *Frankenstein,* Mary Shelley bids a playful adieu to her text and addresses it as if it were now independent from her. She addresses the tale in a fashion that has obvious literary precedent, when she concludes by saying, "And now, once again, I bid my hideous progeny go forth and prosper" (Shelley 1965, xi). This reference to God's creation of Adam and Eve sets up a further series of connections between Mary Shelley's act of writing the story *Frankenstein* and Victor Frankenstein's act of creating the monster. Mary Shelley places herself in the same godlike relation to her text as Frankenstein to his monster, or Coleridge and De Quincey to their autobiographical texts. Both Mary Shelley and Victor Frankenstein, however, create beings that then turn out to have independent wills of their own. Like God creating Adam and Eve, Mary Shelley and Victor Frankenstein create images in their own likenesses that prove disobedient to the will of the creator.

However, Mary Shelley alters God's blessing in a subtle way. Rather than bid her creation "go forth and multiply," she bids it "go forth and prosper." She avoids wishing for her creation the reproduction and multiplication that God bestowed on Adam and Eve, wishing instead for her own "progeny" wealth rather than children. The idea of multiplication and reproduction are destructive ideas both in Mary Shelley's preface and in the text itself. Having created the monster, Victor Frankenstein is horrified by the thought of creating an Eve for his Adam, and thus blocks the possibility of his creation's reproducing himself. By analogy, the possibility of the text as a "hideous progeny" multiplying itself is a horrendous prospect for Mary Shelley herself.

Mary Shelley expresses toward the text as a self-duplicating machine an attitude diametrically opposed to that of Augustine. The thought of her text imitating another, or of someone imitating her text, fills her with horror. Imitation has become a form of transgression, a transgression codified in the law of copyright. The image of a community of texts that I identified in Augustine's text has become completely lost. Literary self-creation, like Frankenstein's creation of the monster, occurs ex nihilo, but it is viewed as a lonely, self-disgusted act.

The monster, like the text, must not be allowed to reproduce itself, as this would of course compromise its "originality" and uniqueness. The autonomous text, like the autonomous individual, is one of a kind and has no future in reproduction. The act of literary creation, expressed as a version of divine creation, is seen as an exercise attended by horror and death. The "progeny" of creation are "hideous" and thus a very mixed blessing on the creator. Literary creation, in fact, seems demonic and depraved.

Mary Shelley associates the act of literary creation with the vocabulary of demonic possession in her preface. The language she uses recalls the supernatural subjects of the Gothic horror tale, as she presents writing as an act guided by dark forces beyond her control. She tells how her "imagination, unbidden, possessed and guided me" (Shelley 1965, x). The act of writing is one of being "possessed" by a horrifying vision, and the aim of the tale is to evoke a corresponding horror in the reader. The language of possession here suggests an uneasy relationship between Mary Shelley and her imagination. Shelley does not control her imagination by an act of will; rather it seems that her imagination controls her. It is not clear whether the text is in fact written by her or by some mysterious external force. Like the monster, the imagination asserts an independent existence of its own, so that the act of creation emphasizes the powerlessness of the author rather than his or her own power. Rather than draw strength from a contemplation and reconstruction of the past in writing, as Wordsworth does in his autobiography, Mary Shelley emphasizes how much of the process lies outside the individual's power. Her relationship to her text is not one of possessor to commodity possessed, but the reverse.

Writing, for Mary Shelley, is bound up with nightmare and horror, yet it is only within the world of nightmare that her imagination can produce a tale that is truly her own, suggesting another side to the issue of possession:

My dreams were at once more fantastic and agreeable than
my writings. In the latter I was a close imitator—rather doing
as others had done than putting down the suggestions of my
own mind...but my dreams were all my own; I accounted for
them to nobody. (Shelley 1965, vii)

Mary Shelley describes the genesis of *Frankenstein* in a dream, thus
marking it as something that is entirely "her own" and not an imitative
act. To be an imitator, to situate oneself within a literary tradition, is seen
by Mary Shelley as something to be avoided. The desire to be original can
only be satisfied in dreams, not in her mundane "writings." For her the
creation of the dream-inspired tale is an original act that is self-consciously viewed as a break from the category of imitation. In writing that
is uninspired by dreams she is crushed by the weight of previous models.
Her creation of *Frankenstein*, like Victor Frankenstein's creation of the
monster, brings an unprecedented and original text into the world, a text
that apparently has nothing to do with any precursors' texts.

The monster himself represents indirectly Mary Shelley's autobiographical text. The monster is not entirely unprecedented, in that he is
composed of the flesh of the dead. Considered as a metaphor for literary
creation, the monster's origins turn the act of writing into a particularly
antisocial activity, that of grave robbing. Even as she claims to be breaking the stifling hold of previous texts, Mary Shelley betrays their unavoidable, if unwelcome, presence as the very material out of which she constructs her own "hideous progeny." Rather than past texts' being sources
of inspiration, they are likened to the dead flesh of past individuals,
brought back to new and gruesome life in the act of writing *Frankenstein*.
Indeed, *Frankenstein* clearly owes a great deal to the conventions of the
Gothic horror tale and is thus not an entirely original or unprecedented
text. It would be surprising if, like God, Shelley really could create ex
nihilo a completely new and unprecedented being. Her ambition to do
so, however, infects the tale with the anxieties that such an idea inevitably
brings with it.

Frankenstein's creation of the monster is an asexual act of creation
that contrasts with the act of procreation implied by Mary Shelley in calling the text her "progeny." Frankenstein undertakes an act of invention
where the result of the action is the production of a creature solely of the
inventor's brain. Frankenstein's dream is essentially of self-reproduction,
an act of self-invention where the result of creation is an extension of the
author's will. In this he represents the ambition behind autobiography,

that of reproducing the author's self in a text. This is, Mary Shelley implies, a self-centered and antisocial ambition. In procreation the connection between parent and offspring is much more ambiguous and asserts a connection between the parent and the child. The result of production through procreation is an independent being with some similarities to, and some differences from, the parent. The monster thus behaves more like one of Victor Frankenstein's offspring than his invention, making demands upon him that he had not foreseen and is unwilling to fulfill. Victor Frankenstein may dream before the act of the intense gratitude and loyalty that his creation will have toward him, but the reality afterward proves quite different.

Victor Frankenstein dreams of a form of creation that surpasses the blood ties of procreation. The monster, as a complete reproduction of the author's personality rather than a child's imperfect copy, is to be tied to his creator more closely than any merely mortal connection. The monster will thus "belong" to Frankenstein completely. Frankenstein states that "no father could claim the gratitude of his child so completely as he would his creations" (26). Frankenstein's act of invention as an act of literary creation is an imperfect form of self-reproduction. The monster is linked to his self but is not a carbon copy of himself. Similarly, Mary Shelley in calling her text a "progeny" implies that, while it is linked to her self, once it goes out into the world through the means of mechanical reproduction it takes on a strange and awful life of its own.

The monster that results from this self-reproduction represents the excluded community, what Harold Bloom calls the "avenging daimon" that results from a narrowing of the social horizon. The avenging daimon returns to haunt the autonomous individual and remind him of his duties to others. Thus, when Frankenstein is on Mont Blanc, experiencing the sublimity of the landscape as a reaffirmation of his self in the tradition of Romantic poetry, the monster interrupts his reverie to remind him of the existence of other individuals who have claims upon his time.

One measure of Mary Shelley's conservatism in this text, however, is the way in which she represents the social in terms of the ideal bourgeois family. As Anne Mellor points out, "Mary Shelley grounded her political ideology on the metaphor of the peaceful, loving, bourgeois family" (Mellor 1988a, 86). Like her reaction against the idea of revolution, her idealized portrait of the De Lacey family shows her fear of the antisocial implications of autobiography. These fears led her to espouse a conservative idealization of the family. There is in fact a comic contrast between the fear Victor Frankenstein expresses of his monster and the monster's very limited and domestic aims. The monster does not wish to overthrow the human social system, but to start his own family. The avenging demon of the social simply wants to re-create the family that Victor Frankenstein is escaping. The family is thus the ultimate form of community in the text.

The primary effect of Victor Frankenstein's act of self-creation is to turn him into a monomaniacal solipsist whose greatest crime is to cut himself off from his family and finally bring about its destruction. His knowledge of the monster's existence becomes for him "an insurmountable barrier between me and my fellow men" (Shelley 1965, 151), and he is plunged into unbreakable solitude. This is an inevitable consequence of an act that is not so much an act of creation as self-creation in which the author's energies, like those of the solipsistic Poet, are directed solely inward. The creation of the monster represents a deliberate turning inward and away from his family, an isolating move that is underlined by the description of the room in which this act takes place.

> In a solitary chamber, or rather cell, at the top of the house, and separated from all other apartments by a gallery and staircase, I kept my workshop of filthy creation. (53)

Like his second abortive act of creation in the remote Orkneys, this original act takes place in a setting that emphasizes how removed Frankenstein is from any human contact. Within a building, but apparently not a part of it, he is separated by "a gallery and a staircase" as well as being "at the top" of the house, apparently without neighbors. Furthermore, his action is antisocially "filthy," something that has no place within the orderly classification of "clean" or socially acceptable acts. It is filthy creation in that his "unhallowed arts" transgress established religious categories that reserve creation for God. The contrast between Frankenstein's filthy creation and natural creation is emphasized by the descriptions of the season during which Frankenstein works feverishly and alone, deprived of contact not only with other human beings but with the very forces of fecundity themselves:

> The summer months passed while I was thus engaged, heart and soul, in one pursuit. It was a most beautiful season; never did the fields bestow a more plentiful harvest...but my eyes were insensible to the charms of nature. (53)

If anything dramatizes the unnaturalness of his occupation, it is this insensitivity to the beauty of the season that provides such an alluring contrast to his own filthy creative act. The task he has set himself is so monomaniacal, engages him "heart and soul" to such a degree that he is led to forget the summer, as well as those "friends who were so many miles absent" (53). The moral repugnance communicated by that word *filthy* seems reserved more for the isolation of his position than anything else. Frankenstein's desire seems to be to cut himself off from anything that might interrupt his solipsistic quest, a desire that is fulfilled by the monster's killing off the members of his family one by one. Whereas the principle of his family is inclusive, its membership growing by appropriating any stray orphans that happen along, Frankenstein's tendency is toward isolation. Frankenstein and his family are thus shown as inimical, each tending toward different states, and it is his family that loses the contest.

Mary Shelley uses the genre of the Gothic to express a dichotomy at the heart of individualism, the potential conflict between one individual's inalienable rights and those of another once the landscape is occupied by more than just one person. Frances Ferguson cites *Frankenstein* as the antitype of the individualist category of the sublime in her essay "The Nuclear Sublime." *Frankenstein* is therefore the antithesis of those Romantic poems that we have seen thus far affirming the centrality of the poet's self, "because it figures the Gothic reversal of the sublime dream of self-affirmation, the fear that the presence of other people is totally invasive and erosive of the self" (Ferguson 1984, 8). For Frankenstein other people threaten his self rather than confirm his sense of self. Although this motive is never consciously articulated, Victor Frankenstein's unacknowledged desire is to rid the world of anyone who has claims on his time and who could threaten his pristine individuality. This is an aim that the monster fulfills for him.

In this antisocial quest Victor Frankenstein joins Robert Walton, who talks about his desire for companionship yet whose quest takes him further away from any human community into the same frozen wastes as Frankenstein himself. Although both Frankenstein and Walton portray themselves as benefactors to mankind thanks to their quests, their energies are in fact directed inward rather than outward. Like the revolutionaries Mary Shelley criticizes, explorers and scientists use idealism as a cloak for self-interest. This is underscored by Walton's description of Victor Frankenstein:

> Such a man has a double existence: he may suffer misery and
> be overwhelmed by disappointments, yet when he has retired

into himself, he will be like a celestial spirit that has a halo
around him, within whose circle no grief or folly enters. (33)

Walton's description of Frankenstein's double nature points out the
growing problem in the Romantic conception of the self that Mary Shelley seeks to overcome. In the locating of Frankenstein's most intense and
powerful experiences within the "inner circle" of his consciousness, a
dichotomy is created between the social and the private selves. The
description I have just quoted occurs within the context of a discussion
between Walton and Frankenstein of their mutual need for "intimate
sympathy with a fellow mind," implying that their aims are primarily
social. Yet, as Walton's words indicate, Frankenstein's energies are predominantly directed inward, not outward. Frankenstein is the embodiment of a consciousness divided between the competing claims of the
social and the private, and the monster is an external symbol for the social
forces that his introspective nature excludes.

In contrast to Frankenstein's inner-directed energies, the monster's
aims are almost entirely social. Where Frankenstein wishes to cut himself
off from his family, the monster's desire is to be accepted into the bosom
of the De Lacey family. The relationship between Frankenstein and his
monster therefore becomes a commentary on the divided nature of
Frankenstein's subjectivity and ultimately a representation of Mary Shelley's ambivalent relationship to literary production.

In the tale *Frankenstein* it is the monster, not Frankenstein or Walton, who most desperately seeks human companionship. The monster is a
perfect example of an autonomous individual, in that he has no family
and no past and is therefore completely free to choose his own identity.
In this he prefigures the later image of the orphan in the Victorian novel,
who similarly is undefined by heredity or parentage and is therefore free
to define his or her own identity. However, like the orphan's, the monster's sole aim is to find a place within society. When the monster says, "I
was dependent on none and related to none" (123), it is a lament rather
than an affirmation of his autonomy.

Mary Shelley through the monster criticizes the ideal of the
autonomous self. The monster's desires, even though he is completely
free from social ties or obligations, are conservative rather than revolutionary. In fact, the contrast between Victor Frankenstein's wild imagin-
ings about the threat the monster poses to humanity and what the reader
knows about the monster's really quite modest ambitions borders on the
ludicrous. As Andrew Griffin says in "Fire and Ice in *Frankenstein,*" the

tale embodies opposites, such as fire and ice, male and female, life and death, but then tries to undercut such dualisms. Ultimately, through the monster, Mary Shelley criticizes a Romantic and revolutionary outlook that polarizes the world into an opposition between self and other:

> The monster's narrative reveals a conservative distrust of Romantic extremes, a Victorian longing for security, society, and self-command, symbolized (as in *Jane Eyre*) by the domestic hearth. (Griffin 1979, 51)

Through the figure of the monster, Mary Shelley criticizes the anti-social implications of the Romantic self in terms similar to those used in the Victorian autobiographies I shall consider in the next three chapters. Rather than view the idea of the autonomous and transcendent self with optimism, Mary Shelley regards its implications with mistrust. Earl Wasserman has characterized the Romantic frame of mind succinctly and well in his study of Percy Shelley when he describes his utopian and revolutionary aspirations:

> The divine sanctions for established institutions had reached their ultimate dissolution in the French Revolution. Instead of being accepted as the dictates of God, the structures and laws of church, state, and society were recognized as the work and responsibility of man, and the Revolution, as the dramatic assertion of man's authority for his own civilisation, opened up giddying possibilities centered in the capacities of man's own nature. (Wasserman 1971, 25)

Where Percy Shelley still feels such "giddying possibilities" opened up for the self on both the individual and the social levels to be exciting, Mary Shelley clearly finds them frightening and incompatible with a sense of human community. Her monster speaks social and political criticism and expresses sympathy for the outcast and oppressed, but does not espouse a revolutionary ideal. He may be an autonomous self, but he is not a revolutionary. Like Wordsworth in his "spot of time" earlier, or like later Victorian writers, Mary Shelley favors individual salvation over collective revolution, reflecting a general reaction against the example of the French Revolution.

Lee Sterrenburg in his essay "Mary Shelley's Monster: Politics and Psyche in *Frankenstein*" has documented the ways in which Mary Shelley incorporates the iconography of the political debate over the French Revolution into her tale, drawing in part upon attacks on the political theories of her father, William Godwin. Godwin's opponents had denounced his theories as "demonic, grotesque, and ghoulish" and likened them to "grave-robbing and trafficking with the dead" (Sterrenburg 1979, 150), accusations Mary Shelley incorporated into her tale. Her story enacts both her own rejection of her father's politics and a general reaction against revolutionary and utopian thought. As Sterrenburg says:

> Mary Shelley translates politics into psychology. She uses revolutionary symbolism, but she is writing in a postrevolutionary era when collective political movements no longer appear viable. Consequently she internalizes political debates....Her narrative re-enacts the monster icon, but it does so from the perspective of isolated and subjective narrators who are locked in parricidal struggles of their own. (145)

Sterrenburg here has isolated a problem that faced both Percy and Mary Shelley, and suggests the ground they share in common, despite their different attitudes to the revolutionary implications of the self. Both believe ultimately in the social uses of the imagination, and both criticize an approach to writing that emphasizes the self to the exclusion of the wider social horizon. However, thanks in part to the legacy of the French Revolution and in part to the gradual definition of art in terms of subjective experiences, both find themselves unable to imagine a wider community. Just as Percy Shelley gestures toward a vision of human sympathy in his preface but cannot represent it in his poem, Mary Shelley writes a psychological drama, not an overtly political drama. The monster, although he criticizes social conditions, learns of society through books and observing a single family, the De Laceys, who are themselves political outcasts on the fringe of society. Rather than write a novel that portrays her society directly, she creates a story that involves, as Sterrenburg points out, "isolated and subjective narrators" who thirst for, yet cannot find, a sense of meaningful connection with a wider community.

The problem faced by Mary and Percy Shelley here was common to all nineteenth-century autobiographies written in the wake of the French Revolution. No matter how committed writers were to changing the social structure of Britain, the widespread fear of social upheaval led them to repress the imaginative representation of broad social change. What they ended up representing was change imagined in essentially psycho-

logical, not political, terms. British culture lacked a coherent revolutionary ideology, as Perry Anderson suggests in "Components of the
National Culture":

> The industrial bourgeoisie, traumatized by the French Rev-
> olution and fearful of the nascent working-class movement,
> never took the risk of a confrontation with the dominant aris-
> tocracy...the result was it never generated a revolutionary ide-
> ology. (Anderson 1969, 220)

Anderson's analysis is borne out by the two texts in question here.
While Percy Shelley may gesture toward social change, he writes poetry
that affirms an individualist, not a revolutionary, ideology. Similarly,
while Mary Shelley's sympathies are with social reform, she is critical of a
revolutionary ideology that she views in terms of individual self-interest.
Both end up affirming repression, via anti-self-consciousness, rather than
revolution.

In *Frankenstein* Mary Shelley captures a feeling that was to domi-
nate Victorian autobiography, the sense on the writer's part that he or she
was isolated from his or her society, and the consequent need to repress
or restrain the self in terms of a wider social ethic. Like Mary Shelley,
these later writers found themselves, however, carrying out a social
debate in psychological terms. They opposed an exclusive concentration
on the self, yet in England after the French Revolution an appeal to wider
social movements was inevitably suspect.

In *Frankenstein* Mary Shelley turns a wider social debate into a portrayal of a single, divided consciousness. In this she creates a plot that has
its most obvious counterpart in Robert Louis Stevenson's *Dr. Jekyll and
Mr. Hyde*. Like the women in many Romantic poems, and very much like
the figure of the Specter of Brocken, the monster that Frankenstein
makes is both part of his consciousness and an autonomous agent.
Frankenstein is shown as a protagonist trying to explain an obscure sense
of connection he feels between his self and an "Other Self" apparently
independent of his will. In *Dr. Jekyll and Mr. Hyde* the debate about the
self is carried on unambiguously within the realm of a single consciousness and is now a drama of "liberation" of one incompatible aspect of the
self from the other. The process of internalization, just beginning in
Frankenstein, is fulfilled in Stevenson's admonitory tale and in the Victorian autobiographies that I examine in the next three chapters.

The terms of the debate about the self thus shift. Where in Romantic autobiography a meeting with self was also potentially a meeting with the other, in Victorian autobiography the self is an unavoidable and falsifying force that must be, yet ultimately cannot be, repressed. The aim of most Victorian novels and autobiographies is, as John Kucich correctly identifies in his study of *Middlemarch* (Kucich 1985), to break out of the cell of egotism and embody a wider social reality. As we shall see, however, the terms in which these debates are carried out indicate that it is impossible for these authors to escape the cell of egotism, and they end up affirming the subjective outlook they seek to transcend.

The implicit call for anti-self-consciousness in the two texts I have analyzed in this chapter prefigures the self-repression that is an explicit part of Victorian autobiography. In the next chapter I will examine three Victorian autobiographical texts, Alfred Tennyson's *In Memoriam,* John Ruskin's *Praeterita,* and Robert Louis Stevenson's *Dr. Jekyll and Mr. Hyde,* in terms of their deployment of repression to create a secret double of the self that symbolizes the autobiographical subject created by the act of writing about the self.

CHAPTER FOUR

FROM ROMANTIC TO VICTORIAN AUTOBIOGRAPHY

RUSKIN, TENNYSON, AND THE LOSS OF NATURE

John Ruskin is the figure who registers most strongly the influence of the Romantic conception of self in the Victorian era. Like Wordsworth, Ruskin experiences moments of epiphany in the presence of landscapes, particularly mountains, and is able to read an image of himself into the landscapes he describes. Certain features of landscape, such as hills and mountains, become charged with especial significance for Ruskin. When he was a child, says Ruskin in *Praeterita*, "the idea of distant hills was connected in my mind with the approach to the extreme felicities of life" (13); for Ruskin, therefore, landscape, as it did for Wordsworth, bespeaks his own psychological condition. As John D. Rosenberg says in *The Darkening Glass*, "*Modern Painters* is the last great statement of the English Romantic renovation of sensibility as the *Lyrical Ballads* is the first" (Rosenberg 1961, 2). However, Ruskin also feels strongly the claims of a wider social horizon, claims that do not allow him to rest content with a solitary communion with nature. Heather Henderson has described the way in which the second half of Ruskin's career as a critic was marked by the conviction that "the only really good and dutiful life...is one of service to others, not of self-indulgent pleasure in lonely contemplation of nature and beauty" (Henderson 1989, 105). Ruskin tries to move beyond a self-enclosed view of the world to social criticism, and in his writings progresses from the appreciation of art and nature in *Modern*

Painters to the social criticism of *Unto This Last*. This social agenda is, however, subverted by his individualist premises.

Wordsworth claimed in *The Prelude* that his love of nature led to a love of man, a claim that in chapter 1 I suggested was inaccurate. For Ruskin, however, such a claim would be valid, for his aesthetic appreciation of art and nature really did lead to a form of criticism that addressed wider social concerns. Rosenberg sums up the evolution of Ruskin's thought succinctly when he says that "the love of nature, which first led Ruskin to the study of art, here leads him to the study of man; the study of man leads him in the closing chapters of *Modern Painters* to the criticism of society" (Rosenberg 1961, 2). As Rosenberg indicates, Ruskin's love of nature gave way to social criticism. However, Rosenberg's formulation is a little too neat, as Ruskin's last work, *Praeterita*, does not fit his description. The course of development implied by Rosenberg's description would suggest that Ruskin's later writings were all works of social criticism, but this is not the case.

Ruskin's later works, beginning particularly with *Fors Clavigera* and culminating with *Praeterita*, are increasingly overtly autobiographical. Ruskin described *Fors Clavigera* as "letters on the state of J. Ruskin, Esq.," admitting their largely self-referential nature. By the time of *Praeterita* he had given up addressing any issue wider than that of his self and its history. In the preface to his autobiography he describes his motives for writing as purely selfish:

> I have written therefore, frankly, garrulously, and at ease; speaking of what it gives me joy to remember at any length I like...and passing in total silence things which I have no pleasure in reviewing. (1)

With disarming honesty Ruskin admits that his autobiography is completely self-referential and that he writes only for his own pleasure. All sense of a wider social horizon is lost in this narrowing of focus. Ruskin also claims that he has written *Praeterita* with no guiding principles, claiming, "I think my history will, in the end, be completest if I write as its connected subjects occur to me, and not with formal chronology of plan" (12). Ruskin is here making a virtue of necessity, in that he seems unable to organize his narrative under any guiding rubric, depending instead upon the free associations generated by memory. In its structural repetition and re-visions, *Praeterita* is the prose equivalent of Tennyson's *In Memoriam*, a poem that has a loose, cyclical pattern but seems overall to obey no particularly stringent "formal chronology of plan." Like Ruskin, Tennyson disavows the attempt to create an overarching chronological narrative for his autobiography. Characterizing *In Memoriam* as "brief lays of Sorrow born," Tennyson describes how his personified Sorrow cannot write a more extended narrative:

> Nor dare she trust a larger lay
> But rather loosens from the lip
> Short swallow-flights of song, that dip
> Their wings in tears, and skim away (48.13–16)

Unlike *The Prelude*, both *In Memoriam* and *Praeterita* make no attempt to provide a coherent chronological framework for their narratives. Both work rather by repeating key ideas and recombining them in different ways through repetition and echo. Similarly, Ruskin's *Praeterita* is organized by recurring motifs, as Ruskin's attempts to organize his memories by chronology are thwarted by the pressure of associations forcing their own, inner logic upon him. For reasons I will explore in this chapter, neither Ruskin nor Tennyson could write an autobiography that followed a "formal chronology of plan."

The diminishment of horizon implied in the preface to *Praeterita* is for Ruskin a sign of his defeat in his fight against what he termed "the pathetic fallacy," the reading of the world in terms of self. The pathetic fallacy, like anti-self-consciousness in John Stuart Mill's *Autobiography*, signals Ruskin's attempt to use repression to reign in what he sees as dangerous tendencies toward solipsism and social isolation. In *Modern Painters* he claimed that "the temperament which admits the pathetic fallacy is...that of a mind and body in some sort too weak to deal fully with what is before them" (Ruskin 1903, 7.388). The artist should therefore exercise strength of mind in seeing accurately, not by imposing his own associations on what is before him. Ruskin here speaks of the necessity of the division of inner and outer, the separation of the mind from that which is external to it. For Ruskin to write an autobiography bespeaks a relaxation of will, a loss of determination in his struggle against what Wordsworth in *The Prelude* before him had called "the abyss of idealism" (4.463). This is a condition of completely self-enclosed solipsism, in which the individual is unable to perceive anything beyond a reflex of his own desires. As I will show in the course of this chapter, in his descriptions of landscape in *Praeterita* Ruskin betrays just the kind of weakness of will that he criticized in the pathetic fallacy.

Ruskin crusaded in the years before *Praeterita* against the self-enclosed mind-set he associated with the pathetic fallacy:

> Let him stand in his due relation to the other creatures and to inanimate things....But let him cast off this relation...all diseases of mind leading to fatalest ruin consist primarily in this isolation. (Ruskin 1903, 7.388)

Like Freud in the quotation from *Civilization and its Discontents* in my Introduction, Ruskin assumes that a strict separation of inner and outer is necessary to mental health. He characterizes the confusion of these boundaries in terms of disease. It is typical of Ruskin that when describing the pernicious effects of the pathetic fallacy he should talk in terms of a relation to "inanimate things" rather than other people, as it is primarily the natural landscape that he finds most appealing, not his fellow men. As Ruskin says in *Praeterita*, thanks to his solitary upbringing as a child, "what powers of imagination I possessed...fastened themselves on inanimate things" (28). Ruskin later admits that his upbringing may have had pernicious effects; he says that he gets "distinctively, attached to places, to pictures, to dogs, cats and girls" (392) but does not experience *friendship* in the way others do. Musing on the absence of the word "friendship" in his autobiography, Ruskin says:

> Without thinking myself particularly wicked, I found nothing in my heart that seemed to me worth anybody's seeing; nor had I any curiosity for insight into those of others....And I never expected that they should care for *me*, but only that they should read my books. (393)

Ruskin had previously lamented that, thanks to his rigorous and solitary upbringing, he "had nothing to love" (35). Ruskin exhibits a deeply ambivalent attitude to his parents' stringent control of his early education, vacillating between appreciation and resentment. On the one hand Ruskin credits his lack of toys and companionship as a child with granting him acute powers of observation (12). On the other hand, Ruskin feels that he had never been taught how to interact with other adults, and feels deeply "the want of social discipline" in his upbringing (36). He therefore feels that he is cut off from the social life of other adults and can relate only to inanimate objects. His experience of natural landscapes, and his writing of books about these experiences, compensates for his sense of social isolation.

Like Wordsworth, Ruskin embodies his sense of community through nature, not people. Ruskin in his close attachment to natural landscapes is a kindred spirit to Wordsworth, in that, although his intellectual sympathies led him to espouse social criticism, his emotional allegiance was to an idealized vision of nature. He insists upon a Wordsworthian sense of the autonomy of natural forces, arguing that seeing them in self-referential terms is to lose hold on the most fundamentally important presence in human consciousness. His vehemence on this point originates in his intense imaginative identification with nature as a surrogate for human intimacy. Ruskin's fear that nature is being corrupted by the industrialization and urbanization of Britain in the late nineteenth century therefore threatens his very sense of identity.

Ruskin felt that he and his fellow Victorians had lost contact with nature. This feeling became particularly acute later in his life, so that in such lectures as "The Storm-Cloud of the Nineteenth Century" Ruskin presents an apocalyptic vision of a British landscape that he and his fellow Victorians had polluted beyond redemption. In an earlier lecture, "The Art of England," Ruskin linked his own career from the first volume of *Modern Painters* on to the increasing industrialization and pollution of the British landscape:

> But it has been my fate to live and work in antagonism to the instincts, and yet more the interests, of the age; since I wrote that chapter on the pure traceries of the vault of morning, the fury of useless traffic has shut the sight, whether of morning or evening, from more than the third part of England; and the foulness of sensual fantasy has infected the bright beneficence of the life-giving sky with the dull horrors of disease, and the feeble falsehoods of insanity. (Ruskin 1903, 33:267)

This is in many ways an idiosyncratic reaction on Ruskin's part to the industrialization of the British landscape; his references to "the foulness of sensual fantasy" and "the feeble falsehoods of insanity" have more to do with Ruskin's own deteriorating psychological state than with social change. Raymond E. Fitch has used the "Storm-Cloud" lecture as the focal point from which to characterize the development of Ruskin's thought toward increasingly esoteric and self-referential uses of myth (Fitch 1982, 14). As I have argued elsewhere (Danahay 1991), this lecture represents projections of Ruskin's own sexual anxieties and fears of social upheaval onto the landscape.

For Wordsworth the landscape functioned as a mediated representation of his sense of self; however, nature was also a sufficiently autonomous category to act as an "anchor" that rescued Wordsworth from the abyss of solipsism. For Ruskin and Tennyson, nature is no longer as accessible in their textual self-representations. Ruskin's failing crusade against the "pathetic fallacy" and his self-referential uses of landscape in *Praeterita* show to what extent nature had lost its power for him. In *Praeterita* Ruskin represents nature as a lost Eden.[1] He describes how as a young adult he "felt for the last time, the pure childish love of nature" (204), an experience that came to him only when he was in solitary communion with nature away from any visible sign of human presence. Solitude was necessary in order to enjoy a neo-Wordsworthian epiphany:

> In myself, it has always been quite exclusively confined to *wild*, that is to say, wholly natural places, and especially to scenery animated by streams, or by the sea. The sense of the freedom, spontaneous, unpolluted power of nature was essential in it...but the feeling cannot be described by any of us that have it. Wordsworth's 'haunted me like a passion' is no description of it, for it is not *like* a passion, but *is* a passion; the point is to define how it *differs* from other passions. (205)

Although Ruskin differentiates himself from Wordsworth here, the experience he is describing is a typical Romantic lonely communion with nature. For Ruskin, however, the possibility of "pollution" comes between him and his solitary contemplation of scenery "animated" by water. Where nature could function as a surrogate community for Wordsworth, Ruskin felt that nature was becoming increasingly inaccessible to him because of literal pollution and his own increasingly disordered passions, leading to the "fatalest ruin" of complete isolation. Similarly, for Tennyson in *In Memoriam,* nature either has become an alien force, as in the famous reference to "nature red in tooth and claw," or has become derealized to the point of insubstantiality.

The hills are shadows, and they flow
From form to form, and nothing stands
They melt like mist, the solid lands
Like clouds they shape themselves and go. (123.6–9)

Tennyson's vision of a melting landscape is inspired in part by Lyell's geologic discoveries and a vertiginous sense of the immense age of the earth, as Eleanor B. Mattes has noted (Mattes 1951, 73–86). Lyell's discoveries affected not only Tennyson's sense of nature, however, but also, as in Ruskin's case, his sense of identity. Lyell called geology "the autobiography of the earth," underlining the deep association between the landscape and the autobiographical subject in the nineteenth century. Tennyson, too, reads personal significance into the landscape. However, nature for Tennyson has become a "phantom," a "hollow echo" of Tennyson's own sorrow (3.8), and is no longer an autonomous force in its own right.

One problem facing both Ruskin and Tennyson in representing nature as an autonomous force is that in Britain in the second half of the nineteenth century most people, including Ruskin and Tennyson, experienced nature through the lens of the suburbs. As Ann Bermingham points out, nature for the Victorians was the site of recreation, a diversion from the stresses of urban existence (Bermingham 1986, 159–60). Tennyson's nature is a garden, not a wilderness. In *In Memoriam* Tennyson describes Hallam leaving the "dust and din and steam of town" (89.8) and enjoying a picnic with Tennyson with "the wine-flask lying couch'd in moss" (89.44) in a landscape viewed as a diversion from the vicissitudes of urban life. Similarly, Ruskin's earliest memories are of the suburban environment of Herne Hill. Both writers felt they were losing contact with nature as an untouched "wilderness," as Ruskin's insistence on a "wild" and "unpolluted" scenery shows, thanks to the increasing urbanization of the English landscape. Ruskin's crusade against the pathetic fallacy is in one sense a reaction against the defoliation of the landscape. It also registers, however, the extent to which the loss of the landscape symbolized for both Ruskin and Tennyson the creeping disease of solipsism.

Tennyson's description of nature as a phantom recalls the personification of the Specter of Brocken in Coleridge's poetry. As in Coleridge's poetry, death as the most extreme metaphor for change is viewed as a threat to the continuity of Tennyson's sense of identity and precipitates a search for some overarching principle that will guarantee the self's transcendence. The insubstantiality of the landscape mirrors Tennyson's sense of his own precarious identity. As with Coleridge, Tennyson looks on nature and the ghost of Hallam as phantom presences that elude definition but may ultimately embody a principle of continuity that will rescue him from unsettling changes, especially the ultimate transformation of death. Heather Henderson has remarked in Ruskin's case how he "feared...the many deaths and transformations" taking place around him, and thus tried to present himself as "unchanged" (Henderson 1989, 91). Tennyson registers a similar fear in his reaction to the death of Hallam. Both writers try to assert the continuity of their identities in the face of the transformations of both death and social change.

Tennyson reads Hallam into nature, but only to make both Hallam and nature into mirrors for his sense of self; Tennyson "finds his own vast shadow glory-crown'd" (97.3) in the landscape. *In Memoriam* records an autobiographical process similar to Ruskin's account in *Praeterita* of "the effect on my own mind of meeting myself, by turning back, face to face" (69). Ruskin is more obviously gazing at himself in a mirror in his contemplation of his past as a metaphorical "face" that can gaze back at him as he looks into the mirror of his text (221); Tennyson mediates his image through Hallam and nature. Tennyson records his perception of the landscape as moments of self-recognition:

> What find I in the highest place,
> But mine own phantom chanting hymns?
> And on the depths of death there swims
> The reflex of a human face. (108.9–12)

The face reflected here is not named by Tennyson, and it hovers ambiguously, like the rest of *In Memoriam*, between a vision of Hallam and a version of Tennyson himself. Hallam, like Dorothy Wordsworth in Wordsworth's poems, comes to serve as a mediating link between the masculine author and an image of the self. These figures serve as antidotes to the isolation both Ruskin and Tennyson feared. Hallam becomes almost a substitute for God in some of the stanzas of *In Memoriam*, Tennyson referring to Hallam as "half-divine" (14.10) and claiming that "God and Nature met in light" in his face (111.20). As Alan Sinfield points out, however, Tennyson by "projecting his love onto eternity forgoes the human contact which was its motive force" (Sinfield 1986, 118). Thus Tennyson's deep fear of loss of contact with both nature and any sense of community, which the idealized figure of Hallam is supposed to counteract, is only reinforced by his turning Hallam into a transcendent image of himself. Tennyson's *In Memoriam* therefore exhibits what Ruskin would have termed the pathetic fallacy. Tennyson "sees himself in all he sees" (97.4) and thus turns all phenomena into an aspect of himself.

The pathetic fallacy quotation above is couched in terms of an objective imperative to "him" that emphasizes the apparent objectivity of

Ruskin's stance. Ruskin eschews the first person here. Ruskin tries to excise from his prose any suggestion of falsifying subjectivity, in keeping with his rejection of the pathetic fallacy. However, all of Ruskin's works can be seen as implicitly autobiographical, as Jay Fellows has argued persuasively in *The Failing Distance*. Ruskin turns his private concerns into public crusades. Just as he turns his own desire to stand in a due relation to nature into a universal concern in the quotation I give above, converting "I" to "he," his works of social criticism can be seen as indirect accounts of his own psychological state. His account of the history of the relationship between the landscape and its inhabitants from classical to modern times in *Modern Painters* can be seen as a public version of his own attitude to nature from childhood to maturity. His description of the loss of religious faith in Venetian society in *The Stones of Venice* parallels his own loss of faith. Similarly, of course, *In Memoriam* has been read as a drama of Tennyson's loss of faith and rediscovery of a vague, diffuse spirituality.

In writing his own autobiography at the end of his career, Ruskin finally succumbs to the lure of the solipsism against which he crusaded so fervently. This sense of defeat begins to emerge toward the end of *Fors Clavigera* when Ruskin characterizes his loss of will in metaphorical terms, describing himself as "vacillating, foolish, and miserably failing in all my conduct in life...I, a reed shaken with the wind" (Ruskin 1903, 8.425). His speaking of himself as a "reed shaken with the wind" shows Ruskin's sense that he has lost control over his life, a frightening feeling of powerlessness that emerges very strongly in his next work, *Praeterita*. Rather than try to resist the pathetic fallacy and order his narrative, Ruskin claims in his preface that he will write "garrulously and at ease" and, like the reed, allow the buffets of fortune to determine his course. At the end of *Fors Clavigera* Ruskin already shows signs of giving up his resistance to a self-enclosed solipsism, and he makes this renunciation explicit in the preface to *Praeterita*.

My reading of his prefatory remarks, then, presents Ruskin as an essentially defeated sensibility. Linda Peterson in her discussion of *Praeterita* in *Victorian Autobiography*, however, reads Ruskin's words in the preface as an active rejection of "the traditional demands of spiritual autobiography." Peterson asserts that Ruskin is avoiding "the introspective and often painful methods of the genre" (Peterson 1986, 61) in concentrating only on what it gives him joy to remember and deliberately defying his parents' religious aspirations for him in not writing a spiritual autobiography. However, while Ruskin may be trying to eschew the more painful aspects of introspection, he is not just rejecting the model of spiritual autobiography; he is renouncing any conscious control over his narrative whatsoever. In keeping with his portrait of himself in *Fors Clavigera* as a "reed shaken with the wind," in *Praeterita* he is a writer without any conscious desire other than to repress what it does not give him joy to remember.

Peterson is right to maintain that Ruskin wished to avoid the more painful aspects of introspection. His resistance here, however, is part of his more general and lifelong resistance to self-consciousness, a resistance that led to severe self-repression. As Peterson says, Ruskin objected very strongly to the egotistical implications of spiritual autobiographies such as Bunyan's *Grace Abounding*, particularly the exclusive concentration on "the relations of the deity to his own little self" (Peterson 1986, 61). Ruskin directs just this kind of criticism toward himself in *Praeterita*, referring frequently to his past self as conceited and self-centered. Ruskin says that "by the time I was seven years old...[I] began to lead a very small, perky, contented, conceited, Cock-Robinson-Crusoe sort of life, in the central point which it appeared to me...that I occupied in the universe" (27). The adult Ruskin implicitly criticizes the solipsistic tendencies of his younger self. Ruskin's frequent descriptions of himself as "selfish" and his dislike of Bunyan's *Grace Abounding* are aspects of his doctrine of anti-self-consciousness, his deliberate repression of his self in favor of wider social or ethical imperatives. This anti-self-consciousness doctrine marks Ruskin's inheritance of another aspect of the Romantic self, as Rosenberg points out:

> To perceive the animate artistry of nature the artist must lose his awareness of self and become a mere 'mirror of truth...passive in sight, passive in utterance'. Here Ruskin is faithful both to his personal experience and to his Romantic heritage, to Wordsworth's 'wise passiveness' or Keats' 'negative capability', the capacity to submit to experience in order to record it more accurately and richly. (Rosenberg 1961, 14)

Rosenberg has in mind the moment Ruskin describes in *Praeterita* of sketching a small aspen at Fontainebleu, when he cites the doctrine of the artist "losing his awareness of self." As Ruskin sketched this tree, his conscious control suddenly seemed to fall away, and the lines of the tree asserted their own design, so that "with wonder increasing every instant, I saw that they 'composed' themselves, by finer laws than any known to men" (285). In claiming that the lines of the tree "insisted on being traced," Ruskin denies that the desire to order his perception comes from within, suggesting rather that it was an impulse from an almost animate nature. Ruskin is here remaining faithful to the ideal that led to his rejection of the pathetic fallacy, in that the artist allows nature to guide his hand, thus preserving the autonomy of natural forces from any falsifying effects of his self-consciousness. Ruskin's ideal is a negation of self in the act of perception. In a revealing passage Ruskin turns himself into a *camera obscura*, a machine designed to imitate what it sees faithfully without the intervention of human consciousness:

> In blaming myself, as often I have done, and may have occasion to do again, for my want of affection to other people, I must also express continually, as I think about it, more and more wonder that anybody had any affection for *me*. I thought they might as well have got fond of a *camera lucida*, or an ivory foot rule: all my faculty was merely in showing that such and such things were so. (425)

As in the quotation above in which Ruskin laments his lack of close friendships, Ruskin tries to excise himself from the picture and turn himself into a mere observer or an "innocent eye." He at this point sounds very close to Mill's claiming that he never "estimated himself at all," thus repressing any sign of self-consciousness. In this he is close in spirit to the experience Tennyson attempted to embody in *In Memoriam* in which "individuality itself seems to dissolve and fade away into boundless being" (Hallam Tennyson 1899, 168). Both Ruskin and Tennyson valued experiences that seemed to promise the erasure of self-consciousness.

While Ruskin's ideal may be that the artist should "lose his awareness of self," this is not in fact what happens in *Praeterita*. In contrast to Ruskin's description of the aspen "composing itself," there are several descriptions of landscape in *Praeterita* that bespeak the presence of a very strong subjectivity that finds expression despite the author's self-repression. If we juxtapose to the description of the aspen composing itself Ruskin's earlier description of the road from Paris to Geneva, a road that he traveled many times with his parents and that became an important symbol for him, we can see how a description of landscape can become an indirect emblem for Ruskin's subjectivity.

> Far retiring, I said,—perhaps a mile into the hills...permitting the main road from Paris to Geneva to serpentine and

zigzag capriciously up the cliff terraces with innocent engineering, finding itself every now and then where it had no
intention of getting to, and looking, in a circumflex of puzzled level, where it had to go next. (149–50)

This description of the road from Paris to Geneva is remarkably similar to the drawing from a youthful piece of literature on "Harry's new
road" reproduced in the early pages of *Praeterita* (45) and suggests that
what Ruskin is giving here is a symbol charged with personal significance.
The description of a winding road, which serpentines and zigzags "capriciously" up a hill, is a way for Ruskin to represent to himself an image of his
life, just as Wordsworth used the image of a river in *The Prelude*. This beautiful piece of anthropomorphizing of the road from Paris to Geneva stands
as a perfect image for the process in Ruskin's autobiography whereby he
follows a narrative thread and then stops "in a circumflex of puzzled level,"
having reached a point that he apparently did not predict. Just as the aspen
he sketched seemed to compose itself, Ruskin's narrative follows its own
logic, apparently independent of its author. I say "apparently" because
there is a design behind *Praeterita*, just as there was in his sketch of the
aspen. It is just that Ruskin denies the presence of a shaping, controlling
self that orchestrates his memories. He practices implicitly what John Stuart Mill explicitly termed "anti-self-consciousness" in his autobiography.

The "innocent engineering" of the road stands for the way in which,
if there is a design behind *Praeterita*, the author keeps it steadfastly hidden from himself. This phrase sums up what an embattled position Ruskin
holds in his "innocence." The position of naiveté or innocence is maintained at the cost of a refusal of the knowledge of the engineering, the
design that it takes to construct the narrative. Ruskin through innocent
engineering tries to keep alive the sense of mystery and wonder that
informs the text. Ruskin wishes to preserve "the innocence of the eye," as
he puts it elsewhere (Ruskin 1903, 5.561), but this innocence is achieved
through a refusal of self-knowledge. The childlike innocence he wishes to
recapture must be won by denying the knowledge of the mature adult.
The innocence he maintains here is linked to the duplicity embodied in
Dr. Jekyll and Mr. Hyde, a duality resulting from self-repression.

Heather Henderson has remarked on the role of "an unconscious
strategy of duplicity" in *Praeterita*, in which Ruskin apparently promises
that his narrative will progress according to a plan, only to disappoint the
reader (Henderson 1989, 73–74).[2] Henderson remarks on the existence
of "two selves" in the autobiography, and of two narratives, one overt

and the other covert (69, 92). Henderson here is reacting to Ruskin's use of repression, and describing the duplicity of a narrative in which consciousness is at war with itself.

Although Ruskin embodies himself indirectly in his descriptions of landscape, he is led by his desire to overcome subjectivity to deny the shaping presence of his own consciousness. In his commitment to anti-self-consciousness Ruskin represses his self out of fear of falling into the pathetic fallacy. However much he may deny the falsifying presence of his self-consciousness, however, it remains an important force in his prose. Ruskin is led by his fear of solipsism to deny his connection to the image of himself in the text in the same way that Dr. Jekyll in Stevenson's tale denies his connection to his double. In these texts, the self is a force that must be suppressed or denied.

"Innocent engineering" best illustrates the distance between Wordsworth and Ruskin. Where Wordsworth spoke of "wise passiveness," he also stressed that people "half create / What they perceive," so that perception and memory are mixtures of both passivity and activity. Ruskin emphasizes only the passivity of the artist's position, apparently suppressing any role for the self in creation. This passivity takes on a disturbing aspect in *Praeterita,* in that Ruskin is unable to order his narrative and, like with the road from Paris to Geneva, finds himself led to points that he did not realize he was going to reach. His description of himself in *Fors Clavigera* as a reed buffeted by the wind is also apt for *Praeterita,* in that his autobiography betrays a collapse of his will. This is particularly evident in the difficulty he has in beginning and ending his episodes, a difficulty that is for him a source of some frustration. Wordsworth in *The Prelude* could point to the transcendence of his memories across time as a source of inspiration, the difficulty he has in defining his self being a token of its limitlessness:

> Hard task to analyze a soul in which,
> Not only in general habits and desires,
> But each most obvious and particular thought
> Not in a mystical and idle sense
> But in the words of reason deeply weigh'd
> Hath no beginning. (2.232–27)

Wordsworth is struggling here to describe a mystical conviction of his self's transcendence. His insistence on "particularity" and "reason" shows that such a conviction does not sit easily with his empiricist faith in the measurability and tangibility of all phenomena, but he nonetheless draws hope and inspiration from his inability to name the origin or the end point of his sense of self. For Ruskin, however, the inability to find beginnings or endings for his narrative is far more troubling, as he admits, "How to begin speaking of [L'Hotel du Mont Blanc], I do not know; still less how to end" (402).

For Ruskin the inability to find a way to begin or end his descriptions attests to a loss of control over his own narrative. Elizabeth K. Helsinger in "The Structure of Ruskin's *Praeterita*" points out that there are eight separate beginnings in *Praeterita*, as Ruskin finds each apparent new thread does not bring with it an expected culmination (Helsinger 1979, 96). Ruskin is simply unable to distinguish "beginnings" and "endings" because everything seems connected to everything else in his life. Ruskin finds he is unable to impose a coherent chronological or narrative form on his memories, as his apologies to the reader show:

> In my needful and fixed resolve to set the facts down continuously, leaving the reader to his reflections on them, I am slipping a little too fast over the surface of things. (253)

> The thoughts come too fast upon me, for before Joanie said this, I was trying to recollect.... (513)

The first of these quotations comes from a quarter of the way through *Praeterita*, the second from the end, and they show that it became more and more difficult for Ruskin to preserve the sense of his autobiography as an ordered narrative directed at an audience outside of himself. In the first quotation Ruskin acknowledges that he may be leaving his reader behind and resolves to "know, or at least try to guess" what his reader is thinking. The fact that he qualifies his attempt to "know" by saying he will try to "guess" shows how far he is beginning to doubt his ability to write anything that does more than give himself pleasure. He is losing his sense of a wider audience for his words. By the closing pages his horizon has narrowed to himself alone, and his sense of a division between his past and present breaks down. He more and more frequently uses the present rather than the past tense.

Ruskin, rather than finding difficulty asserting the connection between a past and a present self, seems on the contrary increasingly to have difficulty in keeping them apart. When he looks back on his past self, he does not discover difference between past and present, only identity:

> Looking back from 1886 to that Brook shore of 1837, whence I could see the whole of my youth, I find myself in nothing changed...in the total of me I am but the same youth, disappointed and rheumatic. (206)

The boundaries between past and present, between private and public, and between inner and outer, that Ruskin tried to maintain by dint of an unremitting self-repression break down in *Praeterita*. Ruskin's use of water imagery in the text records this most dramatically, as he reworks a Romantic motif.

The reference to the "brook" here recalls Romantic imagery of the river or stream as the course of a life, but in Ruskin's case the idea of flow and change implicit in this metaphor seems inappropriate. The river, like the journey, could dramatize a process of gradual development through time, whereas there is no change or development in Ruskin's narrative. As Helsinger points out, water motifs are found throughout Ruskin's text (Helsinger 1979, 87). She argues that their effect is to link the chapters in such a way as to suggest that there is no change or development, just the gradual accretion of metaphors for Ruskin's sense of self, just as in *In Memoriam* there is no obvious chronological development, rather a repetition of key experiences. Thus "The Springs of Wendel" at the beginning of the book links up with the images of water in the final chapter, binding the young and the old Ruskin together and stressing the identity between past and present rather than the difference between them. As Helsinger says, Ruskin's complaints of "shapelessness, isolation, lost ways, and unreached goals go on to imply a criticism of the linear view of life as progress or achievement" (Helsinger 1979, 96), a criticism that is also represented through imagery. In such an autobiography there can be no discrete beginnings or definite culminations, as there would be in a spiritual autobiography that embodied the ideal of progress.

Both Ruskin and Tennyson resist the pull toward completion and thus thwart the narrative progress of their autobiographies. *In Memoriam* in its "short swallow flights of song" eschews a connected biography of Hallam or any chronological account of Tennyson's own development. Ruskin's narrative begins, meanders, then begins again, but reaches no apparent narrative climax. In their desire to resist the extinction of individuality in death, they represent in their texts a self that apparently transcends time rather than one that is trapped within a linear sequence. They represent an attenuated version of Wordsworth's transcendent self, a self that defies the ultimate change of death. The most moving image for this process occurs in the final pages of *Praeterita*.

In the final water image in *Praeterita* Ruskin describes the depiction in a stained glass window of the miracle of water turning into wine, an image irradiated and transformed by sunlight. Ruskin describes the conversion of the pure, innocent water representing youth into the mature wine of the adult, but it is a change that occurs instantaneously rather than through a long maturation process. This image symbolizes indirectly the course of Ruskin's life and his conviction that he has been in some sense deeply changed by his experiences, but in this miraculous tableau any idea of a gradual process is lost in a spectacular, instantaneous transformation. This image symbolizes a change that takes place outside of time rather than within it. This timeless image of change does in fact show a "dramatic development of identity," but so dramatic as to be miraculous.

The image of the water glowing into wine is a mystical and antirational solution to the incompatible convictions that Ruskin holds about himself, the two selves referred to by Henderson. Ruskin's text, like other Romantic and Victorian autobiographies, abounds with dualisms. Stasis versus change, emblematized by the mixing of flowing images of water and of crystalline stasis (54, 57), is one such dualism. The other and most fundamental dualism is the pull of an isolated, meditative existence versus the career of a social reformer. Ruskin repeatedly refers to himself as "monkish" and to his existence at Herne Hill as taking place in a walled Eden, cut off from the rest of society. He is drawn to such Edens, but also finds them "sweetly selfish" (28). In a dialectic of desire and the repression of that desire, he notes that within the walls of the Herne Hill Eden "*all* the fruit was forbidden" (26), but this only made the fruit all the more desirable when his parents had a "harvest festival" and he was allowed to taste the result (40). The fruits of Eden having been forbidden, therefore, only made them twice as attractive. This is the positive side to his enclosure in the Eden of Herne Hill, an enclosure he credits with making Ruskin the child into Ruskin the adult art critic.

However, "the evil consequence" of his parents' raising him in isolation and cutting him off from other children was that "when affection did come, it came with violence utterly rampant and unmanageable, at least by me, who never before had anything to manage" (35). The enclosing walls of his Eden, therefore, kept out temptation, but when Ruskin was finally exposed to temptation his desire exploded with uncontainable force. The references to walled Edens represent Ruskin's ambivalent attitude to desire and the repression of that desire.

Helsinger gives several examples of what she calls "Ruskin's landscape of desire" (Helsinger 1979, 102), pointing out moments in *Prae-*

terita where landscape becomes an indirect emblem for his own desires. Ruskin maintains his innocence by repressing his knowledge of the desire he represents in his landscapes. The repeated Eden images in *Praeterita* point to the narrative of the fall that underlies Ruskin's view of his own development. Ruskin's fall occurs when he meets the beautiful and accomplished Domecq girls and he is plunged into his own "foulness of sensual fantasy":

> Virtually convent-bred more closely than the maids them-selves, without a single sisterly or cousinly affection for refuge or lightning rod, and having no athletic skill or pleasure to check my dreaming, I was thrown, bound hand and foot, in my unaccomplished simplicity, into the fiery furnace, or fiery cross, of these four girls,—who of course reduced me to a mere heap of ashes in four days. Four days, at the most, it took to reduce me to ashes, but the Mercredi des cendres lasted four years. (169)

Ruskin identifies himself as victim in this passage. He compares himself to a novice from a convent, a martyr thrown to the lions, and Christ on the cross. Desire enters the domestic tranquility, and his mother has no idea that "her house was on fire" (171). Sexuality is repre-sented as a fearful, violent force that wrecks the self-enclosed existence of Herne and Denmark Hills. The one thing Ruskin cannot do here is acknowledge himself as a desiring subject; the force of desire acts upon him from outside. He does not acknowledge directly that he had any sex-ual desires of his own. The girls are a "furnace," and he is burned by them, not by the heat of his own desire.

Ruskin projects his desires into landscapes, paintings, crystals, and prepubescent little girls; his anthropomorphizing of crystals in *Ethics of the Dust*, for instance, dramatizes his deeply divided attitude to the girls to whom he is lecturing as potentially sexual beings. Ruskin consistently reads his own divided subjectivity and repressed desires into inanimate nature. In a letter to Effie Gray during their courtship, Ruskin equated her with an attractive but dangerous landscape:

> You are like a sweet forest of pleasant glades and whisper-ing branches—where people wander on and on in its playing shadows they know not how far—and when they come near the centre of it, it is all cold and impenetrable....You are like

the bright—softly swelling—lovely fields of a high glacier cov-
ered with fresh morning snow—which is lovely to the eye—
and soft and winning on the foot—but beneath there are
winding clefts and dark places in its cold—cold ice—where
men fall and do not rise again. (James 1947, 68)

In this letter the woman is turned into a natural landscape, but one
that contains hidden dangers, especially "below." Ruskin's problems with
the "fiery furnace" of his own sexuality lead him to represent Effie Gray
here as a glacier who will quench him so that he cannot "rise again." The
sexual symbolism in this landscape needs no underlining. The important
point here is that Ruskin's relationship to both women and nature is subverted by desire. Because of his own ambivalent sexuality, he must
attempt to excise any taint of "the foulness of sensual fantasy" both from
women, by seeing them as little girls, and from nature, by trying to erad-
icate pollution and returning to an Edenic landscape. Ruskin betrays a
deep fear of female sexuality.

The amazing thing about Ruskin and his fellow Victorians is the
extent to which they used repression and yet seemed unaware of it. To
contemporary commentators such as myself, Helsinger, or Peterson, the
duplicity involved in repressing desire and yet exhibiting it so nakedly in
other forms seems remarkable. As Linda Peterson has remarked, *Praeterita* is so overwhelmingly self-repressive that critics have been led to
wonder "about Ruskin's awareness of his repression and especially about
his self-consciousness in *Praeterita* of his depiction of that repression"
(Peterson 1986, 66). Yet for Ruskin and other Victorians repression was a
tool in the construction of their subjectivity that they could not acknowledge because it would threaten their innocence.

Ruskin admits at one point in *Praeterita*, "As I look deeper into the
mirror, I find myself a more curious person than I had thought" (221).
The autobiographical text for Ruskin has explicitly become a mirror
rather than a disguised vehicle for self-representation like the landscape.
There is a naive quality to Ruskin's surprised self-scrutiny, a lack of self-
consciousness that implies that in writing his autobiography he is discovering things about himself as the text unfolds. Ruskin is "innocent" of his
own designs, but it is an innocence that, like his "innocence of the eye,"
must be maintained at the cost of a willed ignorance. It is this self-denial
that leads to the contradictory images of himself that we find throughout
Praeterita and the pervasive sense of self-repression to which Peterson
refers. When Ruskin experiences desire, he loses this innocence and thus

his direct communion with nature. He enters the world of "The Storm Cloud of the Nineteenth Century," where nature is infected and distorted by the presence of desire. Ruskin would like to erase himself as the desiring subject and thus idealizes a situation in which he is "observing without being observed" (156). He would like to avoid the pathetic fallacy, the confusion of his inner desires with the outer landscape, by becoming invisible. He would like, as he admits, to become a *camera obscura* who simply records what he sees. On the other hand, he is a man with desires and cannot help representing them, whether he acknowledges them directly or not. This leads to his anguished relationship to both landscapes and women. Both women and landscapes function as metaphorical mirrors for Ruskin's divided subjectivity, in which desire and repression produce a split subjectivity.

The two selves in Ruskin's *Praeterita* are therefore a product of the masculine split subject who uses a feminized other to represent his own conflicted sexuality. The use of repression, and the creation of a dual or divided narrative, links *Praeterita* and *In Memoriam* to an important trope in nineteenth-century fiction, the double or doppelganger. The most famous Victorian representation of this double existence and its links to repression is of course Robert Louis Stevenson's *Dr. Jekyll and Mr. Hyde*. The common thread running through *In Memoriam, Praeterita,* and *Dr. Jekyll and Mr. Hyde* is the construction of the subject as divided; this division is expressed in terms of "duplicity," a view of duality that implicates it in lying and secrecy.

"A PROFOUND DUPLICITY OF LIFE": REPRESSION AND THE SPLIT SUBJECT OF VICTORIAN AUTOBIOGRAPHY

Is there no baseness we would hide?
No inner vileness that we dread?
—In Memoriam 51.3–4

Victorian male autobiographers betray what Robert Louis Stevenson in *Dr. Jekyll and Mr. Hyde* termed a "profound duplicity of life" (78). While defining themselves as unitary and single selves, in the sense proposed by Wordsworth as discussed in chapter 1, Victorian authors actually portray a deeply divided and conflicted subjectivity that betrays the effects of repression. The connotations of secrecy and lying in Stevenson's phrase indicate how Victorian subjectivity was implicated in an attempt to mask the falsifying effects of this self-repression. The result was the familiar Victorian characterization of subjectivity in terms of a "double consciousness," an experience of a bifurcating and self-divided interiority at odds with its own being.

The term *duplicity* links Victorian subjectivity to guilty secrets. Recent works on Victorian literature have linked this sense of secrecy in *Dr. Jekyll and Mr. Hyde* and *In Memoriam* to "heterosexual panic" and the articulation of the category of "homosexuality." As Richard Dellamora points out, *In Memoriam* "celebrates desire between men short of sexuality," but the representation of male desire became increasingly problematic as the century wore on (Dellamora 1990, 17). Similarly, Elaine Showalter has linked *Dr. Jekyll and Mr. Hyde* to Robert Louis Stevenson's attractiveness to his male friends (Showalter 1990, 107). While the tension between male affection and the articulation of a homosexual identity informs both texts, this is not in my reading the origin of the motif of the double. Rather, the double has its origin in the idea that individuals can have an inner and private existence that conceals the subject's desires from public scrutiny. The Victorian subject can thus have an inner life that could mask deviance and crime. The actual "crime" in *Dr. Jekyll and Mr. Hyde* is never revealed; the text's cardinal sin is secrecy itself. Similarly, in *In Memoriam* Tennyson's anxiety is not that his desire for Hallam is potentially homosexual, but that he could reveal some "inner vileness," a secret "baseness," in the public medium of language. This vileness is more diffuse than a specific fear of revealing a too-intense attachment to another male. If anything, it is more bound up with the sin of pride than any sexual transgression.

In Memoriam is, after all, more about Alfred Tennyson than Hallam. It is an autobiography, not a biography, and expresses Tennyson's diffuse sense of his own identity rather than details about Hallam. Hallam becomes a kind of mirror for Tennyson, a double onto whom Tennyson projects his own face. Like Dorothy Wordsworth in "Tintern Abbey," Hallam becomes a screen for the projection of Tennyson's sense of self. This is a method that Stevenson turns into the plot of *Dr. Jekyll and Mr. Hyde* when the protagonist's desires take on an independent life and start roaming London of their own accord. Mr. Hyde becomes Dr. Jekyll's "inner vileness" personified.

Both *In Memoriam* and *Dr. Jekyll* exclude the feminine in their representations of the masculine subject. *In Memoriam* focuses on the bond between two men and places Tennyson in the roles usually occupied by mothers or brides. The narrative of *Dr. Jekyll* notoriously excludes women, representing instead a society in which the primary bonds are between bachelors who, if they are sexual, studiously repress any evidence of the fact. Both texts repress the presence of the feminine in constructing the split subject of Victorian masculinity.

Mr. Hallam and Mr. Hyde therefore have a great deal in common. Dellamora sees Tennyson's lines "I sometimes hold it half a sin / To put in words the grief I feel" (5.1–2) as denoting Tennyson's ambivalence about revealing "an embodied affective intimacy that so far exceeds normal experience...that the bond becomes something to conceal from the eyes of the mundane" (Dellamora 1990, 35). However, the "sin" here is more unlocalized than Dellamora suggests, and echoes the innumerable times that Tennyson associates the word *crime* with trying to express in words some ineffable inner psychological state that should not or cannot be embodied in the public medium of language (see for example section 27, line 8; section 72, line 18; section 85, line 61). Like Dr. Jekyll, Tennyson feels there may be a secret aspect to his inner life that it would be a crime to express in public. Victorian autobiography is thus implicated in the idea of secrecy as the sign of an inner life that both guarantees the subject's individuality and links the subject to antisocial practices.

As a Victorian reworking of the Frankenstein myth, *Dr. Jekyll and Mr. Hyde* reveals an underlying suspicion that the autonomous, private self is an antisocial force that, if given public expression, would erupt in violent and criminal acts. The story of *Dr. Jekyll and Mr. Hyde* suggests that to repress the autonomous self is a social duty, but one that is achieved at great cost. Similarly, Ruskin's autobiography *Praeterita* reveals the effects of his lifelong self-repression in his sense of duplicity or doubleness. The model of subjectivity represented in these apparently dissimilar texts by Stevenson, Ruskin, and Tennyson is in the final analysis the same, based upon the Victorian sense of a self-divided subjectivity that is expressed through doubleness or duplicity.

In Stevenson's tale, the socially responsible and professional Dr. Jekyll is threatened by his totally self-centered and destructive internal antithesis, Mr. Hyde. Just as Ruskin embodies a fundamentally divided consciousness, Stevenson portrays his protagonist as divided into two incompatible versions of a single self. *Dr. Jekyll and Mr. Hyde* is a tale of the refusal, and consequent return, of the repressed forces of the psyche that embodies the same kind of anti-self-consciousness as that carried out by Ruskin in *Praeterita*.

In my reading of *Dr. Jekyll and Mr. Hyde* I do not see Hyde as an "evil" character. Rather, he is completely self-centered, like Ruskin's childish self at Herne Hill, and thus represents a perverse sort of innocence. It is Hyde's total indifference to social values, rather than any inherent evil, that makes him such an alluring, and at the same time repellent, character for Dr. Jekyll.

Like the Romantic anti-autobiography *Frankenstein, Dr. Jekyll and Mr. Hyde* is a fictional tale that comments upon the antisocial potential of autobiography. Victorian autobiography as represented by *Dr. Jekyll and Mr. Hyde* involves a denial of self-consciousness, a deliberate attempt to suppress self-knowledge. Jekyll's inability to reconcile himself to the existence of Hyde is a denial of an aspect of his own character. Dr. Jekyll shows a refusal to acknowledge, rather than inability to explain, the connection between himself and his double: Dr. Jekyll exclaims, "He, I say— I cannot say I" (98). Jekyll calls Hyde "he" even though he realizes that the first-person pronoun would be equally appropriate when discussing his double. Jekyll sets up the fiction of Hyde as a person independent of himself and "even called and made myself a familiar object in my second character" (85). However, Jekyll here knows he is practicing a form of self-repression. He is guilty of confusing the bounds of his ego by ascribing desires he knows originate within himself to another person.

In becoming Hyde, Jekyll becomes a younger version of himself, but this is a fraught and guilty return to the past. Jekyll says, "I felt younger, lighter, happier in body; within I was conscious of...a solution of the bonds of obligation, an unknown but not an innocent freedom of the soul" (82). When Jekyll becomes Hyde, he, like any autobiographer, returns to his past and the freedom and exuberance of his youth. However, Hyde's freedom is not purely innocent, even if it is childlike in its selfishness. Just as Ruskin criticized his past self as selfish and solipsistic, Hyde as a younger version of Jekyll finds "his every thought and action centered on self" (87). Just as Ruskin criticized the solipsism of his youthful self, yet saw this past in Edenic and alluring terms, so Dr. Jekyll both abhors and finds attractive the self-centered freedom he experiences in the guise of Mr. Hyde.

This turning inward and backward to a younger self is thus represented as an achievement of freedom at the cost of denying the social "bonds of obligation." Autobiography here is represented, as it is in *Frankenstein*, as a guilty denial of social obligations. To write about the self is to exclude a wider social horizon and thus to evade one's social responsibility. The younger, "free" self gradually erodes the will of the social self in *Dr. Jekyll and Mr. Hyde*, until the divided self becomes single in its selfishness. The plot of the tale records a process where the distinctions between the older, professional self and the younger self gradually erode, until Jekyll becomes trapped in the body of the younger, self-centered Hyde and commits crimes against society, acting out his antisocial nature.

Like Ruskin's autobiography, *Dr. Jekyll and Mr. Hyde* portrays a consciousness divided into incompatible versions of self, one antisocial and childlike in its selfishness, the other mature and socially responsible. It is with the crisis of Hyde's murder of the M.P. that the two halves come together and Jekyll can finally see his life as a whole. He then acknowledges the connection between himself and Hyde that he had previously denied.

> A mist dispersed...the veil of self-indulgence was rent from head to foot. I saw my life as a whole: I followed it up from the days of childhood...through the self-denying toils of my professional life, to arrive again and again, with the same sense of unreality, at the demented horrors of the evening. (94)

Dr. Jekyll experiences within himself a split between the antitheses of "self-indulgence" and "self-denial," completely incompatible antisocial and social impulses. Like *Frankenstein*, *Dr. Jekyll and Mr. Hyde* polarizes the self into diametrically opposed halves. The murder, the antithesis of the professional work of the doctor as a healer and saver of lives, brings the contrast between Jekyll and Hyde to crisis point. With this murder the self-denying professional Dr. Jekyll and the self-centered Mr. Hyde are reconciled, as Jekyll acknowledges a coherence and unity in a life that had hitherto been marked by "incoherency" (84), that is, by both an inability to see his life as a whole and an inability to express the connection between himself and Hyde ("He, I say—I cannot say I"). With the murder he can at last admit that his persona as Mr. Hyde is part of his self, and can articulate the connection between "he" and "I."

Stevenson, in representing the "incoherency" of Dr. Jekyll's autobiography, sets up a fictional counterpart to the difficulty Ruskin and Tennyson had in ordering their autobiographical narratives. Dr. Jekyll voices the suspicion that "man will ultimately be known for a mere polity of multifarious, incongruous and independent citizens" (40), suggesting that his autobiography should be the story of a whole crowd of selves. Helsinger in her article on *Praeterita* says suggestively of Ruskin's autobiography that "in place of a single life, Ruskin discovers many different lives, each with its own time scheme" (Helsinger 1979, 95). Ruskin's and Dr. Jekyll's autobiographies are thus marked by a similar "incoherency" where one would expect unity. They represent the masculine subject, however, not as multiple but as divided or split into two incompatible versions of the self.

The division of Dr. Jekyll into incompatible versions of self is signaled by contrasting images of freedom, or the breaking of bounds, and restraint. For Jekyll to become Hyde is both a gaining of freedom and an entering into a bondage, creating an ambiguity as to whether the idea of "bonds" appropriately characterizes the social, self-denying, professional self or the antisocial, sensual self. Jekyll says, "I could...in a moment, like a schoolboy, strip off these lendings and spring headlong into the sea of liberty" (41). The respectable Dr. Jekyll can return to a schoolboy-like past state, an Edenic condition like Ruskin's selfish days at Herne Hill, and become the unfettered and self-centered Edward Hyde. In doing this he springs into a "sea" of liberty. The idea of a sea, however, expresses a loss of identity that is in some respects a fearsome experience. This fear is also expressed when Jekyll describes falling into "slavery" to Hyde (84), so that this liberty is also an enslavement. The implied contradiction here between freedom and restraint is overtly expressed by Utterson's description of Jekyll's home as "that house of voluntary bondage" (45), the volition implied by "voluntary" contrasting with the "bondage" that Dr. Jekyll's act of will produces.

The phrase *voluntary bondage* expresses what I refer to in the next chapter as "subjected autonomy." It suggests the interplay of autonomy and repression in these Victorian texts. *Voluntary bondage* suggests a self-imposed restraint that counteracts the threat of the autonomous will. Stevenson's ambivalent attitude toward autonomy comes across most forcefully in this phrase. Voluntary bondage is not a condition to be avoided, but the steady state of Victorian subjectivity.

This ambivalent attitude to liberty and constraint marks *Dr. Jekyll and Mr. Hyde* as a meditation upon the status of the autonomous individual. Stevenson fears that the autonomous, self-enclosed individual is inimical to the bonds of the community, yet he also finds the image of the free self appealing. Just like Ruskin, he is both attracted to and repelled by the image of the solipsistic individual. Mr. Hyde is a personification of the capacity of the individual to withdraw from social ties into himself and thus to conceal his inner life from public scrutiny. Mr. Hyde inhabits a realm beyond public reality and the laws of society and is therefore, in Stevenson's terms, absolutely free. Because the hidden aspect of Dr.

Jekyll's personality has no place in the workaday world, Hyde is seen as a completely autonomous, unfettered individual. As Jekyll says, he "does not even exist" and is thus "quite apart from normal laws" (87).

The implication of *Dr. Jekyll and Mr. Hyde* is that Mr. Hyde is the truest expression of Dr. Jekyll's personality. Rather than the persona of the respectable physician being the authentic aspect of Dr. Jekyll's personality, it is Mr. Hyde who is seen as the most powerful. The plot therefore enacts the inevitable exposure of the "hidden" antisocial self and the ultimate death of Dr. Jekyll. The plot is a Victorian nightmare, in that the inner life of the individual, not accessible to public scrutiny, is ultimately bound up with crime and deviance. Indeed, individuality, if it is defined as the degree of the personality's deviance from public norms, can very easily be defined as criminal, as it was by De Quincey in his autobiographical texts. *Dr. Jekyll and Mr. Hyde* as a detective story moves inexorably toward exposure of this "hidden" life in Dr. Jekyll's autobiography. Autobiography is thus connected with the revelation of an inner life that would best be kept secret but erupts into the public realm through writing. The hidden, private, and imaginative self is seen as much more potent than the public self, and accordingly breaks through the public mask in violent and extreme ways.

There is no logical reason why the absolutely selfish Mr. Hyde should commit murder, as it gains him nothing. Stevenson is through murder expressing a fear that the autonomous self is innately inimical to social bonds. Murder is the most extreme antithesis to social behavior, especially the healing function of a doctor, and is an act that precipitates the confession with which the tale ends. The same fear that the self is innately antisocial motivated Ruskin's crusade against the pathetic fallacy and his resistance to encroaching solipsism. For this reason, both texts attempt to repress the autonomous self, and express contradictory images of freedom and constraint. While the autonomous self may be free, it must be repressed and contained, lest it break all social bounds.

Whenever the persona of Jekyll gives way to that of Hyde, he feels "a solution of the bonds of obligation" (48) that had previously restricted him. "Pleasure" is thus seen as a guilty emotion, one that is inimical to the "position" of an eminent doctor, so that when Jekyll becomes Hyde he loses the prestige of the title "Dr" and becomes "Mr." The position of a doctor in society is presented as a special one. Because of his "duty" to heal, he is in some way implicated more closely in bonds of obligation than other people and has a more pressing social commitment. Jekyll's "fall" into the persona of Hyde is thus seen as particularly reprehensible.

This fall in position is intimately bound up with anxieties about language itself. The text signals covert anxieties about language through such signs as Utterson's name; the strong, silent lawyer is actually marked by the degree to which he does not "utter" or express his being through words. His communication is carried on by extralinguistic means. Hyde himself has an "unexpressed" deformity that people cannot name. Part of his horror is that he embodies that which should not be spoken, and elicits from people expressions of rage and hatred that they would normally repress. To express oneself in language, to body forth visibly as Hyde does the repressed aspects of the individual, is therefore fraught with violence and danger. Similarly, in *In Memoriam,* revealing emotion is associated with sin and crime (see for example section 5, lines 1-2; section 27, line 8; section 18, line 85). Stevenson's text is itself divided, as it at once gives expression to dark misgivings yet argues the necessity for repressing those secrets toward which it gestures. Stevenson's text itself both reveals and conceals, enacting its own duplicity or doubleness.

That Stevenson has summed up a prevalent Victorian model of subjectivity is confirmed by the degree to which overt autobiographies embody a similarly divided or double self. Both Mill and Ruskin were able to lead double lives, in which their intellectual and emotional lives were separate, and in their autobiographies suppressed or edited out those aspects of their lives that did not fit their public image. The prevalence of this type of division is attested to by the Victorian insistence upon "sincerity," the correspondence of word and thought. This insistence upon sincerity was an uneasy acknowledgment of the way in which words could often conceal as much as they revealed. J. H. Newman referred to these as "unreal words" (Newman, 54), and Ruskin as "masked words" (Ruskin 1903, 18:67), and what they both had in mind here was a growing sense that people increasingly masked their selves. Victorians used words to conceal aspects of their inner lives from public scrutiny, and thus led double lives.

Dr. Jekyll and Mr. Hyde is the classic expression of this guilty Victorian doubleness. The idea of doubleness as duplicity or secrecy is the main concern of the autobiographical narrative that concludes the tale:

> Hence it came about that I concealed my pleasures; and when I reached years of reflection, and began to look around me and take stock of my progress and position in the world, I stood already committed to a profound duplicity of life. (78)

Jekyll is here expressing in fictional terms the common Victorian experience of a profound contradiction in the experience of a self. Stevenson's description here recalls strikingly Edmund Gosse's assertion that he discovered his individuality when he realized he could keep a secret from his father. At this point he becomes aware of a doubleness within himself that allows him to carry on a "dialogue of the mind with itself." Victorian subjectivity in this model, then, is predicated upon a radical self-division and self-conflict that is deliberately repressed in the presentation of a unitary self.

Dr. Jekyll's inner life is connected through "Mr. Hide" with secrecy and concealment. It is the ability to conceal secrets that Edmund Gosse stresses in his autobiography *Father and Son* as confirming his own individuality and freedom from his father's authority.

> I had found a companion and a confidant in myself. There was a secret in this world and it belonged to me and to a somebody who lived in the same body with me. There were two of us, and we could talk with one another...it was in this form that the sense of my individuality suddenly descended upon me. (30)

Like Dr. Jekyll's doubleness, Gosse's double consciousness is located within a single body and is implicated in duplicity. As in *Dr. Jekyll and Mr. Hyde,* "individuality" means not that the individual is single, but rather that he is double and can thus set up a self-enclosed and self-sufficient system that makes him autonomous. Like Dr. Jekyll and his duplicity, this autonomy is bound up with the ability of the individual to conceal a private or inner meaning from the outside world. To be an individual is, paradoxically, to be double.[3]

When Utterson and Poole finally break into Dr. Jekyll's chambers, one of the things they find there is a mirror:

> Next, in the course of their review of the chamber, the searchers came to the cheval-glass, into whose depths they looked with an involuntary horror. But it was so turned as to show them nothing but...their own pale and fearful countenances stooping to look in. (64)

Showalter says of this mirror that it "testifies not only to Jekyll's scandalously unmanly narcissism, but also to the sense of the mask and the Other that has made the mirror an obsessive symbol in homosexual literature" (Showalter 1990, 111). Rather than symbolize "unmanly narcissism," this mirror in the very heart of Jekyll's private realm stands as a sign of the repression of autobiography as solipsism. Ruskin looks in the mirror and finds himself more "curious" than he had thought, and Utterson and Poole look in Jekyll's mirror and find only their own faces. The mirror links Utterson and Poole, and by extension all Victorian males, to Mr. Hyde as the repressed other of their psyches, the secret half of their double lives. They look with "involuntary horror" at the mirror because of their fear of what it will reveal. They fear expressing their own "inner vileness" if they look too deeply into the mirror.

In the final analysis Mr. Hyde, as a metaphorical mirror in the text, is a sign of the repressed half of the Victorian male's double existence, but a sign without specific content. We can fill in the other with a range of impermissible desires from homosexuality to masturbation, but ultimately Hyde's significance is that he represents the other as mirror, the other as bearer of the self's desires. The horror of *Dr. Jekyll and Mr. Hyde* lies in its imagining a double life in which the repressed other returns with redoubled force and takes over the respectable public persona. As Showalter says, Utterson sees in the mirror "the image of the painfully repressed desires that the cane and the axe cannot wholly shatter and destroy" (Showalter 1990, 111).

Dr. Jekyll and Mr. Hyde, however, comes down finally on the side of repression. Dr. Jekyll brought about his downfall by trying to separate his double consciousness; if only, like Utterson, he had continued to simply repress his desires rather than express them, there would have been no tragedy. The text creates an ideal image of the masculine subject as self-divided and, if not happy, at least respectable. The smooth functioning of society and the preservation of the bonds of obligation, depends upon the repression of the self-centered, antisocial tendencies that Mr. Hyde expressed. So long as repression works, society is safe. Duplicity is ultimately a way of life for the Victorian male.

The experience of individuality as duplicity also informs the autobiographies of Mill and Ruskin. They both remained deeply attached to their fathers while feeling themselves politically estranged from them. Both suppress criticism of their fathers in their autobiographies. As we shall see in the next chapter, Mill and Gosse use their fathers as symbols of authority against which they oppose their conceptions of self. They ascribe to their fathers the function of limiting and suppressing the desire for autonomy from social restraint.

Like Ruskin and Stevenson, Mill and Gosse reveal themselves to be fundamentally divided on the question of the freedom or autonomy of the self as opposed to the call of social duty. Both profess to believe in the freedom of the individual, but the roles their fathers play in their autobiographies belie this professed admiration for the individual's sovereignty. They both feel that the self must be repressed through anti-self-consciousness in order to avoid extremes of solipsistic introspection.

Paradoxically, then, the attempts of Victorian autobiographers to repress their self-consciousness end up affirming their isolation. They write texts that radically subvert their attempts to address communal values. It is precisely the sense of how far the social had been excluded by the emphasis upon individual autonomy that led writers to stress the need for community, or what Stevenson termed "the bonds of obligation." However, in dramatizing the need to repress the autonomous self, Victorian authors actually subvert their own social agendas. As we shall see in the next chapter, repression helped deepen the inward space of the writing subject, and in the process marginalized the social. The repression of the self, which I describe in the next chapter in terms of "subjected autonomy," actually helped produce the subjectivity that informs Victorian autobiography and helped insulate the Victorian masculine subject from the contingent forces of the social.

NOTES

1. George Landow in *Victorian Types, Victorian Shadows* has suggested that *Praeterita* is structured around a series of lost paradises and Pisgah visions that serve as compensations for his sense of loss (Landow 1980, 230).

2. I had written this chapter long before reading Henderson's analysis; this is therefore one of those serendipitous examples of two critics actually agreeing in their evaluation of a text.

3. "Individual" means "that which cannot be divided."

CHAPTER FIVE

SUBJECTED AUTONOMY IN VICTORIAN AUTOBIOGRAPHY: JOHN STUART MILL AND EDMUND GOSSE

In "Revolutionary Action: 'Until Now,'" Michel Foucault proposes a startling definition of humanism as "subjected sovereignty." This definition has profound implications for this study, naming as it does a structure of consciousness that underlies the subjectivity represented in Victorian autobiography. This subjectivity is expressed in the form of "subjected sovereignty" most forcefully by John Stuart Mill in his *Autobiography* and Edmund Gosse in *Father and Son*. Foucault uses the term *subjected sovereignty* to characterize the political message of humanism:

> By humanism I mean the totality of discourse through which Western man is told: "Even though you don't exercise power, you can still be a ruler. Better yet, the more you deny yourself the exercise of power, the more you submit to those in power, then the more you increase your sovereignty." Humanism invented a whole series of subjected sovereignties: the soul (ruling the body, but subjected to God), consciousness (sovereign in a context of judgment, but subjected to the necessities of truth), the individual (a titular control of personal rights subjected to the laws of nature and society), basic

freedom (sovereign within, but accepting the demands of an
outside world and "aligned with destiny"). In short, humanism is everything in Western civilization that *restricts the desire
for power.* (Foucault 1977, 221)

Although Foucault does not make this explicit, he opposes the idea
of subjected sovereignty to the idea of revolutionary action. Subjected
sovereignty is thus a way of aborting the possibility of revolution by limiting the scope of autonomy. Subjecting oneself to a repressive regime is
an antidote to revolution, just as repression was the antidote to the antisocial aspects of the psyche in Stevenson's *Dr. Jekyll and Mr. Hyde* as I
discussed in the previous chapter. This higher authority in the Victorian
period was often expressed in terms of a social "duty" to others.

I adapt Foucault's term in this chapter and render it as "subjected
autonomy." Within the terms I am advancing in this study, subjected
autonomy is the Victorian solution to the dilemma of the autonomous
individual. Conceiving of the individual as potentially antisocial and violent if left unchecked, Victorian autobiographers create within their texts
a higher authority with which to repress the autonomy of the self. While
overtly proclaiming the absolute freedom of the individual, authors such
as John Stuart Mill and Edmund Gosse actually depict a form of subjected autonomy in which the individual cedes the subject's autonomy to
a higher authority.

Both Mill and Gosse show a distinct uneasiness at the possibility of
a "desire for power" within themselves and go to great lengths to project
their own desires onto other figures. Like Frankenstein creating his monster, the authors of these texts cast their fathers in their own image, dis-
placing desires with which they do not feel comfortable onto figures of
authority. In particular both writers betray their ambivalence toward
power conceived of in terms of authority, and use their fathers as a way of
expressing their ambivalence. Through their fathers they create a subjectivity that accommodates itself to the desire for power represented as an
"outside" force that impinges upon the "inner" world of the son. The
power relations within the text are thus distributed in a profoundly
authoritarian manner, contradicting directly their espousal of the freedom
of the individual to fashion his or her own inner existence.

Subjected autonomy in Victorian autobiography thus leads to some
peculiarly and strikingly self-divided texts, like those of Ruskin and
Stevenson in the previous chapter. As Heather Henderson (1989,
121–22) has noted, there are striking similarities between Ruskin's *Prae-*

terita and Gosse's *Father and Son*, despite the fact that Gosse was born some thirty years after Ruskin. Gosse is in many ways a Victorian preserved in amber into the Edwardian age. Gosse deploys repression in his text in a way that links him both with Ruskin and with Mill.

In the previous chapter I used the term *duplicity* to characterize Victorian double consciousness. Ruth Hoberman has also used the term *duplicity* in an article on Gosse's *Father and Son*. Hoberman analyzes Gosse's "narrative duplicity" in ways that parallel my analysis in this chapter. She touches briefly upon the duality that informs Gosse's text between "Gosse as artist, creating an aesthetically self-conscious narrative...[and] as naturalist, studying himself as a specimen" (Hoberman 1988, 304). In this chapter I will analyze in more detail the double and self-contradictory nature of Gosse's narrative, a duality that is played out in terms of the conflict between father and son and between authority and autonomy.

Both Mill and Gosse overtly espouse the autonomy of the individual, yet both authors in their texts enact the subjection of that autonomy to a determining authority. In both texts their autonomy is subjected to the law of the father, against whom they apparently rebel. However, both writers in fact depict a subjectivity that is deeply dependent upon the constraining force of the father both to define the self and to limit its unsettling autonomy. While they espouse complete autonomy, they embody subjected autonomy. Furthermore, both writers use subjected autonomy to produce the subjectivity represented in the text. The apparent repression of self in their texts actually leads to an intensification of self-consciousness. While they apparently follow a program of anti-self-consciousness, both writers actually use repression to create the inward territory of the writing subject.

Both Mill and Gosse deny the centrality of their selves to their autobiographies. Mill concentrates on other people as "influences" in his life, while Gosse represents his text as primarily a portrait of his father. Gosse in his preface to *Father and Son* even goes so far as to deny he is writing an autobiography at all. In both cases, however, this apparent concentration on the other rather than the self masks a unilateral definition of the other in terms of self, as it did in the texts that I examined in the previous chapter.

I understand repression in these texts as productive of a certain subjectivity, and furthermore productive of a subjectivity that is profoundly antisocial. In this I am drawing upon the model of repression in Michel Foucault's *The History of Sexuality* (1980), in which he suggests that far from being simply oppressive, repression helped produce a discourse about the sexual. Similarly, in the texts I examine in this chapter, far from counteracting subjectivity, anti-self-consciousness in Mill and Gosse's texts actually engendered an autonomous subjectivity that negated any social influence.

While authors such as Mill and Gosse represent their motives as social, their social agendas are actually undercut by the repression they employ. It is precisely through the presentation of consciousness as divided that they achieve this end. The texts record a conflict that is located within a consciousness that achieves its autonomy by representing subjectivity as a matter of a purely internal contest of conflicting desires for power. In John Stuart Mill's "mental crisis," for instance, the crisis is represented as a conflict between voices that both have an internal origin. Mill's self-conflicted struggle focuses attention exclusively upon the workings of his own mind, detaching it from any social context.

Mill represents himself as a reformer of society, but his attempts at reform are undercut by this representation of subjectivity. Mill in my account in this chapter sounds very much like George Eliot in Kucich's study of Victorian fiction. Kucich points out that Eliot viewed herself as a social novelist, but that in her novels she actually depicts "a deepening of inwardness, and a rejection of fusional tendencies" (Kucich 1987, 116). Kucich's description of the inner conflict of George Eliot's heroines echoes my description in this chapter of the conflicted subjectivity that both Mill and Gosse depict in their autobiographies:

> They [Eliot's heroines] combine within themselves impulses that seem at first to exclude and contradict each other: the pressure of "personal," self-interested desire, and the pressure of destabilizing, "impersonal" repression....These "personal" and "impersonal" energies eventually form a dynamic that enlarges selfhood in isolation from the inconclusive, fragmentary world of the other, engaging it instead in an inward struggle between passions and repressions that are equally affirmed. (117–18)

The internal dynamic of repression in both Mill's and Gosse's autobiographical texts affirms their individuality. Mill carries out a "dialogue of the mind with itself" that insulates him from the very society he wishes to address, and Gosse finds his individuality when he experiences himself as two identities that could commune with each other in secrecy. Both writers therefore represent their subjectivity in terms of an internal self-division that insulates them from the social.

Furthermore, the way in which the authors represent this divided subjectivity implicates them in wider social distributions of power even as they stress their autonomy. The profoundly authoritarian cast of the subjectivity they embody contradicts their emphasis upon individual liberty. The important role that fathers play as the other in these texts suggests that the issue of authority is central in both cases. Both Mill and Gosse, despite their espousals of the cause of the sovereign individuality of the self, write texts in which they ascribe authority to an external figure, not to their selves. The father is thus an authoritarian presence who actually helps create the son's subjectivity. In other words, the subjectivity these authors represent is dependent upon an authoritarian regime to create the sense of an inner realm of autonomy.

Both authors obfuscate the true source of authority in the text. As Mill himself admits in the early draft of his autobiography, "I acquired a habit of leaving my responsibility as a moral agent to rest on my father, my conscience never speaking to me except by his voice" (Mill 1961, 184–85). By a form of veiled ventriloquism, Mill uses the voice of his father in place of his own conscience, so that his self-repression appears to have an external source. This repressive force actually originates from within Mill himself.

The father's role in this form of self-representation acts as a force against which Mill and Gosse can define themselves indirectly, and thus they need not assume responsibility for their own desire for power. The indeterminacy of self in this form of autobiography, in which the father is cast as the other, betrays an uneasiness about the idea of the autonomous self. Although both men claim to be in favor of a completely autonomous self, the situation they depict in their autobiographies belies their theoretical statements about this sovereign self.

John Stuart Mill's *Autobiography* in this is perhaps one of the most fascinating of all nineteenth-century autobiographies. It is the record of a man who writes about himself even while overtly denying that he is the source and subject of his text. Mill refers to his text as a "biographical sketch" (Mill 1924, 1), not an autobiography. This is an apt characterization of his text, because he goes into great biographical detail, particularly about his father and Harriet Taylor, rather than describe his own consciousness. There are therefore in his text many "biographical sketches" of people close to Mill rather than overtly autobiographical sketches. In this Mill adopts a strategy of anti-self-consciousness similar to John Ruskin's, insisting that his own self "falls away" in his descriptions of others.

One of the most important terms for Mill's description of his life is the idea of education. Mill uses the word *education* as another form of anti-self-consciousness. He claims that his autobiography is of interest not "as being connected with myself" but as the "record of an education which was unusual and remarkable" (Mill 1924, 1). The words *unusual* and *remarkable*, however, recall the terms that I suggested in my Introduction are essential for the ideology of autobiography. They suggest the unique and unprecedented nature of the self.

Mill thus describes his "education," not his self, as "remarkable" or "unprecedented," as a way of arguing for his own originality, but in apparently selfless terms. The word *education* in Mill's text is also "selfless," in the sense that he represents himself as the passive recipient of "influences" that shaped his character. He does not suggest that he consciously took part in his education, nor does he suggest that the aim or effect of education is to encourage independence of spirit. He therefore denies any control over the formation of his adult self by his characterization of education as an essentially passive process on his part. This aspect of Mill's self-presentation is described well by James Olney in his study of the *Autobiography* in *Metaphors of Self*:

> Oddly enough, but also characteristically enough, Mill in his self-presentation claims almost no part in his eventual achievement: that intellectual accomplishment, as he describes it, was almost entirely a matter of influence from others, an influence that was paternal for some quarter of a century, and uxorial thereafter. (Olney 1972, 235)

It is indeed characteristic of Mill that he should present himself in such a way as to deny any active role in the formation of his own character. However, I wish to suggest that we should not take this self-deprecation at face value, because it obscures the role Mill actually plays in his autobiography. Mill in fact possesses a very strong sense of self, despite his protestation to the contrary. In passages such as this he is presenting a form of subjected autonomy, in which his development is shown as being controlled by external forces.

Thanks to his upbringing Mill shows a distinct aversion to acknowledging his own desires as part of his self, and goes to elaborate lengths to avoid any charges of egotism. Reacting to the impression people had of him as "greatly and disagreeably self-conceited," he says:

> My state of mind was not humility, but neither was it arro-
> gance. I never thought of saying to myself I am, or I can do,
> so and so. I neither estimated myself highly or lowly: I did not
> estimate myself at all. (Mill 1924, 23)

In these few lines, Mill essentially carries out a disappearing act and
represents in synechdochal from the process at the heart of his autobiography. Rather than try to define his "state of mind," he says what it was not,
and then carries out the process of self-denial to the point where he claims,
"I did not estimate myself at all." Like Ruskin, he tries to erase the presence of his self-consciousness. If we are to believe Mill here, he was unable
as a young man, and presumably was still unable when writing these lines
as an adult, to imagine himself as a distinct object of thought. So invisible
is his self that it eludes all categories and inhabits some shadowy realm
between "humility" and "arrogance," "high" and "low." This makes it
inconceivable that anyone could ever have suspected him of conceit.

As will become clear, however, the people to whom Mill was
responding were not completely wrong. Although Mill does try not to
"estimate" himself at all, and suppresses any evidence of self-consciousness, his self is in fact the most important unifying presence in his autobiography. Mill is extremely self-conscious, but he represents this self-consciousness indirectly. Through strategies of indirection and displacement
Mill represses his self-consciousness as an apparently selfless exercise. As
will become clear, such self-repression has exactly the opposite effect, so
that Mill's text is informed almost exclusively by his own sense of self.

My account of the extreme importance of Mill's sense of self in his
autobiography apparently contradicts the most famous consequence of
his mental crisis, his formulation of an idea akin to Carlyle's anti-self-consciousness doctrine. My description of Mill's strategy does not contradict
Mill's own statements, however, if one understands "self-consciousness"
specifically as introspection, not just as self-awareness. In his mental crisis,
Mill becomes suddenly and disastrously introspective and is abruptly
made aware of himself as a distinct object of thought. He had claimed he
did not estimate himself at all, but his crisis occurs when he tries to do
just that, and he consciously takes stock of his position. Mill characterizes
his mental process at this point as a dialogue, as he turns back in upon
himself to ask himself a direct question:

> In this frame of mind it occurred to me to put the question
> directly to myself: 'Suppose that all your objects in life were

realized...would this be a great joy and a happiness to you?'
And an irrepressible self-consciousness distinctly answered,
'No!' (Mill 1924, 94)

Mill is not usually thought of as having a flair for the dramatic, but
he certainly exhibits one here. Rather than report his intellectual processes
directly, as he usually does, he casts his thoughts as a mental drama, an
exchange between two voices. This is Mill's version of double consciousness, and it represents a striking way of avoiding direct definition of his
self. Rather than say "I felt" or "I thought," Mill turns the process into an
interrogation by a voice apparently external to his own consciousness that
addressees him as "you." Even the reply does not come from Mill's "I." It
is an "irrepressible self-consciousness," an uncontrollable eruption independent of his own will that he suggests he would repress if he could, but
that proves too strong.

Mill here enacts an internal drama of self-interrogation and self-
mastery. What he gives here is a brief moment in the unfolding drama of
his use of anti-self-consciousness. He presents his subjectivity in terms of
a conflict between impersonal forces. This representation of subjectivity
as self-conflicted helps reinforce Mill's self-consciousness rather than
repress it. His self-consciousness is an almost irrepressible force that stimulates the counter strategy of anti-self-consciousness. The net effect of
this self-conflict is to reinforce the importance of his self-consciousness.

Mill's mental crisis is precipitated when his habitual self-repression
breaks down. He becomes aware of the connection between his own
desires and the apparently objective reformist ideals that he had hitherto
cherished. He sees the other, the ideal of reform through which he usually represented himself to himself, in terms of self, and entirely in terms
of his own happiness. It seems strange that a question such as the one
Mill poses to himself should have this effect. Rather than find the
prospect of the realization of his reformist ambitions comforting, he is
plunged into depression. One thing that will become obvious from my
discussion in this chapter is that when Mill thinks of the prospect of
"reform," he is indirectly discussing his sense of self. When he thinks
about the reform of society he is supposedly thinking of the "greatest
happiness" but is in fact thinking of his own happiness. When he imagines the achievement of his goals of reform, he is in a peculiar way thinking of his own death. To achieve on earth the kind of state he envisages
seems a secular version of Heaven, and the prospect of the loss of self
involved in the achievement of this end is particularly depressing.

Introspection for Mill turns him into a "paralysed intellect" (Mill 1924, 167). His anti-self-consciousness doctrine, then, should be understood as an antidote to introspection, not as expressing a complete antipathy to all self-consciousness. Mill turns into an explicit theory the method he uses throughout the *Autobiography*, the technique of using an ideal image of himself, apparently independent of his own will, as an external means of expressing internal states of feeling. This translation of self into other is what he particularly valued in poets such as Tennyson and Wordsworth. Mill praised Tennyson for his "power of creating scenery in keeping with some state of human feeling," so that landscape became an indirect expression of the perceiving consciousness's emotions (Mill 1965, 134). This ability to embody internal states through the mediation of external images is the method that also underlies his anti-self-consciousness doctrine:

> Those are only happy (I thought) who have their minds fixed on some object other than their own happiness; on the happiness of others, on the improvement of mankind...followed not as a means, but as an ideal end. (Mill 1924, 100)

As his mental crisis makes clear, the word *happiness* for Mill has simultaneously a general and a personal significance. It is only when it occurs to Mill to ask himself directly whether he is happy that he experiences depression. Usually he can think of his own happiness in terms of a universalized vision of the well-being of all mankind. Mill thus embodies his own internal emotion in the external image of "the improvement of mankind."

In this method, "ideal ends" help move the prospect of reform pleasantly away from the imperfection and struggle of actual social change and make it an alluringly distant object. "Happiness" loses its specificity in such a project and becomes a limitless vision of one's own potential and that of society for a vague "improvement." Reform thus becomes a way of representing personal happiness as a selfless and ultimately unrealizable ideal. As Burton Pike has argued, abstract ideals such as history and progress take the place of God as guarantors of individual identity and transcendence in Victorian philosophy, just as the ideal of "reform" provides a "transcendent" force in Mill's life here:

> Belief in the omnipotence of History gave much of European thought in the nineteenth century a sense of universal

structure, which relieved the individual of providing his own....Thus History, serving as a cultural divinity, provided the nineteenth-century autobiographer with an ideal external support for his individual problems with time and identity. (Pike 1976, 330)

The "ideal end" of reform is Mill's "cultural divinity," helping him solve his own problems with his identity and mortality. Although Mill represents his anti-self-consciousness doctrine as a move away from his former state of mind, it is really an intensification and methodologizing of a tendency already implicit in his relation to the world, his tendency to read the other in terms of self. Ideal ends are thus an indirect way of representing his own transcendence through his own particular cultural divinity.

Mill uses the words *object* and *ideal end* to describe his method of anti-self-consciousness. Both are words that resonate with particular force for him. The word *object* for Mill, as I suggest in chapter 2 it did for Coleridge, fuses the subject with an object that renders it back in an objectified other. *Object* is Mill's term for the other, that force apparently external to the self that is in some way connected to it. Mill describes his self in terms of a single object that reflects back at him his sense of self, for instance, when he claims, "I had what might truly be called an object in life. My conception of my own happiness was entirely identified with this object" (Mill 1924, 92). An object in his life for Mill fills the horizon and gives unity to his identity. By confusing his own happiness with that of the external object, Mill is able to avoid the kind of introspection and self-analysis that precipitated his mental crisis. Coleridge's words about "hope without an object" that Mill quotes in his description of his mental crisis (98) therefore speak directly to Mill's experience of losing sight of any external object by which to define himself. To lose sight of an object in life is to be plunged into depression.

Bentham's philosophy provides the most important other or object in the first phase of Mill's autobiography. Bentham's philosophy and later Harriet Taylor and the poetry of Wordsworth and Coleridge allow Mill to represent his sense of self indirectly through their mediation as the other. They represent the possibility of transcendence in human terms for Mill, just as the Specter of Brocken did for Coleridge and De Quincey. Their transcendental possibilities emerge most clearly when Mill describes the effect on him of reading Bentham's *Treatise on Utilitarianism* by saying, "I felt taken up to an eminence from which I could survey a vast mental domain, and see stretching out into the distance intellectual results beyond all computation" (Mill 1924, 46). Mill uses an unusually mystical and transcendent vocabulary to describe his feelings here, suggesting a religious apotheosis. This is Mill's version of the Romantic transcendent self. Where he usually discusses limits, Mill here describes a feeling of limitlessness and power. Bentham's system gives him a "domain," his own realm which he alone can rule. Characteristically, this domain is both mental and social, an inner and outer realm. He moves from a discussion of the "practical improvements in human affairs" that Bentham's system suggested to its effect on his own sense of self. Bentham's philosophy gives him a way of investing his sense of self in a program for the reform of society. The effect of his reading of Bentham's text is dramatic. Just as he experiences a sense of power over a mental domain, he also describes a feeling of control over his own life.

> When I laid down the last volume of the Traité, I had become a different being. The "principle of utility"...fell exactly into place as the keystone which held together the detached and fragmentary component parts of my knowledge and beliefs. It gave unity to my conception of things (Mill 1924, 47)

The effect of Bentham's philosophy as Mill describes it here is essentially that of giving him what Coleridge termed "unity of Being." Mill thus ascribes his sense of self to an external force and denies his own role in providing this unity. Bentham's book "gives" Mill his unity, just as it gives him his power. Through the principle of utility Mill is able to aggrandize his own sense of self and read it in terms of a concern for the greatest happiness of all rather than in terms of his own desire.

Mill here represents himself in terms of subjected autonomy. Bentham's philosophy is the greater determining force within which Mill can now construct his subjectivity. Bentham's philosophy fulfills the same role as religion. Thanks to Bentham, Mill now has "a creed, a doctrine, a philosophy" that, like any religion, mediates the poles of a determining deity and an apparently autonomous individual possessing free will.

Mill's description of his reaction to Bentham's philosophy reaches a climax in which he conflates power, self, and his reformist ambition to change the world.

> This appearance of superiority to illusion added to the effect which Bentham's doctrines produced on me, by height-

ening the impression of mental power, and the vista of
improvement which he did open was sufficiently large and
brilliant to light up my life, as well as to give definite shape to
my aspirations. (Mill 1924, 47–48)

In Mill's description it is ambiguous whether the "vista of improvement" refers to the potential for his own individual or a general social
progress, a telling conflation of his own desire and his apparently selfless
zeal for reform. Thus the "mental power" he describes could equally be
applied to self-improvement or to improvement of society. It seems that
Bentham, temporarily as it turns out, gave Mill a philosophy in which he
could see his own capacity for logical thought as able to effect momentous change. Mill feels that through the principle of utility he can escape
the confines of a deterministic outlook that would radically limit the
potential for meaningful human action.

By reading his own self in terms of a larger "vista," by seeing society
as the arena for the playing out of his own desire, Mill is able to feel he
has a "definite shape" to his life. The conflation of self and other in this
passage helps us to understand the peculiar force of Mill's mental crisis, a
crisis that seems almost incomprehensible if the connection between
Mill's sense of self and his reformist agenda is not recognized.

Just as Mill sees Utilitarianism as a form of religion, he likens his
"loss of faith" in the Benthamite program to the state of mind "in which
converts to Methodism usually are when smitten by their first 'conviction
of sin'" (Mill 1924, 94). Mill's experience is then not as unusual as it first
seems, being a Utilitarian version of the common crisis of faith experienced by many Victorians. Mill simply loses faith in Utilitarianism as an
ideal end or object in his life and gives in to a solipsistic reading of his life
in terms of self. Mill temporarily loses his faith in his cultural divinity.

Mill's crisis marks a swing of his mental pendulum away from a
transcendent ideal of self back to a deterministic view of self. The idea of
the limited nature of his self expresses itself in various indirect ways in his
Autobiography—for instance, by spoiling his love of music. Although Mill
claims he loved listening to music, he finds his enjoyment of it marred by
an odd fear. He is "tormented by the thought of the exhaustibility of
musical combinations" (87). Mill is conscious of the strangeness of such
an idea, and the rather peculiar associations it has for him, so he goes on
to make explicit the connection between this feeling about music, his
sense of self, and his reformist ideals:

> For though my dejection, honestly looked at, could not be
> called other than egoistical, produced by the ruin, as I
> thought, of my fabric of happiness, yet the destiny of mankind
> in general was ever in my thoughts, and could not be sepa-
> rated from my own. I felt that a flaw in my life, must be a flaw
> in life itself. (102)

Mill's self-diagnosis here is impressive, as he directly names the connection between his self and his plans for reform. He links his conception
of "the destiny of mankind in general" directly with his own happiness. I
do not mean to suggest in my remarks on the connection between Mill's
self and his view of society that he was in some way misguided or under-
hand. Mill is himself implicitly aware of the disadvantages of identifying
oneself so closely and vicariously with one's conception of society as a
whole. Mill is a classic example of a Victorian philosopher coming up
against a dichotomy within the idea of an autobiographical relation
between the individual and the world. As in the case of George Eliot, this
is an example of the ideology of self-reflexiveness distorting what Mill
clearly meant to be a sincere attempt to improve the lot of his fellow men.

Mill's crisis, so intimately connected as it is with his most fundamental conception of himself, comes to affect every aspect of his life, from
his hopes of the future to his appreciation of music. Even his enjoyment
of well-loved books is now informed by a fear of the exhaustibility and
limits of his self, by the feeling that something in him had "worn out."
His depression blocks his normal method of reading, which is to see the
text in terms of self. Reading Wordsworth's poetry, however, once again
allows him to read a text in self-referential terms. Thus, when he relates
his experience of reading Wordsworth as an antidote to his depression, it
is in terms of a confusion between his own state and that described in the
poetry.

> What made Wordsworth's poems a medicine for my state
> of mind, was that they expressed,not mere outward beauty,
> but states of feeling....They seemed to be the very culture of
> the feelings, which I was in quest of. In them I seemed to
> draw from a source of inward joy. (Mill 1924, 105)

Mill moves in these lines from "outward beauty" to "inward joy,"
thus confounding inner and outer through Wordsworth's poetry, just as
he did in equating landscape and human emotion in his praise of Ten-

nyson's poetry. Mill's method of reading poetry is to read the poem as the other in terms of self. It is ambiguous in Mill's description whether the source of his inward joy is located within his self, is somehow located in the poem, or originates in Wordsworth's own self. It is not clear precisely whose inner self Mill is referring to here. Wordsworth's poems speak for Mill here, just as the voices he used to describe his crisis spoke for him, so that he did not have to use the first person. Just as in the description of his crisis Mill uses the quotation from Coleridge's "Dejection" to speak for him, he uses Wordsworth's poetry here.

This strategy could be seen as either humble or egotistical. He could be implying that Coleridge and Wordsworth describe his state better than he ever could, or that the poems can be subsumed under his own personal crisis. Whatever interpretation we put upon Mill's statement that Coleridge's poem "exactly described my case" (Mill 1924, 94) he distances the description of his own mental state from himself by using another person's words to describe it.

The effect for Mill of reading Wordsworth's poetry is to reconstitute the intersection between his own desires and those of a reformation of society. Wordsworth's poetry represented for Mill an ideal other onto which he could inscribe his own desires and have them rendered impersonal and illimitable. Wordsworth reconnects Mill's sundered self-image and his projects for reform by once again allowing him to conflate his own individual happiness and general social happiness. Not only does he find a source of "inward joy" in Wordsworth's poetry, this "joy" was one "which could be shared by all human beings" (Mill 1924, 104) and thus was not limited to himself alone. This joy becomes the basis for a renewed vision of the limitless possibilities of reform as he discovers in Wordsworth's poetry the vision he had once found in Bentham's philosophy.

> A source of inward joy...which had no connexion with struggle or imperfection, but would be made richer by every improvement in the physical or social condition of mankind. From them [Wordsworth's poems] I seemed to learn what would be the perennial sources of happiness, when all the great evils of life have been removed. And I myself at once better and happier as I came under their influence. (104)

By turning Wordsworth's poems into this "influence," Mill is able to rediscover an other apparently outside his self that once again embodies his inner existence. He rediscovers the happiness he lost in asking himself directly whether he would be happy if he ever achieved his reformist goals. Wordsworth's poems, like Harriet Taylor later in the *Autobiography*, apparently divert Mill's attention from himself once more by providing him with an image of a transcendent self that has no bounds or limits. As in Bentham's philosophy, Mill once again represents his own happiness in terms of general social happiness. Wordsworth's poems become "perennial," inexhaustible ideals that stave off the world of "struggle" or "imperfection." Like Utilitarianism as an ideal end, Wordsworth's poems are comfortably removed from any contact with real social conditions. Wordsworth gives him once more a utopian and panoramic view of the scope for reform, the achievement of which is pleasantly distant.

It is in this context that Harriet Taylor makes an appearance as a deus ex machina, reintroducing into his life a mystical element he had lost in his crisis of faith. Harriet Taylor is an external figure to whom Mill can ascribe aspects of his own character. She can thus replace the figure of his father, whom Mill had both admired and secretly resented. Gertrude Himmelfarb in "The Other John Stuart Mill" has pointed out that Mill in his *Autobiography* has conflated two crises, one that did indeed concern Bentham's philosophy and an earlier one that concerned his assertion of independence from his father (Himmelfarb 1975, 115). It is when reading the passage in Marmontel's *Memoires* on the death of a father that Mill first feels a thawing of the paralysis that afflicted him following his mental crisis. When reading Marmontel's text, as he did when reading Wordsworth's poems, he is able to express his own feelings about his father through the mediation of a text as other. His reading of Marmontel, and his consequent imaginative identification with the son who takes over from his dead father, is the first stage in his break with his father's authority and his rejection of his father's philosophical outlook. It is with his discovery of Harriet Taylor that his assertion of independence from his father is completed. However, Mill does not achieve autonomy in this process. He merely replaces one authority figure, his father, with another, Harriet Taylor.

Harriet Taylor becomes one of the "influences" in his life that helped "to shape the character of my future development" (Mill 1924, 132), taking her place alongside his father, Bentham, and Wordsworth. Characteristically, Mill speaks of "formation" of his own self by powers beyond him, returning to his model of education as a passive and selfless exercise. Mill does not represent himself as taking command of his own fate. He consistently chooses external authorities to whom he can ascribe his sense of self. He described feeling completely hopeless after his mental crisis because "there seemed no power in nature sufficient to begin the formation of my character anew, and create in a mind now irretrievably analytic, fresh associations with any of the objects of human desire" (98). Mill does not suggest that in this crisis he could draw upon some source of inner strength. He sees the situation entirely in terms of some external authority changing his character for him, not he himself actively seeking a cure for his depression. Implicitly blaming his father for "making" him what he now was, an analytic but unfeeling man, he merely invokes some other "power in nature" to remake him, as if he were clay to be molded to the specifications of another's will. Mill presents himself here as completely the creation of forces beyond his control. It is as the "power" external to himself who could "remake" him that Harriet Taylor makes her appearance in the *Autobiography*. He turns her into a semidivine presence in his life.

The hyperbolic language with which Mill describes Harriet Taylor makes it clear that he is describing an idealized image of her and ascribing to her powers and potential similar to those he found in Bentham's philosophy. He turns her into another "cultural divinity" in his life. Taylor provides the external object that Mill lost during his mental crisis, and thus provides his life with shape and substance in the way that Bentham's philosophy had previously.

> My objects in life are solely those which were hers; my pursuits and occupations those in which she shared, or sympathized, and which are indissolubly associated with her. Her memory is to me a religion, and her approbation the standard by which...I endeavour to regulate my life. (Mill 1924, 170)

Harriet Taylor provides the new object for Mill after his crisis of faith in Utilitarianism. She becomes for him an ideal and transcendent object in life, an image ideal enough to fulfill his program of anti-self-consciousness. He can ascribe his own desires to her, as he did to the idea of reform, and avoid introspection. She gives shape to and "regulates" his internal life. Mill turns her into an authority that controls his inner existence.

Rather than represent the situation in terms of self-control, Mill ascribes his process of self-regulation entirely to her. After her death, the influence of her idealized image is even more potent than her living presence was becoming overtly a "religion" in the way that Bentham's philosophy was a religion to him previously. As a religion she is clearly untainted by any human imperfections and can become a repository for all of Mill's most cherished values.

Mill's autobiography therefore records not his gradual assertion of autonomy from his father, but his discovery of a more palatable regime under which to live. Mill through Harriet Taylor carries out the same sort of ventriloquism as with his father. Mill presents himself as morally passive, not as a moral agent. He leaves his "responsibility as a moral agent" to his wife instead of to his father, ascribing to her the authority that properly resides within himself. It should be clear that I find this blurring of the boundaries of Mill's self deeply disturbing and consider it to be ultimately an evasion of moral responsibility.

Mill is following the tactic I ascribed to Wordsworth's "Tintern Abbey" in my Introduction; he imposes his masculine desire onto the figure of the woman and turns an apparent meeting with a female other into a meeting with a version of his self. Ruth Hoberman has described a similar tactic in Gosse's use of women in *Father and Son*. She points out that Gosse exploits the paradoxical Victorian image of woman and uses it to represent his own "narrative duplicity":

> He allies his childhood self with images of imprisoned and yearning women, of women threatened by rape and then rescued by lovers. In doing so he reflects and takes advantage of his culture's ambivalent view of women as at once passive victims and threateningly powerful temptresses. In women, in other words, Gosse finds a neat analogy for his own paradoxical position as victim and victor, as rebel against and invoker of established authority. (Hoberman 1988, 307)

Gosse identifies with women, in other words, in terms of the way in which they reflect back to him his own double consciousness. The women in Gosse's text, like Harriet Taylor in Mill's *Autobiography*, thus become signs of the identity of the male subject. They act as metaphorical mirrors for the masculine subject's own divided subjectivity. This divided identity in the case of both Mill and Gosse is bound up with their identification with women as representatives of values to which they owe theoretical allegiance, in Gosse's case fiction and storytelling as counterauthoritarian forces. Their ultimate identification, however, is not with women but with their fathers as masculine models. Both Mill and Gosse define themselves as men in ambivalent relationships with their fathers as authority figures whom they simultaneously emulate and reject.

In its discussions of his difficulties with his father and the program of education he had to suffer at his father's hands, Mill's *Autobiography* recalls strongly the subject matter of Edmund Gosse's *Father and Son*. Gosse's text, like Mill's, apparently records the son's gradual assertion of independence from his father's authority. It is open to question, however, just how independent Gosse is at the close of the narrative, and this ambiguity raises troubling questions similar to those implicit in Mill's *Autobiography*.

Gosse, like Mill, asserts his belief in the right of individuals to fashion their own inner existences free from external authority. However, Gosse as much as Mill portrays a situation in which some form of external authority is essential to the autobiographer's sense of self. Gosse does not replace his father with some other authority figure, but it becomes clear in the narrative that without the memory of his father's presence, Gosse has nothing to say about himself. Gosse's sense of self is thus determined by the memory of his father as an authority, and his identity is defined solely in terms of his resistance to this authority.

Gosse suggests that the discovery of his individuality was connected with a crisis of authority and faith. Previously he had believed that his father was infallible and omnipotent, in fact that he was "a deity." With the discovery of his ability to deceive his father, Gosse finds his unquestioning faith shaken:

> The theory that my Father was omniscient or infallible was
> now dead and buried....My Father, as a deity, as a natural
> force of immense prestige, fell in my eyes to a human level.
> (Gosse 1982, 30)

Gosse says that he discovered his "individuality" at precisely the same time as he came to doubt the single most important external image of authority in his life, that of his father. Like Mill losing faith in Utilitarianism, Gosse is forced to see his life in terms of self in losing his father as a transcendent other. The crisis here, then, is one of the location of authority, since his father has now ceased to be the omniscient legislator he once was, just as Mill lost faith in his father and his Utilitarian philosophy.

At the moment Gosse asserts himself in opposition to his father's authority, he discovers within himself a profound ambiguity or doubleness. Gosse's rebellion against his father and the system of religion he represented reaches a "culmination" in a fit of hysterics in which he "lost all sense of self-control." This description implies that Gosse at this moment experienced a loss of self. Rather than a loss of self, however, this episode is described by him as an extreme state of "double-consciousness" in which he experienced himself as divided into two incompatible aspects of self: "While this was proceeding, I was conscious of that dual individuality of which I have already spoken, since while one part of me gave way, and could not resist, the other part in some extraordinary sense seemed standing aloof, much impressed" (34). Gosse at this moment experiences an extreme sense of self-contradiction between the aspect of himself that "gives in" and the part that resists his father's influence. His self bifurcates into two fundamentally irreconcilable versions, one that asserts its own authority and ability to define itself, and another that accedes to an external authority willingly. It is to the resistant inner core that Gosse attributes his strongest and most vital sense of self, ascribing to it the continuity of his "innate and persistent self":

> Through thick and thin I clung to a hard nut of individuality, deep down in my childish nature. To the pressure from without I resigned everything else...but there was something which I never resigned, my innate and persistent self....I was always conscious of that innermost quality which I had learned to recognize in my earlier days in Islington, that existence of two in the depths who could speak to one another in inviolable secrecy. (140)

Gosse translates what as a child he had seen as a distinction between his self and his father as the other into a purely internal dialectic, a doubleness located within his own consciousness. It is doubtful, however, just how far this doubleness is a true dialectic, since Gosse is unable to define the nature of the kernel of the resistant self. Gosse's defense is "secrecy," but it is a secrecy without a specific content. Gosse cannot say what attributes his central self has, as its only characteristic is resistance to the "pressure from without" of his father's will. His innate and persistent self is merely a "nut" of resistance, a stubborn refusal to do something rather than a positive assertion of an alternative existence. Gosse says he preserved a portion of himself despite his resigning "everything else, my thoughts, my words, my anticipations, my assurances" (140). What exactly could be left over after this resignation of self-control is not clear.

The doubleness that he represents here is an internalization of the interplay of coercion and resistance that characterized his relationship with his father. Gosse's double consciousness here does not represent an escape from or a complete rejection of his father's authority, as he would like to suggest by naming it "individuality." What he does here rather is to replicate his relationship with his father on the level of internal consciousness. Gosse defines himself in terms of the back-and-forth between a dominant and a resistant self, selves that become locked in an incessant mutual antagonism. Gosse links this consciousness with the idea of secrecy, because it in effect sets up a self-contained system that insulates him from the need for contact with anything beyond himself. He is able to isolate himself from his father in exactly the same way as his father isolated him from boys of his age. His relationship with his father thus becomes a model for his own sense of self.

The fact is that his father, and his system of religion, are seen both as defining, in the sense of giving shape to, and as constraining and imprisoning Gosse's self. Without the presence of his father's authority, Gosse loses all sense of himself as a distinct individual. Gosse oscillates between resistance to and appreciation of the way in which the pressure on him by his father to "testify" helped him to become aware of his own identity. His father insisted that Gosse talk to him about the state of his soul and his standing in God's eyes, and also testify in public as to whether or not he was in a state of grace. Gosse was pressured by his father into making public the state of his innermost soul.

Gosse describes feeling in such situations "like a small and solitary bird, caught and hung out hopelessly in a glittering cage" (39). The image of the cage is for Gosse a metaphor for his father's presence, as it is when he says, "I was still but a bird fluttering in the net-work of my father's will" (208), and it registers Gosse's ambivalence about his father's authority. On the one hand the cage clearly imprisons him, but on the other hand it also gives him definite boundaries that help him to define his sense of self. Without his father's presence his sense of self is "undulating and shapeless" and lacks the distinct outlines it has when he experiences the "isolation" that his father induces in him.

In writing his autobiography, Gosse is still under the influence of his father and his father's injunctions to define and make public his inner self. Even though he says that he "must not define too clearly...the blind movements of a childish mind" (144), this is in fact what he attempts in *Father and Son*. His father's "postal inquisitions" later on in the book demand that he "define the exact outlines of what is so undulating and shapeless" (208), and without them he loses the sense of himself as a distinct object of thought necessary to write autobiography. He may resent his father's insistent questioning, but it is only by re-creating his father's presence in his autobiography that he can recapture the sense of the boundaries of his own self. It is thus impossible for Gosse to write directly about himself. Without his father as a mediating force, as the other that helps define his self, he cannot write his own autobiography.

Gosse's narrative comes to an end when he finally breaks from his father's influence and moves away. This silence is predicted within the text by the way in which, whenever he leaves his father's presence, he finds nothing to write about in his life. When he finally finds friendship with boys his age, he finds nothing to record, so bound up is his self-image with the solitude and isolation he feels in his father's presence, and he reports, "Once more I have to record the fact that...precisely as my life ceases to be solitary, it ceases to be distinct" (157).

This period of the loss of the "distinctness" of his sense of self coincides with a period when his father ceased the minute surveillance of previous years, thanks to his second marriage. Whenever Gosse does not feel the pressure of his father's will, he loses his sense of identity and merges with the crowd. His self is defined entirely in relation to his father and in terms of isolation and solitude, so that he loses all sense of himself as distinct when his life "ceases to be solitary." Similarly, the impetus to write comes from his father, so that he loses all desire to define himself when away from his father. He may be happy when his father is not around, but he is also unable to find anything about which to write during such times. He says of such periods, "The result was that of this happy little breathing-space I have nothing to report...a brief interval of healthy, happy child-life, when my hard-driven soul was allowed to have, for a little while, no history" (56–57). By calling these times "intervals," Gosse suggests that they are abnormal interruptions of the usual tenor of his existence. These intervals of happiness away from his father have no "history" because Gosse no longer has the need to make "reports" on the condition of his self. Gosse's own ambivalence about his relationship to his father is most acute in this area, as his father's presence stimulates him even as he resists it. He describes how the knowledge that his father would later ask him for a detailed account of his activities "gave me the habit of concentrating my attention on what was going on in the course of our visits, in case I might be called upon to give a report" (95). Without his father's presence he has nothing to report and thus possesses no history. The need for self-definition is gone, and he loses all sense of himself as a distinct personality. His sense of self becomes like his memories of all his happiest times, "vague" and "pale and shadowy."

Although Gosse apparently wishes to break out of the solitary, isolated condition that he characterizes as his childhood, when he ceases to feel isolated he loses all sense of himself as an individual. Gosse's attempt to represent himself as an individual in a wider social context is therefore subverted by his definition of himself. He returns obsessively to his relationship with his father because it is only in opposition to the "network" of his father's will that Gosse can experience his self as a distinct entity. Without this relationship he simply melts in with the crowd and can find nothing to write about.

Gosse's text ends with a plea for the right of all individuals to fashion their own "inner existence" free from external pressure. He claims at the end of his autobiography that he asserted "a human being's privilege to fashion his inner life for himself" (40). Yet Gosse's text depicts a self that is deeply dependent upon external pressure for its self-presence, a self that, when not reacting against an external authority, has no substance. Although he represents his autobiography as a record of his gradual emancipation from his father's tyranny, he makes it clear within the text that without reconstructing his father's presence through memory he would not be able to write at all. He can only talk about himself by talking about his father.

The very capitalization of the word *Father* in *Father and Son* indicates that within the text the figure of his father resonates with some force above and beyond the usual sense of the word. His father is a symbol of authority on both the individual level and the social level, being an image for any kind of "external pressure." Gosse makes it clear in his preface that he feels himself alienated from his contemporaries, thanks to his upbringing, and that he defines himself in opposition to the social movements of his time. Just as he defined himself in opposition to his father's will as a child, he now defines his identity as alienated from his own era. His sense of self is constituted within the framework of a resistance to authority, both in relation to his father and in relation to society, and the text of *Father and Son* embodies the tension between his sense of rebellion against this authority and his dependence upon it. This is an authority that Gosse implicitly confirms even while denying its legitimacy.

John Stuart Mill also links his autobiography to wider philosophical and social issues when he closes his *Autobiography*, and he does so in terms that help illuminate the deeper issues that lie behind both texts. Reverting to a discussion of his mental crisis, Mill introduces the doctrine of determinism in his thought, saying that "the doctrine of what is called Philosophical Necessity weighed on my existence like an incubus" (Mill 1924, 118). The idea of necessity is the antithesis of the vision of the transcendent and infinitely perfectible self that Mill derived from Bentham's philosophy. Determinism reminds Mill of his own mortality. His fear of determinism is akin to his fear that the number of possible musical combinations was finite and exhaustible, and he opposes to it an idea of unlimited individual free will.

> I saw that though our character is formed by circumstances, our own desires can do much to shape those circumstances; and that what is really inspiriting and ennobling in the doctrine of free-will, is the conviction that we have real power over the formation of our character. (Mill 1924, 119)

It may be a "really inspiriting" aspect of the doctrine of free will that it allows the idea of the formation of one's own character, but Mill's account of the formation of his self is, as we have seen, represented entirely as if his personality were formed by powers external to himself. Mill may profess theoretical allegiance to the ideal of the autonomous individual, but his autobiography enacts a plot entirely different from the one that would correspond to the idea of free will. His autobiography is fundamentally deterministic, in that his chief intention is to set limits on the self, and not to portray the self as a free agent. Like Gosse at the end of *Father and Son*, he may espouse the cause of the individual, free to shape his or her own inner life, but this is not the model of the self that informs his text.

Mill, in discussing the doctrine of necessity, professes allegiance to the ideals of "the rights of individuality" (Mill 1924, 179) and the "sovereignty of the individual" (180). The idea that the individual is sovereign, that is, a law unto his or her self, is a potentially revolutionary ideal. It implies that the individual is free to question and reject any authority external to the self. It is clear to me from reading their autobiographies that both Mill and Gosse are deeply divided about this issue. Both believe in theory that individuals should be free to shape their own fates, but both also experience a need within themselves for the presence of an external authority to regulate and order their internal existences. For this reason the figure of the father as the other is particularly important for both men. Their relationships with their fathers, or with other authority figures in Mill's case, become an arena within which to act out their ambivalence about the doctrine of the sovereign individual's free will and their need for an authority figure to control and regulate their lives.

Instead of the sovereignty of the individual, these texts represent what I term "subjected autonomy." The apparent zone of freedom they create is circumscribed within an authoritarian regime that legitimates a circumscribed exercise of will. Mill and Gosse both identify strongly with women in their texts, but also implicitly relegate the ideals that women embody to a subordinate position within Victorian patriarchy. This comes across most clearly in Gosse's *Father and Son* when in the preface to the text he insists that his autobiography is fact and not fiction. As Ruth Hoberman points out, "Gosse as subject claims the right to fiction, self-invention, and imaginative freedom, yet as narrator echoes his naturalist father's faithfulness to literal 'fact', producing not a novel...nor even, according to him, an autobiography, but a slice of life" (Hoberman 1988, 304). While Gosse on one level may idealize fiction as a "feminine" and liberatory mode, he ultimately comes down on the side of hard, masculine facts. Both Mill's and Gosse's texts construct a masculine subjectivity in which women function as a sign of the values that the male narrators apparently espouse but actually marginalize. The narrators actually identify with their fathers as symbols of authority rather than with women as symbols of imagination. These texts do not portray the liberatory individualism that they profess to value, but a much more conservative subjected autonomy in which the subject constructs himself in the image of his father.

CHAPTER SIX

"DIALOGUE OF THE MIND WITH ITSELF": MATTHEW ARNOLD AND MONOLOGISM

In his preface to the 1853 edition of his *Poems,* Matthew Arnold criticized Victorian poetry for being too preoccupied with morbid and introspective states of mind, in which suffering found no vent in action. Arnold was criticizing a certain form of subjectivity, that of the autobiographical subject examining the mysterious origins of his or her sense of identity, to the exclusion of all else. Arnold criticized autobiographical poetry that he saw as betraying the beginnings of the modern "disease" of the "dialogue of the mind with itself" (Arnold 1965, 591). Like Ruskin, Arnold saw the increasingly self-referential character of Victorian literature in terms of pathology; where Ruskin saw the pathetic fallacy as a sign of disease, Arnold diagnosed the dialogue of the mind with itself as the sign of excessive introspection. Arnold's phrase *dialogue of the mind with itself* is a strikingly appropriate description of the procedure in his autobiographical writing. His formulation helps underscore the problematic relationship between the writing subject and a wider universe of social discourse that marks both his and other autobiographical texts in the nineteenth century. Using Arnold's phrase and the theoretical insights of M. M. Bakhtin, I will map the ways in which Arnold's autobiographical writings actually embody the dialogue of the mind with itself that he criticized in his 1853 preface.

I wish to first give the conventional account of what Arnold is saying in his preface, then suggest a different reading of this much-quoted phrase that I believe has broad implications for Victorian autobiography generally. Victorian poetry in Arnold's terms is weakened by the dialogue of the mind with itself, which betrays the effects of a creeping solipsism. Arnold argues that Victorian poetry, rather than indulge in introspective states of mind, should be motivated by some more outwardly or socially directed agenda. In the conventional reading of his words, then, Arnold is shown as eschewing the subjective in favor of the objective or social. The reverse is actually the case, as I will make clear.

In the conventional approach the phrase *dialogue of the mind with itself* is construed as a laudable reaction *against* excessive self-consciousness. Arnold seems to be arguing for what Bakhtin characterized as the "dialogic" imagination, an imagination that actively engaged its social milieu and reflected in its language an engagement with the social conflicts of its day. While much attention has been paid to texts that exhibit a "dialogic" imagination, I wish in this chapter to propose that Arnold's texts betray the workings of the "monologic" imagination.[1] Bakhtin contrasts the "polyglossia" and "semantic openendedness" of dialogic forms such as the novel with the impulse toward "monoglossia" in other genres, particularly highly conventional poetry. While not subscribing to Bakhtin's implicit denigration of poetry in favor of prose, I find that his comments help elucidate the repression of the social at work in Victorian autobiography. To choose to write autobiography in the Victorian period was to deliberately eschew fiction in favor of an apparently more objective form, as John Stuart Mill and Edmund Gosse make clear in the opening remarks to their autobiographies. Gosse begins his autobiography in the following manner:

> At the present hour, when fiction takes forms so ingenious and so specious, it is perhaps necessary to say that the following narrative, in all its parts, and so far as the punctilious attention of the writer has been able to keep it so, is scrupulously true. (Gosse 1982, 5)

Gosse is anxious to differentiate his text from works of the imagination, but his very anxiety at the "ingenious" forms fiction could take betrays his concern that the distinction may not hold. Similarly, John Stuart Mill stresses that his desire is to "document" and provide an objective "record" of an unusual education. (Mill 1924, 1). Mill and Gosse stress the "monoglossia" of autobiography over the "polyglossia" of fiction.

Both Mill and Gosse betray an anxiety about language's indeterminacy and a desire to bring it under the strict control of the monologic imagination. Mill and Gosse chose to write autobiographies as a deliberate strategy to distance their texts from fictional autobiographies, and to insist that, even though they are writing about themselves, the texts are dictated by truth. They represent themselves as truthful, unitary subjects.

Mill and Gosse are here giving expression to a desire that Bakhtin links to politics, particularly the creation in the nineteenth century of a bureaucratic nation-state. Bakhtin terms the language connected with such forces "unitary." This language is the vehicle of "the forces that serve to unify and centralize the verbal-ideological world" and establish a stable version of "correct usage" in the face of the instability and mutability of language's "heteroglossia" (Bakhtin 1985, 270). A unitary language "gives expression to forces working toward concrete verbal and ideological unification, which develop in vital connection with the processes of sociopolitical and cultural centralization," so that language itself records the social and political changes in its environment (271). Mill and Gosse, like Arnold, wish to use the unitary and documentary language of autobiography rather than the polyglossia of fiction.

Similarly, Arnold exhibits anxiety when faced with the indeterminacy and heteroglossia of language. David Riede has termed this Arnold's "betrayal" by language, in that, despite his efforts to contain it, signification always exceeded his control. In his conclusion Riede briefly invokes Bakhtinian terms to characterize Arnold's relationship to language:

> In general, the effort to reduce the 'heteroglossia' of a multitudinous language to a unified poetic utterance that excludes the untamable associations of other levels and types of discourse is an attempt in language to reflect a unified and authoritative ideology. It is, in short, an attempt to erect a monolithic 'culture' against anarchy, a unified ideology... against multitudinousness. (Riede 1988, 211)

Arnold's attempts to control the heteroglossia of language led him to idealize the centralized French bureaucratic system. In such essays as "A French Eton" and "The Literary Influence of Academies," Arnold shows a blend of the characteristic British distrust of centralized systems, which were equated with tyranny, and a desire to emulate the centralized French system of education and the Academie Française. As I have argued in "State Power and the Victorian Subject" (Danahay 1992),

Arnold's identification with monologism as opposed to heteroglossia led him to further the interests of the bureaucratic nation-state in England.

This is not to say that what is in question here is some simple binary opposition between centripetal and centrifugal tendencies, or the mono-logic and the dialogic. All language, Bakhtin emphasizes, participates in these competing and conflicted tendencies, so that no text is entirely monologic or dialogic.

> Every concrete utterance of a speaking subject serves as a point where centrifugal as well as centripetal forces are brought to bear. The processes of centralization and decen-tralization, of unification and disunification, intersect in the utterance....Every utterance participates in the "unitary lan-guage" (in its centripetal forces and tendencies) and at the same time partakes of social and historical heteroglossia (the centrifugal, stratifying forces). (Bakhtin 1985, 272)

The opposing centripetal and centrifugal tendencies are therefore potential within all texts, and no text is univocally monologic or dialogic. It is possible, however, to privilege one form over the other, as Victorian autobiographers do in their insistence upon their status as truthful, uni-tary subjects. Part of the anxiety behind Gosse's preface is his awareness that, while he stresses the unitary aspects of language, the boundary he wishes to create is unstable. He privileges unitary language and promotes the monologic imagination, just as Arnold does, but his text betrays the repressed presence of heteroglossia.

In Arnold's prose and poetry it is the unitary language of monoglos-sia that is privileged, not the dialogic imagination. In his remarks on the dialogue of the mind with itself, Arnold is apparently insisting that poetry be written in active engagement with the social and ideological conflicts of his time. The opposite is true. In his poetry and prose alike Matthew Arnold actually tries to disengage his utterances from the political and social struggles of his time and insist on their lack of participation in het-eroglossia. He, like other Victorian autobiographers, gives voice to the centripetal and unitary voice of his age, not to the dialogic voice of the novel.

Like John Stuart Mill, who sketches a program of anti-self-con-sciousness in his *Autobiography*, Arnold in his preface apparently criticizes the excessive self-involvement and introspection of his age. Arnold's phrase *dialogue of the mind with itself,* however, betrays that deepening of inwardness that I have described in previous chapters. Far from express-ing a desire to suppress the self in favor of the social, his poetry and prose, like John Stuart Mill's *Autobiography* and Gosse's *Father and Son*, mask a strategy of self-representation that privileges the autonomous individual at the expense of a wider community. Victorian autobiographers try to limit their horizons through the monologic imagination, reducing het-eroglossia as far as possible to the single subject of the autonomous self.

Arnold's characterization of literature as a "dialogue" of the mind with itself, rather than a monologue, implicitly raises the possibility of writing as a social encounter. The use of the term *dialogue* raises the spec-tral possibility of community and ideals of human intimacy. However, the gesture toward the social implied in the term *dialogue* is rapidly undercut by the addition of the words *with itself*. The phrase *dialogue of the mind* could be construed to mean the dialogue between the minds of different individuals. Arnold's "dialogue" actually takes place within a single mind, so that "monologue" would in fact be a more accurate description of the process he is describing. Arnold's phrase describes a situation akin to Gosse's discovery of himself as a split subject who can carry out a private, self-enclosed dialogue with another aspect of himself.

The situation here is best illustrated by poems such as "The Buried Life," where an apparent desire to initiate dialogue, in this case with a lover, modulates into a purely self-referential epiphany. The poem opens with an expression of a desire to "unlock the heart, and let it speak" (Arnold 1965, 13). The poem begins with a lament on the impossibility of expressing emotion in language, or even of naming that emotion to oneself:

> Light flows our war of mocking words, and yet,
> Behold, with tears mine eyes are wet!
> I feel a nameless sadness o'er me roll.
> Yes, yes, we know that we can jest,
> We know, we know that we can smile!
> But there's something in this breast,
> To which thy light words bring no rest,
> And thy gay smiles no anodyne. (1–8)

The poem begins with an image of language as heteroglossia. The narrator's use of "war" in the opening line invokes images of conflict. Although this is a mock battle, and language is being used to jest, the poem represents words being employed in a social give-and-take that involves the participants in an effort at intersubjective communication.

This image of social exchange is quickly subverted, however. Arnold proceeds to redirect the poem away from its apparent social agenda into a self-directed, introspective mode. The words being used are "light," implying that they are superficial and do not reach the inner depths at which Arnold is hinting. Whereas language is equated with jests and smiles, Arnold links his own emotions to a supposedly more weighty and meaningful sadness, his tears standing as mute testimony to the strength of his feelings. In the contrast between "light" words and Arnold's emotion, the cards are clearly stacked in favor of Arnold's melancholy.

The true theme of Arnold's poem is announced by his title, "The Buried Life." The opening image of social exchange is simply a pretext. The knowledge that this poem seeks has nothing to do with another person's true feelings, but solely with Arnold's own. Arnold gestures toward a "nameless" emotion, a private "something" that public language cannot define. This "something" just like the "something" that Wordsworth could not name in "Tintern Abbey," is the self imagined as a private, secret interiority. Arnold's poem is saturated with metaphors implying depth or extension. These metaphors represent Arnold's attempt to represent an interiority that by definition cannot be embodied in language because it is predicated upon its uniqueness and originality. If Arnold or Wordsworth were able to name the "something" within them it would in their view no longer be unique or individual. Individuality is an excess of interiority that exceeds the representational capacities of language.

"The Buried Life" is a monologic poem. Its true subject, far from being the desire to "read" the "inmost soul" (11) of the unnamed love, is Arnold's introspective interest in the lineaments of his own interiority. Arnold is primarily interested in unearthing his own "buried life." This is made clear later in the poem:

> But often, in the world's most crowded streets,
> But often, in the din of strife,
> There rises an unspeakable desire
> After the knowledge of the buried life. (45–48)

Arnold at this point sets up the same opposition between the autonomous, private individual and the social as Wordsworth did in *The Prelude*. The desire for knowledge of the "buried life" of the individual is represented as a reaction against the "crowded streets" and the "din of strife" of the city, and by extension as a rejection of the social generally. Like Wordsworth in *The Prelude*, Arnold uses the interiority of the autobiographical subject as a retreat or refuge from the heteroglossia of the social. An idealized image of the country here is opposed to the city, and nature imagined as a refuge from the social. As the quotations from Bakhtin and Williams in my Introduction pointed out, however, nature has by this time become a backdrop for the autobiographical subject, a private landscape that bespeaks the presence of the perceiving subject. The same process is at work in paintings of nature, as Bermingham has argued in *Landscape and Ideology*. Arnold gestures toward a landscape of "meadows" and "hills" (90–97) toward the end of the poem, but in an entirely conventional language that refers primarily to Arnold's subjectivity, not to an autonomous nature.

Arnold's language is typically impersonal when he describes the desire for "knowledge of the buried life." He says that this desire "rises," apparently spontaneously and without conscious control on his part. Like John Stuart Mill in his "mental crisis," Arnold is here representing his own desires in impersonal terms. It is Arnold himself who desires this knowledge, but he does not acknowledge this desire as originating within himself. His desire is "unspeakable." It is "unspeakable" partly because his originality makes it impossible for him to represent his inner existence in language; it is also unspeakable because, like the subjectivity represented in *In Memoriam* and *Dr. Jekyll and Mr. Hyde*, it is associated with secrecy and concealment.

Gorge Levine has suggested that all Arnold's writings are "autobiographical fictions" (Levine 1983, 473) that betray Arnold's unspeakable desire for knowledge of the "buried life." Following Levine's lead, I read both Arnold's poetry and prose as representing the presence of Arnold as autobiographical subject. Just as in "The Buried Life" Arnold moves from the apparently social desire for communication to an entirely self-referential epiphany, so in his other writings the heteroglossia of language is replaced by monologism. "The Buried Life" replaces the attempt at monologue with an unnamed interlocutor with a dialogue of Arnold's mind with itself. Rather than discover what the other is thinking in "The Buried Life," Arnold's gaze "sinks inward" (86). Arnold's poem thus represses the presence of the other, and affirms instead the centrality of Arnold's self. This is Arnold using monologism in the way described by Bakhtin in *Problems of Dostoyevski's Poetics*:

> Ultimately, monologism denies that there exists outside of it another consciousness, with the same rights, and capable of responding on an equal footing, another equal I (thou). For

the monologic outlook (in its extreme or pure form) the other remains entirely and only an object of consciousness, and cannot constitute another consciousness. (Bakhtin 1984, 318)

Bakhtin's definition of monologism accurately captures the movement of Arnold's thought in such poems as "The Buried Life" and "Dover Beach" in which the initially ghostly and insubstantial interlocutor is simply an object of Arnold's consciousness and, like the landscape, is subsumed under monologism. However, as will become clear, Arnold's self is also a ghostly and insubstantial presence. Arnold carries even further the derealization of the subject that in chapter 2 I discussed in the context of Coleridge's poetry and De Quincey's prose.

The self that Arnold embodies in his poetry is insubstantial and isolated, yearning for contact with an autonomous other that is permanently inaccessible. Arnold in his poetry creates a solipsistic cocoon that effectively insulates the self from contact with anything beyond itself. In his poetry he represents the extreme of self-enclosure that writers from Wordsworth on feared and tried to overcome through anti-self-consciousness.

To illustrate just how far we have come from the celebration of the single self in Wordsworth's poetry, I would like to compare Arnold's "Resignation: To Fausta" with Wordsworth's "Tintern Abbey." About "Resignation" Leon Gottfried has suggested in *Matthew Arnold and the Romantics* that it "has so many points of contact with 'Tintern Abbey' that it may almost be considered a reply to it" (Gottfried 1963, 19). Gottfried in the appendix to his book lists some of these "points of contact," such as the presence of a sympathetic woman figure, the role of landscape, and the autobiographical exercise of memory. Gottfried asserts that Arnold's treatment of these themes makes him an "anti-Romantic" (207). This is to a certain extent true, but if we analyze in some detail these points of contact, we will find that, although Arnold tries to be an anti-Romantic, he in fact affirms the Romantic autobiographical sensibility he is trying to overcome.

The most striking difference between the two poems as autobiographies is the status of memory. For Wordsworth memory was a storehouse of epiphanic moments that stood outside the course of time. In revisiting these moments, as in revisiting a landscape after five years' absence, he could reestablish contact with his past and affirm the continuity of his self despite temporal boundaries. Through memory he establishes a "timeless" continuity of self that links past, present, and future into a new unity.

Just as the "lofty cliffs" that he sees once more "connect / the landscape with the sky," so Wordsworth's memory "connects" past and present in the poetic re-creation of the scene. This continuity backward in time allowed him to extrapolate the continuance of his self into the future, and ultimately beyond death. For Arnold, memory is a resource that is no longer available to the self. Far from having a restorative function, Arnold's return to a familiar landscape is an occasion for elegy and lament.

> And to stand again
> Where they stood once, to them were pain;
> Pain to thread back and to renew
> Past straits, and currents long steer'd through. (18–21)

To "stand again" amid a familiar scene is an occasion for pain, not joy. Arnold finds no affirmation of the transcendence of self through memory, only a weary confirmation of how much his inner resources have dwindled. He looks upon his past self as if it were dead and beyond recall, the opening motto of the poem introducing immediately the idea of death as a welcome end. Where to revisit a landscape for Wordsworth was to gain an insight into the transcendence of the self through the agency of memory, Arnold stresses endings, death, and limitation. Where in "Tintern Abbey" the connections made by the landscape stand as a metaphor for the creative activity of memory, in Arnold's poem memory is no longer a resource, just as the landscape also proves hostile to the human consciousness.

I argued in chapter 1 that Wordsworth discovered both in the landscape and in the figure of Dorothy an indirect vehicle through which to represent in the poem a residual sense of community. Both these sources of comfort Arnold denies himself. The woman in Arnold's poem is a shadowy and unresponsive figure who, rather than confirm the poet's sense of self, forces him back in upon himself and makes him try to interpret her emotions.

> You listen—but that wandering smile,
> Fausta, betrays you cold the while! (199–200)

Although she listens, the woman is an unflattering audience. Unlike Dorothy she refuses to play the role the poet assigns her, so that he cannot like Wordsworth "behold in thee what I once was." Both nature and the feminine have become inaccessible to Arnold as guarantors of his identity.

The "cold" woman "betrays" the poet, Arnold bringing in the language of unrequited love and the archetypal situation of a man facing his unresponsive lover. The language of betrayal and the unresponsiveness of the woman mark this as a moment similar to that represented in Dante Gabriel Rossetti's "The Mirror," where the central male figure is "betrayed" by the woman when she fails to conform to his expectations. Rossetti's governing metaphor for this situation is that of the image in the mirror that fails to reflect the actions of the poet. Miller and Lesser have suggested in their analyses of men's use of women as objects of representation that such imagery betrays the male search for an "other self" (Lesser 1991, Miller 1991). Rather than find confirmation for the self, the poet is reminded of the liminality and insubstantiality of his self-image. In refusing to conform to the poet's desire, "Fausta" in "Resignation" plays the same role as "Marguerite" in the series of poems addressed to her. She reminds the poet of his own and of everyone else's isolation.

> We mortal millions live *alone*.
> The islands feel the enclasping flow,
> And then their endless bounds they know. (3–6)

Arnold in "To Marguerite—Continued" uses the metaphor of islands in the ocean to represent the distance between himself and the woman. The relationship between himself and his lover, or the lack of any kind of contact that could be the basis for a relationship, becomes a metaphor for the situation of individuals in society as a whole, "the mortal millions" whose most powerful experience is of their own isolation. An intimate relationship produces an acute sense of limitation, not transcendence as it does in Wordsworth's poem.

The woman in these poems, like the woman in "Dover Beach," confirms the poet's failure to find himself, rather than representing the self-affirming presence of a sympathetic audience. Wordsworth imagined himself into the future by envisaging Dorothy remembering him on revisiting the landscape of "Tintern Abbey." The women in Arnold's poetry do not represent any such hope and remain insubstantial figures, barely realized tokens of a presence beyond the self. Their role, like that of the landscape, is to refuse to conform to the contours of the poet's consciousness rather than to reembody it in transcendent form, as Arnold makes plain in "Resignation."

> The world in which we live and move
> Outlasts aversion, outlasts love...

This world in which we draw our breath,
In some sense, Fausta, outlasts death. (215–230)

The landscape in "Resignation" speaks to Arnold of the limits of his self. It reminds him of the insignificance of human consciousness. Arnold denies transcendence to the human self by opposing to it "the far regions of eternal change," regions that define the limitations of human emotion. Arnold represents his self in a way diametrically opposed to that embodied in "Tintern Abbey." In Wordsworth's vision, it was his poetic self that "outlasted" the landscape and even death. For Arnold it is something beyond and alien to the self that outlasts death. This is Arnold's anti-Romantic representation of self, his portrayal of a self determined by forces beyond its control.

However, the lines that I have quoted above finally come down to a conclusion that is not so distant from Wordsworth's as one might at first imagine. What starts in "Resignation" as the admonition that "this world" confirms the limitation of human existence by "outlasting" it, ends up nonetheless affirming the presence of an undefined yet omnipresent "something" that outlasts death. The very same "far regions of eternal change" that define the limits of the self can overcome even what "wipes out man," death. It seems there is some force in the world that is transcendent, even if Arnold does not connect it directly with his self. The use of the word *eternal* here recalls the idea of endless bounds in the lines I quoted above. Arnold, in using the words *endless bounds*, was apparently talking about the isolation and limitation of the individual self, but also signaled his continuing allegiance to a mystical conception of some transcendent force in the human consciousness.

Arnold here is expressing a faith in an omnipresent and omnipotent self, that ungraspable something described by Wordsworth in "Tintern Abbey." His refutation of the Romantic self is thus not total. He betrays in such formulations as *eternal* and *boundless* the continuing existence of an unnamed and undefined something that transcends death in the same way that Wordsworth felt was possible for his self. Arnold retains in his poetry an attenuated version of the Romantic transcendent self.

Arnold's tactic in his poetry is his version of Victorian anti-self-consciousness. Arnold deliberately limits his self-consciousness by using women and the landscape to emphasize its boundedness. However, in much the same way that a larger vision of society became an indirect expression of Mill's self in his *Autobiography*, Arnold's self-repression leads him to express his sense of self in the apparently objective term *this world*. Arnold finds through this vision of the totality of existence confirmation of a transcendent power and a vicarious experience of the transcendence of his self. Arnold therefore betrays an ambivalent attitude toward the idea of Romantic transcendence, both rejecting it and accepting it at the same time. His anti-Romanticism is undermined by a continuing allegiance to the Romantic self.

This ambivalent attitude also marks Arnold's descriptions of the status of his self. Arnold shares with Coleridge a sense of the insubstantiality of his self. As I argued in chapter 2, in Coleridge's poetry references to ghosts or phantoms were metaphors for the precarious existence of Coleridge's self, denoting a presence that threatened to disappear from the public into the private realm and become completely inaccessible to language. Arnold, like Coleridge, uses the vocabulary of ghosts and phantoms to describe his self and its uncertain existence in the social world. He and Fausta in "Resignation" are "ghosts of that former company" (89). The collectivity has been lost, and Arnold and his companion have been turned into phantoms by the passage of time.

Arnold is the Victorian poet who approaches most nearly the neurotic obsession with the loss of self found in Coleridge. Not even Tennyson at his most guilt-ridden can approach the claustrophobic impact of these lines, in which not only the self but all social life is robbed of significance. Arnold in "Growing Old" describes himself as "immured" in himself, trapped by an inability to experience anything directly, even the melancholy that gave rise to the poem in the first place. He is haunted by the suspicion that his self is so insubstantial that he can "feel but half, and feebly, what we feel" (27). Arnold represents the derealization of the subject that Tennyson represented in his descriptions of nature in *In Memoriam*. Even the passionate experience of joy or suffering is lost in this draining of significance, so that the most that can be felt is a vague melancholy. In this Arnold expresses one of the most powerful themes in his poetry, the suspicion that what is beyond his reach is not only a wider reality, but also the very self that has led to this isolation in the first place. This theme he expresses in both "The Buried Life" and "Below the Surface Stream."

Like "Resignation," "The Buried Life" uses the figure of an unresponsive woman to emphasize the inability of even lovers to "reveal / to one another what indeed they feel" and moves on from this to express dismay at the way people are "alien" from one another and doomed to isolation. "The Buried Life" goes further than "Resignation" or even the Marguerite poems, however, by describing how the individual is isolated from his own self, not only from other people:

Fate...
That it might keep from his capricious play
His genuine self, and force him to obey
Even in his own despite his being's law
Bade through the deep recesses of our breast
The unregarded river of our life
Pursue with indiscernible flow its way. (30–40)

Arnold uses the metaphor of the river or stream to represent the course of his life, as did Wordsworth in *The Prelude*. Arnold calls his life "the buried stream," however, suggesting that the sense of the self as a principle of coherence is not open to him as it was for Wordsworth. Arnold describes a situation in which people live without being able to comprehend the reasons for their existence. This is an extreme image of the subject's alienation from the "inner" self, of which only the surface and not its "depths" can be seen. This formulation turns most of Anrold's social life into a "false consciousness," the only true experience being epiphanic moments in which the subject glimpses for a moment the "unregarded river" of the inner life

A bolt is shot back somewhere in our breast,
And a lost pulse of feeling stirs again
The eye sinks inward, and the heart lies plain
And what we mean, we say, and what we would, we know.
(84–87)

The poem moves in these lines from the attempt to communicate with the unnamed female other and turns instead inward. What the poem initially presented as an attempt at dialogue becomes instead a dialogue of the mind with itself as the sundered halves of Arnold's split subject are reunited in a brief moment of self-knowledge. Like Gosse, Arnold finds his individuality confirmed by this secret communion. He substitutes this self-communion for the attempt at human communication represented in the poem's opening scenario of the attempt of a lover to speak with his beloved.

Arnold's escape from the social in a poem like "The Buried Life," however, is subverted by the heteroglossia of language. Even as Arnold maintains that "what we mean, we say," his language eludes his attempts to create a unitary self that is expressed directly and unambiguously in a truthful language. David Riede has documented the dense, uncontrolled intertextuality of "The Buried Life," which echoes both Wordsworth's "Tintern Abbey" and Satan in Milton's *Paradise Lost* (Riede 1988, 181–90). Arnold in "The Buried Life" cannot create the unitary subject to which he aspires, in which self and language correspond on a one-to-one basis. His poem is dialogic despite his efforts to create a pristine monologic text.

An even more striking representation of the split subjectivity implied in "The Buried Life" occurs in "Below the Surface Stream," in which "central stream" of the subject's inner existence flows on completely independently of consciousness. As in "The Buried Life," there are epiphanic moments in which this split is healed:

> And then he thinks he knows
> The hills where his life rose,
> And the sea where it goes. (96–98)

This is a moment in which the "buried stream" is apparently revealed and the individual can see his or her life as a coherent whole. Arnold here is supposedly describing the resolution of the sort of "incoherency" that in chapter 4 I described as marking Victorian autobiography, a subversive sense of how far words as outer public forms have become divorced from the inner subject that uses them. Arnold describes an ideal moment in which "what we mean, we say," a moment in which the individual can not only scan the course of his life and see it as a composite whole, but also express his or her sense of self in language. He is here expressing a powerful autobiographical ideal. This ideal is, however, tempered by his saying that the individual "thinks he knows" his life in its totality. This qualification is made even more emphatic in "Below the Surface Stream" when Arnold describes the "surface-stream, shallow and light":

> Of what we *say* we feel—below the stream,
> As light, of what we *think* we feel. (1–2)

The qualification is even more pronounced in these lines than in those in "The Buried Life." We may *think* we know what we feel, but in fact the self's emotions are as inaccessible as they were said to be in "Growing Old." Arnold's use of *think* in "The Buried Life" implicates even the apparent epiphany he describes in the experience of the "surface" of words rather than the true depths of the inner life that he is apparently plumbing. The metaphors of surface and depth here underscore how the contrast is weighted in favor of the buried life. Language is light and inexpressive, as it was in the opening lines of "The Buried Life," whereas the buried life itself connotes depth and extension. Where Arnold is apparently praising communication and community, he actually privileges experiences of isolation and alienation. The epiphany that ends "The Buried Life" turns an attempt at communication into a radical affirmation of the inwardness of his experience. Arnold's experience bears out Toulmin's contention that once one accepts the existence of an inner self, it becomes impossible to reunite the sundered inward and outer spheres of experience.

By linking his subjectivity and metaphors of depth, Arnold shows his affinity with the models of subjectivity found in Mill's and Gosse's autobiographies. His individuality is confirmed to the extent to which it cannot be revealed in language and to which it possesses an interiority figured through images of an eternal landscape. Like Gosse he finds within himself a kernel of identity that he cannot reveal. This is at once a melancholy and a comforting discovery. Like Dr. Jekyll, Arnold has a "Mr. Hide" who must remain unexpressed. Like Tennyson in *In Memoriam*, Arnold links self-expression to a sense of the impropriety of revealing a secret buried life that should be protected from public scrutiny. His autonomy is guaranteed by this secrecy, but it also leads to images of ghostliness and imprisonment, such as those found in "Growing Old."

Arnold remains committed to the ideal of the autonomous individual. It is here that we find the most striking and disturbing ambivalence. While on the one hand portraying his experience of self as insubstantial and isolated, he on the other hand praises an autonomous self that is independent of all outside forces. This is an ideal he praises in such poems as "Religious Isolation" and "Self-Dependence." "Religious Isolation," far from criticizing the isolation that is introduced in the title, praises the disjunction between the human consciousness and the world and criticizes as childlike the search for a confirmatory presence for the self. It ends on an injunction to its unnamed friend to "live by thy light" and not expect a response from "the earth" (15). Similarly, "Self-Dependence" praises a complete autonomy of being as symbolized in nature by the stars:

> These demand not that the things without them
> Yield them love, amusement, sympathy. (19–20)

This is Arnold in quite another mood than the one we saw in "Resignation." He here uses the fact that nature outlasts human conscious-

ness, and is apparently completely indifferent to it, not as a way of emphasizing the limitations of the self, but as a way of affirming its complete
autonomy. Arnold praises here his version of the autonomous self on the
same grounds as he elsewhere condemned it, making an apparent vice
into a virtue. The stars, the ideal state in this poem, are "self-poised" and
"bounded by themselves." Where the individuals as islands in "To Marguerite" were aware in a pernicious sense of their "endless bounds," here
to be "self-bounded" and self-contained is to set up a benign insularity. It
would appear that here Arnold is reversing his terms and making a virtue
out of what he bemoans in other poems as a judgment by fate or by God.

This would be the case if it were not for the title and subject of the
poem. The poem praises autonomy, but its very premise is Arnold's
demanding and receiving an answer from an apparently indifferent universe. If Arnold himself were as self-sufficient as he would ideally like, he
would not in the first place have to pose the question to which he receives
an obligingly comforting answer. If he were truly self-sufficient, he would
not need to look for an ideal model in nature, and if nature were truly
indifferent, she wouldn't vouchsafe an answer. The title of this poem,
however, is not "Independence" or "Self-Sufficiency" but "Self-Dependence." Arnold is unwittingly undermining his own objective by raising
the idea of dependency upon an external agency in the poem's title, while
overtly criticizing such a damaging limitation on the self. Arnold subverts
his own terms by introducing the idea of dependency in a poem that celebrates independence. Arnold in his notion of dependency here resurrects
very briefly a notion of community. The poem, while it ostensibly praises
autonomy, actually shows how he is dependent upon a sense of an external force, symbolized in the stars. He is not as completely self-sufficient as
he would apparently like to believe.

In these two poems we see Arnold attempting to reaffirm his faith
in the autonomous self and simultaneously overcome the isolation and
alienation he elsewhere admits is attendant upon the sort of autonomy he
praises in "Self-Dependence." His apparent self-contradiction illustrates
graphically the ambivalence he felt toward the Romantic ideals he inherited and his attempts to criticize and go beyond them. In moments such
as these Arnold finds himself defeated by the very terms he uses, and he
ends up affirming the isolation of the self even while trying to surpass it.

Leon Gottfried has summarized Arnold's relationship to his
Romantic forebears in terms of an increasingly self-referential use of
poetry:

If Wordsworth is to bear the responsibility of establishing the poet's own states of mind as the main subject of poetry, Arnold surely is equally responsible for furthering, and further limiting, its establishment in his practice in spite of his intended rebellion against it, and thereby for furthering the divorce between "poetry" and "life" (Gottfried 1963, 21)

As Gottfried, suggests, Arnold continues a process of separation of the inward from the social that was initiated in the Romantic period. Arnold is clearly an anti-Romantic in that he both registers the inheritance of the autobiographical approach to poetry begun in the Romantic period and tries to overcome what he perceived as its limitations. In this very resistance, however, he nonetheless affirmed the self's centrality and the inevitable presence of the falsifying subjectivity he sought to escape. As I have suggested above, his self-repression led him to reinscribe his self in larger and more general terms in "this world," rather than to escape the idea of self altogether. His attempts to make a virtue of the autonomy of self and its consequent isolation were undermined by the very evils he elsewhere expressed so eloquently. By bemoaning and attempting to go beyond the isolation of his self in his poetry, Arnold merely affirmed its condition and made more emphatic the split between individual and social in his poetry.

Arnold's poetry is indelibly marked by a falsifying self-consciousness that he wished to overcome but could not. Like Ruskin, Arnold turned from writing poetry to writing prose, and particularly social criticism, as an antidote to the modern disease of excessive self-consciousness. Arnold's social criticism should be read as an explicit rejection of the autobiographical sensibility expressed in his poetry, an attempt to repress the antisocial implications of individualism in favor of a wider social ethic. Arnold's prose embodies a form of anti-self-consciousness similar to that which I have described as the method behind the prose of Ruskin and Mill. As in his poetry, Arnold in his prose tries to repress the self in favor of the other.

Having said this, however, I must confess immediately that I feel Arnold's prose is undermined by its premises in exactly the same way as his poetry. While he may try to repress his self in his prose, he ends up affirming the self's ubiquitous presence. Arnold uses a constellation of terms to embody the disinterested ideal he opposes to the limited outlook determined by a narrow concentration on self. These terms are *the best self, criticism, culture, the State,* and a host of metaphors based upon

the image of flowing water, metaphors that depict the activity of the critical consciousness. I wish to suggest that, far from being an antidote to
the isolated and alienated self described in his poetry, the self in Arnold's
prose reenacts the same dichotomies, and finds itself trapped by the same
contradictions, as his poetic self. The self in Arnold's criticism, in other
words, is as informed by its Romantic heritage as the self in his poetry.

The most striking aspect in Arnold's description of the critical consciousness in "The Function of Criticism at the Present Time" and *Culture and Anarchy* is the deep confusion between inner and outer. As in
Romantic poetry, in Arnold's prose the two terms keep threatening to
coalesce. Arnold represents in his prose the same liminal position as he
embodied in his poetry, occupying what in chapter 2 I characterized as
the liminal position of the writing subject. Even as Arnold gestures
toward the social function of criticism, he portrays a subjectivity that is
marginal to the very society he wishes to address. He embodies a subjectivity that, like the ghostly presence in his poetry, is alienated from its
social context.

This can best be seen in Arnold's use of water metaphors. In his
poetry Arnold used images of flowing water to express the inner life of
the individual. In "The Function of Criticism" Arnold singles out
Edmund Burke for praise because of his rejection of the French Revolution when others were being swept up by its example, and then goes on
to characterize Burke's thought processes in liquid metaphors when he
says that "it is his characteristic that he so lived by ideas, and had such a
source of them welling up within him, that he could float even an epoch
of concentration and English Tory politics with them" (Arnold 1962a,
267). Arnold gives us a rather peculiar image of Burke "saturating" political thought as if he were a faucet, in fact giving off so much water that he
could "float" an entire epoch like a ship. Arnold turns Burke into a veri-
table fountain. I underline the fact that Arnold is approaching the ludicrous in his description of Burke to emphasize what a powerful image
flowing water was for Arnold. This is the highest praise he can bestow
upon Burke. It is particularly telling that Arnold should resort to water
imagery here, because he is praising Burke in opposition to the example
set by the French Revolution. Arnold says that the French Revolution
was not "a disinterestedly intellectual and spiritual movement" (263) but
one that, rather, moved too precipitously from "the world of ideas" into
"the world of practice" (265). Burke, by implication, represents all that is
opposed to this. He is disinterested and inhabits the "world of ideas."
Arnold is praising Burke, in other words, for his inner qualities, suggest-

ing that Burke's inner life was so powerful as to overcome the barriers to "the buried stream" and emerge as a torrent into the public realm.

Burke, then, turns away from revolution. Just as the political was displaced in Wordsworth's poetry into the personal, so Burke reacts to the social upheaval of his time by recourse to the world of ideas. This world of ideas is divorced from the world of action and represents a pristine inner space from which Burke can resist the social discourse of his time. Arnold praises Burke for possessing inwardness.

The predominance of water metaphors in Arnold's description of Burke signals that what he is praising in Burke above all is inwardness. Arnold is praising Burke for inhabiting that watery realm that in "The Buried Life" he associates with the "genuine self." In his contrast between Burke and the French Revolution, Arnold is underscoring the very dichotomy he bemoans in "The Buried Life," the insurmountable disjunction between the self and its expression in outward reality. Just as in "Self-Dependency" he praised the autonomy of self from outward forces, he praises Burke for his independence from the language that his party used "like a steam-engine," and his ability to "think, to be irresistibly carried...by the current of thought to the opposite side of the question" (Arnold 1962a, 267). Arnold sees inwardness here as a virtue, as he does in "Self-Dependence."

It seems for Arnold that Burke's inner life is so strong that it overcomes the isolation and alienation he elsewhere describes as endemic to the inner life of the modern individual. Burke is able to withdraw into himself and resist the "steam engine" language of his party, becoming the sort of ideally self-dependent figure Arnold praises in "Religious Isolation" and "Self-Dependence." The same terms that Arnold uses to praise Burke and his reaction to the French Revolution, however, can also be used in an opposite sense, as we have seen in the poetry. This is also true in Arnold's prose.

One place where this reversal of terms occurs is in Arnold's criticism of "Empedocles on Etna" in his 1853 preface to his *Poems*. Arnold's comments on "Empedocles" reverse the precedence of the world of ideas over the world of practice, making excessive inwardness a flaw. Arnold, as we have seen, maintains that "Empedocles" was flawed because it was a type of poetry "in which the suffering finds no vent in action...in which there is everything to be endured, nothing to be done" (591). Arnold criticizes "Empedocles" because it represents in a dramatic poem the same disjunction between idea and action that informs his lyric poetry. Empedocles' dialogue of the mind with itself, his excessive inwardness, is therefore a model to be avoided. However, Arnold describes Burke as having much in common with Empedocles when he says, "That return of Burke upon himself has always seemed to me one of the finest things in English literature" (Arnold 1962a, 267).

Arnold praises Burke for the ability to "return upon himself," to withdraw from the realm of action into himself. The return of Burke upon himself is not very far removed from the dialogue of the mind with itself. Burke's example is praiseworthy where Empedocles' is not because Arnold is contrasting the buried stream of inwardness with a reality characterized by steam-engine language. The steam engine here stands for everything that is bad about industrialization and from which the cultured mind instinctively recoils. Eugene Goodheart in *The Failure of Criticism* places Arnold's concern with inwardness within the context of just this type of reaction against mechanization:

> The revulsion from the spiritually vacuous alternative of mechanical civilization produces an inordinate preoccupation with inwardness. This is the unsurmounted legacy of both Romanticism and Protestantism. (Goodheart 1978, 48)

Arnold's commitment to inwardness in opposition to mechanization in the case of Burke leads him to praise what in "Empedocles" he condemned. Although Arnold in his 1853 preface professes a desire to overcome an inordinate preoccupation with the self, he retreats into just such a self-enclosed position when faced with the demon of the steam engine or the example of the French Revolution. Arnold betrays in his prose here the same ambivalence as I described in his poetry. He wishes to "surmount" his Romantic legacy, but so imbued is his language with the ideals of the Romanticism he criticizes that he unwittingly reinscribes them in his vocabulary. As Eugene Goodheart points out, his Romantic and Protestant legacy proves an unsurmountable presence, leading him to affirm inwardness when he elsewhere criticized it.

Arnold stands committed, in his ideal of criticism as exemplified by Burke, to a paradoxical situation. His solution to excessive inwardness and to subjectivity is for subjectivity to overcome itself. So inward is Burke that he overcomes by some magical process the boundaries of his self, transcends them and floats an entire epoch on the sea of thought. Through the idealized image of Burke, Arnold seeks to overcome the profound dichotomies between thought and action, or inner and outer, that inform both his poetry and his prose. Arnold's description of the ideal of culture in *Culture and Anarchy* betrays its alliance with the values he attaches to Burke and inwardness by his use of water as a metaphor once again for the action of thought. Arnold defines "culture" in *Culture and Anarchy* in the following terms:

> Culture being a pursuit of our total perfection by means of getting to know, on all matters which most concern us, the best which has been thought and said in the world; and through this knowledge, turning a stream of fresh and free thought upon our stock notions and habits, which we now follow staunchly but mechanically....And the culture we recommend is, above all, an inward operation. (Arnold 1925, 6)

The "stream" of thought has its origin, as it does in Burke, in that very buried stream that Arnold bemoaned as inaccessible in "The Buried Life." As in "The Function of Criticism," the recourse to inwardness in *Culture and Anarchy* is a reaction against the mechanization of thought and the French Revolution. Arnold adds the further component here of "freedom." Freedom is allied with inwardness, so that it is only within the self, in its far recesses, that the individual can experience true freedom from mechanization.

The problem with defining freedom in terms of inwardness here is that, as in Mill's definition of freedom in *On Liberty*, it stops with the individual. Once one tries to imagine liberty beyond individual rights, one is presented with indissoluble dichotomies between the rights of competing individuals, and between the individual and the state. What is lost in this view is ant notion of rights emerging from a collectivity rather than from individuals. The idea of the social basis of life is lost in the vision of the autonomous and inward existence of individuals.

The free "stream" of thought of culture is a further development of the "free play of mind" (Arnold 1962a, 268) that Arnold praises in "The Function of Criticism" as the hallmark of the critical consciousness. This free play of mind itself leads back to a disguised form of inwardness, because the effect of the critical application of mind is itself to create yet another "current," only this time one that has a public, exterior existence. Arnold says of the free play of the mind that "no other criticism will ever attain any real authority or make any real way towards its end—the creating of a current of true and fresh ideas" (271). By a magical transformation the inner stream of the buried life is turned into the social current of "true and fresh ideas." This current remains in the realm of ideas, how-

ever, not practice. It is still unclear from Arnold's description what concrete effects this new current will have on Victorian society.

Arnold associates a dense cluster of ideas around the image of free-
flowing water, and it is through the imagery of water that we best can
understand what he was trying to accomplish in his use of the terms *culture* and *criticism,* and why he failed. Just as images of flowing water for
John Ruskin represented incompatible versions of self, they do so in
Arnold's prose also. Water represents the inaccessible areas of the self that
alone can escape the pernicious effects of mechanization. Water also
comes to represent the magical relocation of this inwardness from an isolated and deeply private experience into the realm of action. It is thus
through inwardness that Arnold tries to overcome inwardness.

This paradoxical self-overcoming is most evident in his use of the
term *best self.* In his insistence on the idea of the best self in culture,
Arnold tries to overcome the self through the self. Using the term *best self*
does not do away with the narrow self-consciousness Arnold criticized; it
assumes that the individual can carry out some self-surmounting selection
process through which all that is not the "best" in inwardness is simply
jettisoned. There is a mystical and transcendental side to Arnold's conception here that betrays his lingering faith in the transcendent self.

Arnold in *Culture and Anarchy* adds to the terms *criticism* and *culture* the supervening idea of "the State." The state represents for Aarnold
not any concretely imagined system of government, but rather the agency
through which the individual can overcome the isolating boundaries of
his self. Through the state the individual can by a magical transformation
become everything that is the opposite of the fallen "ordinary self." The
state is for Arnold the ultimate expression of the best self, the self that is
connected with everything that is the opposite of egotism.

> But by our *best self* we are united, impersonal, at harmony...
> and this is the very self which culture, or the study of perfec-
> tion, seeks to develop in us; at the expense of our old untrans-
> formed self. (92–93)

For Arnold the individual can be "transformed" from an antisocial
and conflict-prone atomistic self into a member of a harmonious community by the actions of criticism, culture, and the state. To participate in
these terms is to escape the boundedness he criticized in the Nonconformists (13) and achieve a mystical communion that fulfills his ideal of
"eluding sterile conflicts...[and] refusing to remain in the sphere where

alone narrow and relative conceptions have any worth and validity" (Arnold 1962a, 274). This harmony is achieved by a voluntary self-regulation on the part of the individual, who overcomes his self through the ideal of the state:

> We [English] have not the notion, so familiar on the Continent and to antiquity, of *The State*,—the nation in its collective and corporate character, entrusted with stringent powers for the general advantage, and controlling individual wills in the name of an interest wider than that of individuals...we say that a State is in reality made up of the individuals who compose it, and that every individual is the best judge of his own interests. (72)

Arnold is here giving the most explicit and forceful expression in Victorian literature to the ideal that I have in this study termed anti-self-consciousness, the repression of the individual self "in the name of an interest wider than that of individuals" in order to incorporate the antisocial implications of the autonomous individual within the community. The state is for Arnold an "imagined community" in the sense proposed by Benedict Anderson (1991), an idealized image that encourages individuals to represent themselves as citizens of a collective nation-state. Arnold's formulation captures here the self-limiting operation behind anti-self-consciousness and the deeply paradoxical nature of this ideal. The individual voluntarily enters into a bondage, endowing the state with the authority that rightly belongs to the autonomous self. The state is "entrusted" with this power because the autonomous self cannot be trusted to act socially unaided. Like Mr. Hyde, the autonomous self will erupt in antisocial ways if not restrained, so that its freedom of action is defined as a threat that must be contained.

Arnold here is representing the form of subjected autonomy that I have described in chapter 4 in the context of Ruskin's and Stevenson's autobiographies, and in chapter 5 in the context of Mill's and Gosse's creation of their fathers as external authorities to whom they cede their own sovereignty. In subjected autonomy, the freedom of the individual is guaranteed by his or her ceding authority to a regulating authority such as the state. Arnold here betrays most graphically his allegiance to monoglossia. He wishes to bring subjectivity and language under the controlling power of the state, which will neutralize conflict and ensure that social interactions are carried on in harmony. In the state, Arnold embodies a vision of community, but it is a community imagined as an authoritarian corrective to his individualist premises.

Arnold at this moment in *Culture and Anarchy* faces the aporia that has informed all the texts I have studied thus far. He too wishes to overcome the antisocial implications of individualism in the name of a wider social ethic, but his terms do not allow him to imagine anything beyond the individual. By starting with the premise that every individual is endowed with a unique, autonomous self, he then finds it impossible to imagine a wider community. The idea of community, or, in Arnold's terms, the state, can only be the image of the individual writ large. Eugene Goodheart has described this process in his study of the social criticism of Arnold, Carlyle, and Ruskin in *The Failure of Criticism*.

> In short, they [Ruskin, Carlyle, Arnold] wish to overcome the disjunction between man and society which they perceive to be the essential human condition at the present moment by conceiving society as expressive of individual life, when its faculties are in a state of harmony and health....Carlyle and the others seek to transcend the conception of individuality as separate from society, not by remaking the individual to conform to an abstract model of society, but by remaking society to express the full moral and intellectual character of individual life. (Goodheart 1978, 38)

This is an admirably succinct account of Arnold's ideal. As Goodheart says, Arnold's social criticism is founded upon the ideal of the perfectibility of man, hence his emphasis upon perfection in culture. Arnold projects this ideal image of the perfect individual onto the state in order to imagine a redeemed and harmonious self that overcomes the deeply felt dichotomy between self and society. My point is, however, that such a move merely reinscribes the self in larger terms onto an apparently objective and selfless term, as it did in Mill's ideal of social reform. Arnold's solution to the problems of individualism is in the final analysis an irrational faith in the ability of the individual to transcend himself, give up his solipsistic and egocentric ways, and find redemption in a collective ideal that is the self cleansed of its impurities. As Arnold's term *the best self* implies, his ideal does not reject the category of self altogether, rather it embodies an ideal of self-selection, a self-limitation of the individual will in favor of the wider social ethic. His attempts to imagine community are subverted by his premises.

Arnold, like Ruskin and Mill, is in his "best self" trying to reconcile the dichotomy between authority and autonomy, by representing the state in terms of subjected autonomy. No matter how much Arnold may criticize the ethos of "doing as one likes," he remains committed to an individualistic faith in the freedom and autonomy of the self. He divides the world into the inward realm, associated with intellect, metaphors of flowing water, and freedom, and the public realm, which is associated with constraint and restraint. It is this radical dichotomizing of the issues that leads him to the impasse we find throughout his writings, whether poetry or prose. As Leon Gottfried said, for all of Arnold's anti-Romanticism, he himself is guilty of further divorcing poetry and life in the terms he uses. Similarly, Eugene Goodheart's remarks help illustrate how Arnold's conceptions of the self and the state turn the issue into an either/or contrast that can only be overcome through a complete transformation of the ordinary self. In Arnold's terms, either the individual must be remade in the image of society or society must be remade in the image of the self. There is no middle ground. Clearly, within the terms that Arnold uses, the solution he gives is the more humane, but the terms themselves are flawed.

The principal reason for Arnold's difficulty here is a failure of the imagination endemic to nineteenth-century British literature. The writers I study wish to overcome the isolation of the self from a wider society, but they cannot move beyond the individualist ideology within which they think. Arnold espouses in *Culture and Anarchy* an apparently social ethic in his vision of the state. In reality, he is, like the Romantics by whom he is so deeply influenced, promoting a vision of the autonomous and transcendent self that can surmount all bounds. He criticizes the Nonconformists, for instance, for their "special difficulty in breaking through what bounds them" (Arnold 1925, 12), implying that it is possible for the best self to break all bounds. He is, however, as bound by his own ideology as the Nonconformists.

While Arnold in his conception of the self advocates a voluntary self-limitation of the individual, in his remarks on criticism and culture he espouses the ideal of the individual who can, outside the public realm of the state, achieve complete autonomy and self-sufficiency, and thus develop his or her "totality." In his ideal of the "critical consciousness," Arnold gives expression once again to the vision of the transcendent self that first found its expression in Wordsworth's *The Prelude*.

The primary poetic metaphor for this free critical consciousness is the scholar gypsy. This figure combines the intellectual and scholarly attributes of the critic with the lack of self-consciousness and freedom from constraint of the Gypsies. In "Resignation" the Gypsies provide a positive contrast with the jaded self-consciousness of the poet. While the poet experiences pain and an overwhelming sense of the diminishment of personal resources upon revisiting a landscape after ten years' absence, the Gypsies remain impervious to such feelings. Such returns "do not raise / In them the ghost of former days"(37), says Arnold, that is, they do not remind them of the insubstantiality and gradual erosion of the self. In this they are figures embodying anti-self-consciousness, an ideal that, like Mill's Utilitarianism, overcomes determinism and promises immortality for the human soul.

It is the continual recurrence of the Gypsies and the scholar gypsy that guarantees their transcendence. The implication of the poem entitled "The Scholar-Gipsy" is that the scholar who has joined the Gypsy band will forever be a part of the landscape around Oxford. Like the landscape, the scholar gypsy "outlasts death" and enters the realm of the eternal. It is for this reason that Arnold ends the elegy "Thyrsis" with a comforting vision of the scholar gypsy. Arnold mourns the passing of Clough until he connects the memory of his dead friend with the elusive figure of the scholar gypsy:

> Still, these slopes, 'tis clear,
> Our Gypsy-Scholar haunts, outliving thee! (196–97)

The scholar gypsy "outlives" the self, just as this world outlasts human emotions in "Resignation," yet Arnold can through this figure find a vicarious salvation. The scholar gypsy is a figure of autobiography, like the Brocken-Spectre I described in chapter 2. Like the Specter of Brocken in Romantic imagery, the scholar gypsy in Arnold's poems fuses self and other in an ambiguous figure that inhabits both a private and a public realm. Through the figure of the scholar gypsy Arnold is able to find both a symbol of his own salvation and a meeting ground for himself and his memory of Clough. The scholar gypsy symbolizes their joint "quest," a quest that is the critical activity conceived of in pseudoreligious terms.

Arnold in "The Scholar-Gipsy" represents his desire to flee the social context, in this case Oxford University, and enter a timeless realm free from social change. The gypsy scholar is for Arnold a symbol of Wordsworth's single self, as Arnold makes clear when he contrasts the gypsy scholar's existence to his own divided and conflicted subjectivity.

Thou hadst *one* aim, *one* business, *one* desire;
...O life unlike to ours!
Who fluctuate wildly without term or scope
Of whom each strives, nor knows for what he strives,
And each half lives a hundred different lives. (152–69)

The gypsy scholar represents the ideal of a unitary subject, where Arnold's experience of his subjectivity is fragmentary. In a letter to his sister "K," Arnold acknowledged the fragmentary nature of his experience, as opposed to his ideal of a unitary and "whole" self:

> The true reason why parts [of the poems] suit while others do not is that my poems are fragments—i.e. that I am fragments, while you are whole; the whole effect of my poems is quite vague & indeterminate—this is their weakness. (Arnold 1923, 267)

The scholar gypsy functions as an explicit compensation for the divided and contradictory nature of his own subjectivity and the ideal of a unitary and rational self that informs all his writings. The poem also enacts a disturbing desire to escape the social context that contradicts the social agenda of his literary criticism. Like for Wordsworth, his ideal of the single self threatens his social ideals by separating him from the very community he wishes to address.

Wordsworth conceived of *The Prelude* as a preliminary stage for the eventual completion of an epic poem that would incorporate a wider vision of society. This poem was never written. The exercise of the autobiographical consciousness blocked Wordsworth's ability to imagine his society in any other than individualist terms, and the nascent possibility of an alternative vision of society is dropped in his renunciation of his sociological studies in London. The retreat into inwardness that he proposed to himself as a preliminary stage in *The Prelude* in fact blocks his imagination and makes him unable to turn his inner vision into a social vision. The same is true in Arnold's case.

Wordsworth is remembered as a poet for his autobiographical poetry, a poetry that gave voice to the new self-consciousness of the Romantic period. Matthew Arnold, for all his anti-Romanticism, stands committed to the same ideals as Wordsworth. The self that Arnold portrays is certainly more attenuated, more acutely beset by feelings of isolation and alienation, than the Romantic self, but nonetheless Arnold in the final analysis professes allegiance to this self as embodied in the scholar gypsy. Like Wordsworth, Arnold desires to address wider social themes but in his poetry finds himself unable to do so. In his poetry Arnold is primarily remembered for his "radical affirmation of inwardness," so that he "remains very much the modern artist of the buried life" (Goodheart 1978, 34, 48).

In his prose Arnold tries to succeed where Wordsworth failed. He attempts to turn a "radical affirmation of inwardness" and a philosophy based on the autonomous self into a manifesto for society. As I have suggested in my analysis of the similarity between his poetry and his prose, Arnold in his prose tries to turn the vices of inwardness into virtues. Having accepted the category of the autonomous self, he tries to "transform" the self into what he conceives of as its opposite, society. By imagining the perfection of the best self, he tries to overcome the feelings of isolation and alienation to which he gives such powerful expression in his poetry. Arnold asserted that "perfection as culture conceives it, is not possible while the individual remains isolated" (Arnold 1925, 44). Through the idea of perfection and its collateral idea of the totality of the individual, Arnold seeks to overcome the isolation inherent in the idea of the individual. However, Arnold in *Culture and Anarchy* misnames the opposition that lies at the heart of his system, conceiving it in terms of "perfection" as opposed to individualism:

> The idea of perfection as an *inward* condition of the mind and spirit is at variance with the mechanical and material civilization in esteem with us. The idea of perfection as a *general* expansion of the human family is at variance with our strong individualism. (45)

The idea of perfection as an inward condition is in fact in total harmony with individualism. Arnold's ideal of perfection, like Wordsworth's, assumes that the individual withdraws into himself, finds redemption within himself, and moves from there to transform society. This second stage never materializes. Arnold's most treasured vision of community, that of a dedicated band of scholars brought together by their common desire to "do good" to society through their disinterested efforts, never itself surpasses the individualism it criticizes. Arnold describes this group of people in very suggestive terms in *Culture and Anarchy*:

> Therefore, when we speak of ourselves as divided into Barbarians, Philistines, and Populace, we must be understood

always to imply that within each of these are a certain number
of *aliens,* if we may so call them,—persons led, not by their
class spirit, but by a general *humane* spirit, and by the love of
human perfection. (49)

This small band of people is implicated in inwardness by Arnold's
linking them with perfection. These people, through their sense of
inwardness and difference from the masses, are able to achieve, in
Arnold's terms, a classless outlook that transcends their class background.
The term *aliens,* however, recalls Arnold's laments about the isolation of
the individual in "The Buried Life":

I knew they lived and moved
Trick'd in disguises, alien to the rest
Of men and alien to themselves. (20–22)

Arnold here laments the anomie and alienation of modern life, the
apparently insuperable isolation that insulates one individual from
another. Arnold in his prose tries to take the exact same term, *alien,* and
make it into the basis for a sort of benevolent community outside the
competing classes of society. The problem that he diagnoses in "The
Buried Life," however, haunts this ideal, because an alienated individual,
although he may be able to use his estranged position to criticize society
and to gain a critical distance on his alienated self, will not be able to form
a meaningful bond with other alienated individuals. If perfection for
Arnold depends, as he says, upon the individual's overcoming isolation,
then alienation is not a very good basis from which to start.

The vision that underlies Arnold's ideal of criticism, culture, and
the state is not, therefore, antithetical to the strong tradition of British
individualism, as he claims, but is a product of that tradition. It reaffirms
that value resides alone in the individual, freed from the constraints of his
or her social background. It affirms that inwardness and the resulting
experiences of isolation and alienation are the basis upon which the critical enterprise is established. It is only through the extreme and extravagant claims that Arnold makes for culture that he can overcome this
dichotomy at the heart of his philosophy. His faith in the isolated, alien
individual as the bedrock of the critical consciousness is at odds with his
desire to overcome the individual in the name of a wider social ethic.

Arnold's dichotomy is in the final analysis one that besets literary
criticism itself, which has inherited through Arnold from the Romantic

period a profound commitment to individualism, and a mistrust of its implications. It remains committed to an extravagant Arnoldian vision of culture, as Eugene Goodheart rightly points out (Goodheart 1978, 95). If criticism is imagined as a disinterested and classless enterprise, it will inevitably find itself hoisted by its own petard when it tries to address wider social issues. To maintain along with Arnold that the critic is able to take up a disinterested position by virtue of his alienation means that the critic cannot appeal to a wider sense of community on the basis of his vision. The alienated individual by definition cannot communicate through a shared language with anyone who is not him- or herself alienated. The critic, like the scholar gypsy, is doomed to wander the periphery of human existence, appearing only briefly to small, isolated bands of fellow wanderers.

The gypsy scholar, that marginal figure who flees the university to seek after a knowledge outside of its bounds, enters a conventional pastoral landscape reminiscent of the fields within which we ourselves work. The gypsy scholar, who purchases the power of a control over people's minds at the cost of an extreme alienation from the social, is an apt symbol for many aspects of contemporary literary criticism. Like Arnold, the gypsy scholar pursues an object that makes him indifferent to earthly rewards but gives him a compensatory otherworldly power. It is this common "quest" that inspires Arnold's imagination in "Thyrsis":

A fugitive and gracious light he seeks,
Shy to illumine; and I seek it too. (201–2)

"Fugitive" is a displaced adjective here, signaling the larger displacement that lies behind the poem. It is not the light that is fugitive but the gypsy scholar, as he flees the university and any contact with a diseased society. Linking himself with the gypsy scholar's quest, Arnold underlines how the figure in the poem stands for Arnold's own displaced desires, his own covertly expressed wish to escape the present. The gypsy scholar's search for a fugitive light or an otherworldly power represents a desire to escape the contingent forces of the social and historical.

Arnold here is invoking an image that holds powerful sway over contemporary literary criticism. Arnold is making an appeal to what Terry Eagleton has described as "a deracinated cultural intelligentsia whose plea for 'disinterestedness' is a dismissal of the public rather than an act of solidarity with them" (Eagleton 1984, 80). Arnold uses the notion of alienation here as a way of "deracinating" his ideal group of literary critics, but this very alienation also blocks off the avenues of communication between the critic and the public, the body of people to whom he is presumably meant to be doing good. The group of aliens cuts itself off quite deliberately from any class allegiance or socially grounded position. Deracination, one of the primary effects of state-sponsored education, is here turned into the prerequisite for criticism. Like the gypsy scholar, the critic flees the social context of criticism.

It is at this point that the affiliation between criticism and the gypsy scholar becomes clear; like the gypsy scholar, the critic is alienated from the march of time and social change and makes contact only with wandering individuals who glimpse a lonely figure on the margins of existence. Alienation is both the source of his otherworldly power and the cause of a disempowering social isolation that dooms him to wander the peripheries of society. I would suggest that here, in the figure of the gypsy scholar, we have a perfect symbol of the reigning model of the social function of literary criticism.

The ideal espoused by Arnold still informs criticism to this day. By withdrawing into disinterestedness, into inwardness, and away from the realm of the practical, the critic hopes to gain an audience, and thus power over his audience, through the spotless purity of his intentions. The critic aspires to be a free and transcendent consciousness, pursuing the disinterested quest of literary criticism. The literary critic represses his or her social context in performing the act of criticism. The critic writes as a completely deracinated and alienated intellect. However, far from excising the self, such a procedure actually promotes the importance of the individual consciousness at the expense of the social. Rather than join literary criticism and the social context, Arnold sunders the two. As George Levine says of Arnold:

> We give Arnold credit for an idea of culture and of criticism
> that resists the separation of society and art; but the ideal of
> the best self, which permeates all the writing is an ideal which,
> precisely, disengages criticism (and art) from society because it
> is an ideal of the escape from contingency. (Levine 1983, 476)

The desire behind Arnold's poetry and prose is, therefore, an ideal of escape from contingency based upon an individualist ideology of the autonomous self. The vision that underlies Arnold's ideal of criticism, culture, and the state, is a product of an individualist ideology. It reaffirms that value resides alone in the individual, freed from the constraints of his or her social background. It affirms that inwardness and the resulting experiences of isolation and alienation are the basis upon which the critical enterprise is established. It affirms the experience of alienation he embodied in "The Buried Life" as the basis for criticism itself. Arnold's criticism is based upon the same desire to escape contingency as his vision of the gypsy scholar, as George Levine's comments help establish.

The territory to which I am gesturing here has been mapped most thoroughly by Jim Merod in *The Political Responsibility of the Critic.* Merod criticizes the reigning "aesthetic idealism" in departments of English that allows academic writers to "see themselves as executing a kind of work unattached to anything except their own writing" (Merod 1987, 40). This aesthetic idealism allows academic writers to see themselves as "historically 'free' agents whose self-defined activity is not attached to any vested authority beyond their own professional competence" (41).

Arnold's legacy has yet to be completely surmounted. Despite recent attacks on individualist premises such as Elizabeth Fox-Genovese's *Femininsm without Illusions,* the ideal of the deracinated, free intelligence still exerts a strong appeal for literary criticism. Most academics are still gypsy scholars who owe allegiance to an idealized image of the profession more than to any concretely realized community. The masculine model of the free, autonomous self who represses the social context of his writing still holds sway. We are still paying the cost of the Romantic severance of the individual from the community enacted by the redefinition of literary production in individualist terms and the creation of *autobiography* in the late eighteenth century.

Such recent theoretical works as *Changing the Subject* and feminist criticism as Sidonie Smith's *A Poetics of Women's Autobiography* suggest that alternatives to the unitary subject of nineteenth-century autobiography are being formulated. However, the reaction against nineteenth-century individualism is not new. As I will show in my concluding chapter, even though Virginia Woolf overtly rejected the masculine, autonomous subject as part of Victorian patriarchy, she still shows its pervasive influence in her writings. In her images of herself as a writer she continues to represent the kind of autonomous, deracinated self that I have analyzed in Romantic and Victorian autobiographies.

NOTES

1. Most uses of Bakhtin's theories stress the dialogic principle and its applicability to the novel—for instance, Todorov's *Mikhail Bakhtin: The Dialogic Principle* and de Man's "Dialogue and Dialogism." I wish, by contrast, to focus on the monologic principle exhibited in Victorian autobiography.

VIRGINIA WOOLF AND THE PRISON OF CONSCIOUSNESS

Discussing her father's violent rages, which he displayed only before the women in his family, Virginia Woolf analyzed the dynamics of the Victorian male's dependence upon women as a sympathetic audience with her characteristic unflinching severity. Woolf explains that her father "needed always some woman to act before; to sympathise with him, to console him...he had an illicit need for sympathy, released by the woman" (Woolf 1985, 145–46). Woolf shows how her father's fear of his own failure as a philosopher "gnawed at him," but his public, masculine pose made him "hide the need he had for praise" (145). He thus turned to his nearest female relations and coerced them into providing the emotional support he could not find in public. In Woolf's autobiographical writings we find given voice the female side of the dynamic I have been describing in these pages, and Woolf's own refusal to accept the role ascribed to Dorothy Wordsworth or Harriet Taylor, that is, silent bearer of the masculine word. She refuses to subscribe to the construction of women as mirrors for the masculine ego.

Woolf turns her father into the symbol of all that was wrong with patriarchal Victorian society and its exploitation of women. Using the excuse of "genius," her father was allowed to get away with self-centered histrionics that would have been inexcusable in a woman, and that he would not have dared exhibit in the company of male peers. When Vanessa refused to play her role of "part slave, part angel" (146), he became violently incensed. By refusing to play her role, Vanessa was

refusing to supply him with the confirmation of his genius upon which he
depended.

Woolf's memoirs bear a close resemblance to Gosse's *Father and
Son* in the way in which she fashions herself in apparent rejection of the
figure of her father. The similarities are especially evident when she turns
the struggle between herself and her father into a contest between two
different ages rather than just two individuals:

> But from my present distance of time I see too what we
> could not then see—the gulf between us that was cut by our
> difference in age. Two different ages confronted each other in
> the drawing room at Hyde Park Gate. The Victorian age and
> the Edwardian age. (147)

Woolf, like Gosse, generalizes her family drama into a clash
between completely different sensibilities appropriate to different historical epochs. Casting herself as the "Edwardian," she sees her father as representing Victorian repression, prudery, and stifling social manners (150),
a way of behaving that depended upon indirection and silence. Her father
comes to symbolize the horrors of Victorian repression. She paints her
father in his last years as a prisoner within the walls of Victorian social
conventions, and says that his lifelong repression of his feelings isolated
him from those around him.

> The fact remains that at the age of sixty-five he was a man
> in prison, isolated. He had so ignored, or disguised his own
> feelings that he had no idea what he was; and no idea of what
> other people were. Hence the horror and the terror of those
> violent displays of rage....He did not realize what he did. No
> one could enlighten him. Yet he suffered. Through the walls
> of his prison he had moments of realisation. (146)

This description of her father's isolated "prison" of his ego encapsulates the nightmare of complete solipsism that informed nineteenth-century British autobiographies by male writers. Woolf's father becomes
immured in himself, cut off from all intimate contact with others, thanks
to his repression of his own feelings and his unrecognized need for confirmation of his identity from those closest to him. The prison imagery
here recalls Arnold's horror in "Growing Old" at becoming the ghost of
himself, or the images of enclosure in Ruskin's autobiography. Woolf says

that the example of her father convinced her that "nothing is so much to be dreaded as egotism" (147). Her father's egotism helped turn him into the lonely old man she remembers. Woolf rejects Victorian masculine subjectivity in her rejection of her father's isolated and lonely existence

Woolf's rejection of the masculine egotism embodied in her father's violent rages parallels a general modernist rejection of the autonomous self. Woolf, like her fellow modernist T. S. Eliot, overtly rejects the model of the autonomous individual. Jerome Buckley takes the title of his study of nineteenth-century autobiography *The Turning Key* from T. S. Eliot's image of a key locking each individual into the prison cell of the self. Eliot in *The Wasteland* describes the way in which focusing on "the key" only serves to reinforce the isolation of individuals in the prison of their consciousness.

> I have heard the key
> Turn in the door once and turn once only
> We think of the key, each in his prison
> Thinking of the key, each confirms a prison
> Only at nightfall, ethereal rumours
> Revive for a moment a broken Coriolanus. (413–17)

In a symbol that captures the problematic nature of any attempt to go beyond the aporias of individualism, Eliot suggests that imagining the "key" that would release the subject from the prison house of consciousness only affirms the isolation that it is designed to assuage. Eliot suggests that like Coriolanus we are doomed by egotism, and we will slowly starve to death like Ugolino imprisoned with his children in the *Inferno*. Eliot himself sought to escape the consequences of individualism through the "objective correlative" but was obviously acutely aware of the difficulty of such an endeavor. Eliot uses a quotation from F. H. Bradley's *Appearance and Reality* as an explanation of the image of the key and the prison in *The Wasteland*:

> My external sensations are no less private to myself than are my thoughts and feelings. In either case my experience falls within my own circle, a circle closed on the outside; and, with all its elements alike, every sphere is opaque to the others who surround it....In brief, regarded as an existence which appears in a soul, the whole world for each is peculiar and private to that soul. (Quoted in Buckley 1984, 6)

Like Woolf, Eliot viewed the self as a potential prison house if seen in isolation. Bradley's quotation represents people as atomistic individuals, enclosed within the "circle" of their own consciousness. Privacy here is equated with isolation. Eliot takes the circle metaphor and, like Woolf, turns it into an image of the prison of consciousness.

In the image of the key in Eliot's *The Wasteland* and in Woolf's portrait of her father in *Moments of Being*, the individualist ideals of privacy and autonomy are portrayed as potentially leading to complete isolation. Images such as these are further examples of what Rzepka in the context of W. B. Yeats' poetry has called "later poetic manifestations of the solipsistic temptations that beset the Romantics" (Rzepka 1986, 245). They register in the twentieth century the anxieties that beset Romantic authors when writing autobiographical texts. Woolf and Eliot both appear to reject the lure of solipsism and move toward a more socially directed use of autobiography. In Woolf's case this rejection of previous nineteenth-century models is even more pronounced given the added wieght of her anger at the silencing of women by Victorian males such as her father. Like Gosse she attempts to put an oppressive upbringing behind her and declare her autonomy from the Victorian age as a progressive and enlightened Edwardian.

As in Edmund Gosse's case, however, we have to ask to what extent Woolf actually differentiates herself from this nightmarish father figure. While Woolf participates in the general modernist rejection of the Victorian autonomous self, her approach to autobiography has much in common with that of the nineteenth-century texts I have analyzed in this study. Despite her apparent rejection of Victorian narrative models, Woolf does not reject the individualism upon which nineteenth-century British autobiography was predicated. She dichotomizes the individual and the social in ways that recall nineteenth-century individualism. Woolf uses metaphors to describe herself that represent her as an isolated, discrete entity, separated from the external world. Her metaphors for herself imply that she is enclosed within the "circle" of her own consciousness in the way that F. H. Bradley described, and that occasional epiphanic "moments" of experience break through this circle.

For example, Woolf reflects upon the act of writing about her memories and asserts that she remembers in "scenes" that she does not construct but that appear to her apparently of their own volition.

These scenes, by the way, are not altogether a literary device—a means of summing up and making a knot out of

> innumerable little threads....But whatever the reason may be, I find that scene making is my natural way of marking the past. A scene always comes to the top; arranged, representative. This confirms me in my instinctive notion—it is irrational; it will not stand argument—that we are sealed vessels afloat upon what it is convenient to call reality; at some moments, without a reason, without an effort, the sealing matter cracks; in floods reality; that is a scene...that is a proof of their reality. (142)

Woolf represents herself as "sealed off" from reality, as a vessel that is afloat on, but not part of, reality. Only when her sealant is cracked open, in an almost violent manner, does she experience contact with "being" rather than "nonbeing." Experience in Woolf's autobiography is radically discontinuous, erupting into her consciousness unpredictably and without conscious design on her part. Her description of her lack of control over her memories recalls John Ruskin in *Praeterita* disavowing control over his own narrative and presenting himself as at the mercy of forces beyond his control rather than as composing his own life in writing his autobiography.

Woolf says that in writing autobiographically "I see myself as a fish in a stream; deflected; held in place; but cannot describe the stream" (80). As a fish rather than a boat she presumably has more contact with the "stream" of reality, but her description emphasizes once more her lack of power over her narrative. She is borne along by the current, a current she can sense but not describe. Woolf is here describing the limits of her own individualism, which makes the stream of her social environment inaccessible to her. Her sense of her relation to things around her comes only in those moments when her individuality is broken down by the pressure of events.

The image of the boat and its cracking under pressure suggests that Woolf shared Eliot's unease about her potential isolation and entertained a violent fantasy of the self's dissolution as an escape from such complete separation from the social. However, she cannot articulate an alternative within the vocabulary with which she is working. As she complained in such essays as "On Being Ill" and *A Room of One's Own*, the vocabulary with which she worked repressed the body completely, focusing on the mind. She was forced to use a vocabulary that was inhospitable to women's experience, being based upon a masculine image of the self. In *Moments of Being* she presents discontinuous, fragmentary essays that attempt to capture experiences that evade the unitary, coherent subject of masculine autobiography.

Woolf therefore presents her autobiography as a diary rather than as a continuous narrative. Her entries are prefaced by the date and place of composition and begin with references to contemporary events, such as bombing raids on London the night before. She deliberately eschews the pose of disinterested narrator summing up a life from a stable vantage point, acknowledging instead the fluidity of her construction of past events and the way in which her self-representation is affected by contemporary events.

> I write the dates, because I think that I have discovered a possible form for these notes. That is, to make them include the present—at least enough of the present to serve as a platform to stand upon. It would be interesting to make the two people, I now, I then, come out in contrast. And further the past is much affected by the present moment. What I write today I should not write in a year's time. But I cannot work this out; it had better be left to chance, as I write by fits and starts by way of a holiday from Roger. I have no energy at the moment to spend upon the horrid labour that it needs to make an orderly and expressed work of art. (75)

Woolf, like Ruskin before her, "follows no formal chronology of plan," writing her autobiography in the form of diary entries. She is ambivalent about making her autobiography "orderly" and "artistic," because she associates such methods with the "great patriarchal machine" (153) of Victorian society, which formed her sense of herself and which she is trying to reject. Woolf describes her ambivalence toward the Victorian "great patriarchal machine" in terms of her reactions to Victorian masculinity and patriotism.

> Sometimes when I hear God Save the King I too feel a current of belief but almost directly I consider my own splits asunder and one side of me criticizes the other....There was a spectator in me who, even while I squirmed and obeyed, remained observant, note taking for some future revision. (153–54)

Like Gosse before her, Woolf experiences her self as a bifurcated personality, at once acceding to and resisting authority. Both Gosse and

Woolf prefigure the contemporary rejection of the subject as a unified, continuous self. Woolf is far more radical than Gosse in her rejection of this image, because, in addition to the tyranny of an overbearing father, she had to suffer under the stifling regime imposed on women in the Victorian household. Woolf's fiction, especially novels such as *The Years* and *The Waves*, represent a rejection of the formal literary conventions that paralleled the Victorian conception of an autonomous self embodied in a continuous narrative. Woolf participates in the modernist rejection of the self as the *a priori* category of literary representation. She attempts what Elizabeth Abel has termed "the purging of the authorial self" (Abel 1989, 87). In *The Waves*, for instance, she represents a transindividual subject in an experiment that deliberately critiques the conventions of autobiographical fiction. In a novel such as *The Waves* she represents what she refers to in *Moments of Being* as "the waves of these fragmentary feelings" (156).

The self, however, is not dead. While Woolf may have rejected Victorian conventions, she was conscious of the extent to which her writing and her manners had been shaped by her socialization. When she imagines herself as a writer, Woolf still thinks in terms of the isolated author sitting alone in a room, like the image of Charles Reade in his study discussed in the opening pages of this book:

> I want you to imagine me writing a novel in a state of trance. I want you to figure to yourselves a girl sitting with a pen in her hand, which for minutes, and indeed for hours, she never dips in the inkpot. The image that comes to my mind when I think of this girl is the image of a fisherman lying sunk in dreams on the verge of a deep lake with a rod held out over the water. (Woolf 1966b, 248)

Writing is represented here as a quiet, essentially solitary activity. This is an image of introspection, as the "lake" by which the woman writer sits symbolizes the unconscious as a body of water by which the writer waits for a nibble from the unplumbed depths of the psyche. Like Wordsworth in *The Prelude* "incumbent o'er the surface of past time" (4.272), Woolf uses the analogies of boats and water to represent her relationship to memory and the act of writing. Woolf's lake imagery and her uses of stream imagery in *Moments of Being* also show her using metaphors very similar to those in Arnold's "The Buried Life," with the conscious self waiting for moments of revelation that will unite the sundered conscious and unconscious in a deeper, whole version of the self.

Writing is associated with "dreams" and "trances," moods that set the writer apart from mundane reality rather than show her involved in daily activities.

When Woolf defines the necessities for artistic production in *A Room of One's Own,* one of them is "a room with a lock on it" (109), a study like Charles Reade's, into which to withdraw. When she imagines the lives of nineteenth-century women, she considers their lack of a separate room to which to retire as one of the checks upon their creative powers, since "if a woman wrote, she would have to write in the common sitting-room" (69). As the quotation from Margaret Oliphant in my Introduction demonstrates, it was indeed difficult for women to find any time of their own. Woolf herself quotes Florence Nightingale complaining that women had no time of their own. (70). Oliphant, however, viewed writing her autobiography as part of her identity as a mother, and when her last child died she felt that the impetus to write any more of her autobiography had been lost. In the most poignant ending to any autobiography I have ever read, Oliphant links the end of her narrative to the death of her son Cyril:

> And now here I am all alone.
> I cannot write any more. (Oliphant 1988, 150)

Being alone, rather than being the prerequisite for artistic production, for Oliphant means that she can no longer write. I do not wish to romanticize Oliphant's position here; she had to work at a breakneck pace to support her family through her writing, and she wondered whether she would not have been as famous as George Eliot if she had not had to produce novels so rapidly. On the other hand her writing is tied directly to her family life, not separated from it. This is a model of the artist that goes against the grain of our received notions of artistic production.

Woolf herself viewed literary production and maternal reproduction as incompatible. Woolf noted that the one thing that the women novelists she admired had in common "was the possibly relevant fact that not one of them had a child" (Woolf 1929, 69). Although Woolf views the novel as a "relational" form that embodies women's experiences, she views literary production in terms of individuals. Woolf enacts in her texts what Abel has described as the conflict between "biological motherhood" and "literary maternity." She dramatizes the conflict between the pull of the social and the image of the autonomous individual that I have discussed in previous chapters.

Alice Walker in an essay entitled "A Writer Because of, Not in Spite of, Her Children" describes the effect on her of reading a dedication to a novel in which the author thanked her children for "their sweet background noises" (Walker 1983, 67). Walker is amazed that anyone could actually thank her children for their background noise as if it helped in writing the novel. The idea leads her to meditate upon our image of the creative process as an essentially solitary activity.

> The notion that this is remotely possible causes a rethinking of traditional Western ideas about how art is produced. Our culture separates the duties of raising children from those of creative work. I have myself always required an absolutely quiet and private place to work (preferably with a view of a garden). Others have required versions of an ivory tower, a Yaddo, a MacDowell Colony. (69–70)

Like Woolf, Walker thinks in terms of "a room of her own" when it comes to writing, a place of seclusion and quiet separated from the duties of raising children. However, as Walker implies, this involves a cutting off of the writer from other aspects of his or her life. This is the kind of separation of spheres embodied in the portrait *Charles Reade in His Study* and affirmed in nineteenth-century masculine autobiography. The author has to separate him- or herself from the social to write, and embody physically in the isolation of "a room of his own" the kind of distance needed psychically either to write about oneself or to write novels.

Jack Stillinger's *Multiple Authorship and the Myth of Solitary Genius* has documented the extent to which literary production is a social activity. Rather than being composed in solitude, the Romantic and Victorian texts that Stillinger analyzes were the products of "multiple authorship." Stillinger points out that "at present, there is a basic contradiction between the theorists' single-author standard for interpreting and editing, and the way much of our literature has been, and continues to be produced" (Stillinger 1991, 202). Stillinger correctly identifies here the contradiction between images of the author as solitary genius, such as those embodied in nineteenth-century autobiography or even early twentieth century autobiography such as Woolf's, and actual practice. Stillinger also makes the perceptive point that literary critics, whatever their theoretical allegiance, continue to act as if texts had "authors," despite Michel Foucault's questioning of the category of the "author" in "What Is an Author?"

The recent publication of studies such as Stillinger's *Multiple Authorship and the Myth of Solitary Genius,* Paul Smith's *Discerning the Subject,* and the critique of the individual/society dichotomy in Julian Henriques et al.'s *Changing the Subject* suggests that at a theoretical level at least Wordsworth's "single" self no longer functions as a unifying category for contemporary critics. Where in chapter 1 I argued that Wordsworth appealed to his self as a "theme single and of determin'd bounds" (1.640), the self for contemporary theorists looks more like a loose, baggy monster than a unified entity. The contemporary view of the subject is close to Dr. Jekyll's nightmare vision of "a mere polity of multifarious, incongruous and independent citizens" (Stevenson 1981, 40). The subject is viewed as a fragmented collection of ideologies, interpellated by the state and ideological state apparatuses, and ultimately at the mercy of the all-determining social codes of class, race, and gender.

While Wordsworth's unitary self has been deconstructed and the form of autobiography been declared an outdated fiction by myself and other theorists, I would like to conclude by pointing out that life goes on just the same. Bookstores persist in maintaining a section for autobiography separate from fiction; authors continue to write their life histories; and academics blithely continue to put their names on their Curriculum Vitae and their publications, even though they know they are simply ideological constructs. I myself have put my name on this text and provided only a brief nod in the direction of multiple authorship in my Acknowledgments section. At present critical theory seems to have far outstripped critical practice.

This should come as no surprise. Alice Walker's essay indicates what a powerful grip the image of the author as a solitary worker, toiling in the seclusion of his or her study or office, still has on representations of the labor of writing. I chose the painting *Charles Reade in His Study* as the cover for this book because it sums up elegantly the nineteenth-century iconography of the solitary genius retiring to a room of his own to produce texts. While feminism has succeeded in correcting the gender bias of this picture, it still remains true that, like Woolf, we think of a room of one's own as essential for artistic production. Artistic production is imagined as involving a withdrawal from the social into the private and subjective. As I have suggested, the return to the social, which writers from Wordsworth on have seen as the next stage in this process, never occurs, and the overtly social function of all writing, literary criticism included, is subverted by the individualist premise of this image of literary production.

This image of the single, solitary author is the result of two centuries of individualist ideology. Individualist premises inform a host of daily activities from writing a book to signing a credit card slip, from composing a curriculum vitae to filling out a census form. Until laws such as copyright are reformulated to acknowledge writing as a social activity that cannot be classified in terms of individual ownership of a text, books will continue to have single authors, and autobiography will persist as a viable category. As I pointed out in the Introduction, autobiography is just one example of a whole series of categories that are now defined in individualist terms. To proclaim the end of autobiography, or even the death of the author, we need more than just a theoretical revolution that replaces one set of terms with another; we need a social revolution that alters daily practice, not just consciousness.

WORKS CITED

Abel, Elizabeth. 1989. *Virginia Woolf and the Fictions of Psychoanalysis* Chicago: University of Chicago Press.

Anderson, Benedict. 1991. *Imagined Communities: Reflections on the Origin and Spread of Nationalism* Revised ed. New York: Verso.

Anderson, Perry. 1969. "Components of the National Culture." In *Student Power/Problems, Diagnosis, Action* Harmondsworth, England: Penguin.

Arnold, Matthew. 1923. *Unpublished Letters of Matthew Arnold*. Edited by Arnold Whitridge. New Haven, Conn.: Yale University Press.

———. 1925. *Culture and Anarchy*. New York: Macmillan. Reprint. 1929.

———. 1927. "The Preface to the First Edition of the Poems, 1853." In *Matthew Arnold: Prose and Poetry*. New York: Scribner's.

———. 1962a. "The Function of Criticism at the Present Time." In *Collected Prose Works*. Vol. 3. Edited by R. H. Super. Ann Arbor: University of Michigan Press.

———. 1962b. "The Literary Influence of the Academies." In *Collected Prose Works*. Vol. 3. Edited by R. H. Super. Ann Arbor: University of Michigan Press.

———. 1962c. "A French Eton." In *Collected Prose Works*. Vol. 2. Edited by R. H. Super. Ann Arbor: University of Michigan Press.

———. 1965. *The Poems of Matthew Arnold*. Edited by Kenneth Allott. London: Longmans.

Augustine of Hippo. 1960. *The Confessions of St. Augustine*. Translated by John K. Ryan. Garden City, N.J.: Image Books.

Bakhtin, M. M. 1984. *Problems of Dostoyevski's Poetics*. Translated by Caryl Emerson. Minneapolis: University of Minnesota Press.

———. 1985. *The Dialogic Imagination*. Translated by Caryl Emerson and Michael Holquist. Austin: University of Texas Press.

Barrell, John. 1991. *The Infection of Thomas De Quincey: A Psychopathology of Imperialism* New Haven, Conn.: Yale University Press.

Bate, Jonathan. 1992. *Romantic Ecology: Wordsworth and the Environmental Tradition* London: Routledge.

Benstock, Shari. 1988. "Authorizing the Autobiographical." In *The Private Self: Theory and Practice of Women's Autobiographical Writings*. Edited by Shari Benstock. Chapel Hill: University of North Carolina Press.

Bermingham, Ann. 1986. *Landscape and Ideology: The English Rustic Tradition, 1740–1860* Berkeley: University of California Press.

Blanchot, Maurice. 1988. *The Unavowable Community*. Translated by Pierre Joris. Barrytown, N.Y.: Station Hill Press.

Bloom, Harold. 1964. "The Internalization of Quest-Romance." In *Romanticism and Consciousness: Essays in Criticism*. Edited by Harold Bloom. New Haven, Conn.: Yale University Press.

———. 1973. *The Anxiety of Influence*. New York: Oxford University Press.

Bourdieu, Pierre. 1984. *Distinction: A Social Critique of the Judgement of Taste*. Translated by Richard Nice. Cambridge: Harvard University Press.

Buckley, Jerome H. 1984. *The Turning Key: Autobiography and the Subjective Impulse since 1800*. Cambridge: Harvard University Press.

Burke, Edmund. 1958. *A Philosophical Enquiry Concerning the Origin of our Ideas of the Sublime and the Beautiful*. London: Routledge.

Carrithers, Michael, and Steven Collins, eds. 1986. *The Category of the Person: Anthropology, Philosophy, History*. Cambridge: Cambridge University Press.

Coleridge, Samuel Taylor. 1907. *Biographia Literaria*. Oxford: Clarendon Press.

Corbett, Mary Jean. 1992. *Representing Feminity: Middle-Class Subjectivity in Victorian and Edwardian Women's Autobiographies*. New York: Oxford University Press.

Danahay, Martin A. 1986. "Autobiography and Tradition." *A/B: Auto/Biography Studies* 2 (Spring): 15–19.

———. 1990. "Class, Gender and the Victorian Masculine Subject." *A/B: Auto/Biography Studies* 5 (Fall): 99–113

———. 1991. "Matter Out of Place: The Politics of Pollution in Ruskin and Turner." *Clio* 21 (Fall): 61–77

———. 1992. "State Power and the Victorian Subject." *Prose Studies: History, Theory, Criticism* 15:1 (April): 61–83

Dellamora, Richard. 1990. *Masculine Desire: The Sexual Politics of Victorian Aestheticism.* Chapel Hill: University of North Carolina Press.

de Man, Paul. 1977. "The Purloined Ribbon." In *Glyph 1*: 28–50. Baltimore: Johns Hopkins University Press.

———. 1979. "Autobiography as De-Facement." *Modern Language Notes* 94: 919–30.

———. 1989. "Dialogue and Dialogism." In *Rethinking Bakhtin: Extensions and Challenges.* Evanston, Ill.: Northwestern University Press.

De Quincey, Thomas. 1854. *Autobiographic Sketches.* Edinburgh, Scotland: J. Hogg.

———. 1889–90. *The Collected Works of Thomas De Quincey.* Edited by David Masson. Edinburgh, Scotland: Charles & Black.

———. 1948. *Recollections of the Lakes and Lake Poets.* London: J. Lehmann.

———. 1979. *Confessions of an English Opium Eater.* Harmondsworth, England: Penguin.

Derrida, Jacques. 1980. "La Loi du Genre/The Law of Genre." Translated by Avital Ronnel. *Glyph 7:* 202–32. Baltimore: Johns Hopkins Universtiy Press.

Duncan, Carol. 1973. "Virility and Domination in Early Twentieth-Century Vanguard Painting." *Art Forum* 12 (December): 30–39.

Dunning, Stephen N. 1985. *Kierkegaard's Dialectic of Inwardness: A Structural Analysis of the Theory of Stages.* Princeton, N.J.: Princeton University Press.

Eagleton, Terry. 1984. *The Function of Criticism: From the Spectator to Poststructuralism.* London: Verso.

Eilenberg, Susan. 1992. *Strange Power of Speech: Wordsworth, Coleridge, and Literary Possession.* New York: Oxford University Press.

Eliot, T. S. 1952. *Complete Poems and Plays.* New York: Harcourt Brace Jovanovich.

Fellows, Jay. 1975. *The Failing Distance: The Autobiographical Impulse in John Ruskin.* Baltimore: Johns Hopkins University Press.

Ferguson, Frances. 1977. *Wordsworth: Language as Counter-Spirit.* New Haven, Conn.: Yale University Press.

———. 1984. "The Nuclear Sublime." *Diacritics* 14 (Summer): 4–10.

Fisher, Philip. 1981. *Making Up Society: The Novels of George Eliot.* Pittsburgh: University of Pittsburgh Press.

Fitch, Raymond. 1982. *The Poison Sky: Myth and Acopalypse in Ruskin.* Athens: Ohio University Press.

Fleishman, Avrom. 1983. *Figures of Autobiography: The Language of Self-Writing in Victorian and Modern England.* Berkeley: University of California Press.

Foucault, Michel. 1977. *Language, Counter-Memory, Practice: Selected Essays and Interviews.* Ithaca, N.Y.: Cornell University Press.

———. 1980. *The History of Sexulaity.* New York: Vintage.

Fox-Genovese, Elizabeth. 1985. *The Autobiography of Pierre Samuel Du Pont.* Wilmington, Del.: Scholarly Resources.

———. 1991. *Feminism without Illusions: A Critique of Individualism.* Chapel Hill: University of North Carolina Press.

Freud, Sigmund. 1961. *Civilization and its Discontents.* Translated by James Strachey. New York: Norton.

Friedman, Michael. 1979. *The Making of a Tory Humanist: William Wordsworth and the Idea of Community.* New York: Columbia University Press.

Fruman, Norman. 1971. *Coleridge: The Damaged Archangel.* New York: George Brazilier.

Gagnier, Regenia. 1989. "The Literary Standard, Working-Class Lifewriting, and Gender." *Textual Practice* 3 (Spring): 36–55.

Gilbert, Sandra, and Susan Gubar. 1979. *The Madwoman in the Attic*. New Haven: Yale University Press.

Goethe, Johann Wolfgang von. 1971. *Elective Affinities*. Harmondsworth, England: Penguin.

Goldman, Albert. 1965. *The Mine and the Mint: Sources for the Writings of Thomas De Quincey*. Carbondale: Southern Illinois University Press.

Goodheart, Eugene. 1978. *The Failure of Criticism*. Cambridge: Harvard University Press.

Gordon, Peter, and John White. 1979. *Philosophers as Educational Reformers: The Influence of Idealism on British Educational Thought and Practice*. Boston: Routledge.

Gosse, Edmund. 1982. *Father and Son*. Harmondsworth, England: Penguin.

Gottfried, Leon. 1963. *Matthew Arnold and the Romantics*. London: Routledge & Kegan Paul.

Graver, Suzanne. 1984. *George Eliot and Community: A Study in Social Theory and Fictional Form*. Berkeley: University of California Press.

Griffin, Andrew. 1979. "Fire and Ice in *Frankenstein*." In *The Endurance of Frankenstein*. Edited by George Levine and U. C. Knoepflmacher. Berkeley: University of California Press.

Gusdorf, Georges. 1980. "Conditions and Limits of Autobiography." In *Autobiography: Essays Theoretical and Critical*. Edited by James Olney. Princeton, N.J.: Princeton University Press.

Harpham, Geoffrey Galt. 1986. "Conversion and the Language of Autobiography." In *Studies in Autobiography*. Edited by James Olney. New Haven, Conn.: Yale University Press.

Hartman, Geoffrey H. 1964. *Wordsworth's Poetry 1787–1814*. New Haven, Conn.: Yale University Press.

———. 1970a. "The Internalization of Quest-Romance." In *Romanticism and Consciousness*. Edited by Harold Bloom. New York: Norton.

———. 1970b. "Romanticism and 'Anti-Self-Consciousness.'" In *Romanticism and Consciousness: Essays in Criticism*. Edited by Harold Bloom. New York: Norton.

Henderson, Heather. 1984. *The Victorian Self: Autobiography and Biblical Narrative.* Ithaca: Cornell University Press.

Heinzelman, Kurt. "The Cult of Domesticity: Dorothy and William Wordsworth at Grasmere" in *Romanticism and Feminism.* See Mellor 1988c.

Helsinger, Elizabeth K. 1979. "The Structure of Ruskin's *Praeterita.*" In *Approaches to Victorian Autobiography.* Edited by George P. Landow. Athens, Ohio: Ohio University Press.

Henriques, Julian, Wendy Hollway, Cathy Urwin, Couze Venn, and Valerie Walkerdine. 1984. *Changing the Subject: Psychology, Social Regulation, and Subjectivity.* New York: Methuen.

Herdman, John. 1990. *The Double in Nineteenth-Century Fiction.* Basingstoke, England: Macmillan.

Himmelfarb, Gertrude. 1975. *Victorian Minds.* Gloucester, Mass.: Peter Smith.

Hirst, Paul Q. 1979. "Introduction." In *Ownership of the Image: Elements of a Marxist Theory of Law.* London: Routledge.

Hoberman, Ruth. 1988. "Narrative Dulpicity and Women in Edmund Gosse's *Father and Son.*" *Biography* 11 (Fall): 303-315

Jacobus, Mary. 1984. "The Law of/and Genre: Genre Theory and *The Prelude.*" *Diacritics* 14 (Winter): 47–57.

James, W. M. 1947. *John Ruskin and Effie Gray.* New York: Scribner's Sons.

Jay, Paul. 1984. *Being in the Text: Self-Representation from Wordsworth to Barthes.* Ithaca, N.Y.: Cornell University Press.

Johnson, Barbara. 1982. "My Monster/My Self." *Diacritics* 12 (Summer): 2–10.

Judovitz, Dalia. 1988. *Subjectivity and Representation in Descartes: The Origins of Modernity.* Cambridge: Cambridge University Press.

Kessler, Edward. 1970. *Coleridge's Metaphors of Being.* Princeton, N.J.: Princeton University Press.

Kucich, John. 1985. "Repression and Dialectical Inwardness in *Middlemarch.*" *Mosaic* 18:45–63.

————. 1987. *Repression in Victorian Fiction: Charlotte Bronte, George Eliot, and Charles Dickens.* Berkeley: University of California Press.

La Belle, Jenijoy. 1988. *Herself Beheld: The Literature of the Looking Glass.* Ithaca, N.Y.: Cornell University Press.

Lacan, Jacques. 1977. "The Mirror Stage." In *Ecrits: A Selection.* Translated by Alan Sheridan. New York: Norton.

Landow, George. 1980. *Victorian Types, Victorian Shadows: Biblical Typology in Victorian Literature, Art, and Thought.* Boston: Routledge.

Lang, Candace. 1982. "Autobiography in the Aftermath of Romanticism." *Diacritics* 12 (Winter): 2–16.

Langbaum, Robert. 1957. *The Poetry of Experience.* London: Chatto & Windus.

————. 1977. *The Mysteries of Identity: A Theme in Modern Literature.* New York: Oxford University Press.

Lansbury, Coral. 1985. *The Old Brown Dog: Women, Workers, and Vivisection in Edwardian England.* Madison: University of Wisconsin Press.

Lejeune, Philippe. 1975. *Le Pacte Autobiographique.* Paris: Editions du Seuil.

Lesser, Wendy. 1991. *His Other Half: Men Looking at Women through Art.* Cambridge: Harvard University Press.

Lever, Karen M. 1979. "De Quincey as Gothic Hero: A Perspective on *Confessions of an English Opium Eater* and *Suspira De Profundis.*" *Texas Studies in Literature and Language* 21 (Fall): 332–46.

Levine, George. 1983. "Matthew Arnold: The Artist in the Wilderness." *Critical Inquiry* 9 (March): 469–82.

Lewes, George Henry. 1883. *Comte's Philosophy of the Sciences.* London: George Bell & Sons.

Liu, Alan. 1989. *Wordsworth: The Sense of History* Stanford: Stanford University Press.

Loesberg, Jonathan. 1986. *Fictions of Consciousness: Mill, Newman, and the Reading of Victorian Prose.* New Brunswick: Rutgers University Press.

Lukes, Steven. 1973. *Individualism*. Oxford: Oxford University Press.

Lyons, John O. 1978. *The Invention of the Self.* Carbondale: Southern Illinois University Press.

Macfarlane, Alan. 1979. *The Origins of English Individualism: The Family, Property, and Social Transition*. Cambridge: Cambridge University Press.

Mattes, Eleanor B. 1951. *In Memoriam: The Way of a Soul*. New York: Exposition Press.

McGann, Jerome. 1983. *The Romantic Ideology: A Critical Investigation*. Chicago: University of Chicago Press.

Mellor, Anne K. 1988a. *Mary Shelley: Her Life, Her Fiction, Her Monsters*. New York: Methuen.

———. 1988b. "Possessing Nature: The Female in *Frankenstein*." In *Romanticism and Feminism*. See Mellor 1988c.

———. 1988c. *Romanticism and Feminism*. Bloomington: Indiana University Press.

Merod, Jim. 1987. *The Political Responsibility of the Critic*. Ithaca, N.Y.: Cornell University Press.

Middleton, Peter. 1992. *The Inward Gaze: Masculinity and Subjectivity in Modern Culture*. New York: Routledge.

Mill, John Stuart. 1924. *The Autobiography of John Stuart Mill*. New York: Columbia University Press.

———. 1961. *The Early Draft of John Stuart Mill's Autobiography*. Edited by Jack Stillinger. Urbana: University of Illinois Press.

———. 1965. *Mill's Essays on Literature and Society*. Edited by J. B. Schneewind. New York: Collier.

———. 1986. *On Liberty*. New York: Penguin.

Miller, J. Hillis. 1963. *The Disappearance of God*. Cambridge: Harvard University Press.

———. 1982. *Fiction and Repetition*. Cambridge: Harvard University Press.

———. 1991. "The Mirror's Secret: Dante Gabriel Rossetti's Double Work of Art." *Victorian Poetry* 29 (Winter): 333–49.

Miller, Karl. 1985. *Doubles: Studies in Literary History*. Oxford: Oxford University Press.

Miller, Nancy K. 1988. *Subject to Change: Reading Feminist Writing*. New York: Columbia University Press.

Miyoshi, Misa. 1969. *The Divided Self: A Perspective on the Literature of the Victorians*. New York: New York University Press.

Mockford, George. 1984. "Autobiography." In *Destiny Obscure: Autobiographies of Childhood, Education, and Family from the 1820s to the 1920s*. Edited by John Burnett. Harmondsworth, England: Penguin.

Morson, Gary Saul, and Caryl Emerson. 1990. *Mikhail Bakhtin: Creation of a Prosaics*. Stanford, Calif.: Stanford University Press.

Newman, John H. 1868. *Parochial and Plain Sermons*. London: Rivingtons.

Oliphant, Margaret. 1988. *The Autobiography of Margaret Oliphant*. Edited by Laurie Langbauer. Chicago: University of Chicago Press.

Olney, James. 1972. *Metaphors of Self: The Meaning of Autobiography*. Princeton, N.J.: Princeton University Press.

Patterson, Lyman Ray. 1968. *Copyright in Historical Perspective*. Nashville, Tenn.: Vanderbilt University Press.

Peterson, Linda. 1986. *Victorian Autobiography: The Tradition of Self-Interpretation*. New Haven, Conn.: Yale University Press.

Pike, Burton. 1976. "Time in Autobiography." *Comparative Literature* 28:326–42.

Poggioli, Renato. 1975. *The Oaten Flute: Essays on Pastoral Poetry and the Pastoral Ideal*. Cambridge: Harvard University Press.

Pollock, Griselda. 1988. *Vision and Difference: Femininity, Feminism, and Histories of Art*. New York: Routledge.

Prickett, Stephen. 1970. *Coleridge and Wordsworth: The Poetry of Growth*. Cambridge: Cambridge University Press.

Richardson, Alan. "Romanticism and the Colonization of the Feminine." In *Romanticism and Feminism*. See Mellor 1988c.

Riede, David. 1988. *Matthew Arnold and the Betrayal of Language*. Charlottesville: University Press of Virginia.

Rosenberg, John D. 1961. *The Darkening Glass: A Portrait of Ruskin's Genius.* New York: Columbia University Press.

Ross, Marlon B. "Romantic Quest and Conquest: Troping Masculine Power in the Crisis of Poetic Identity." In *Romanticism and Feminism.* See Mellor 1988c.

Rosetti, Christina Georgina. 1979. *The Complete Poems of Christina Rossetti.* Edited by R. W. Crump. Baton Rouge: Louisiana State University Press.

Rousseau, Jean-Jacques. 1959. *Les Confessions* Paris: Editions Gallimard.

Ruskin, John. 1903–12. *The Works of John Ruskin.* Library Edition. Edited by E. T. Cook and Alexander Wedderburn. 39 Volumes. London: George Allen.

———. 1978. *Praeterita: The Autobiography of John Ruskin.* Oxford: Oxford University Press.

Rzepka, Charles. 1986. *The Self as Mind: Vision and Identity in Wordsworth, Coleridge, and Keats.* Cambridge: Harvard University Press.

Schlenker, Barry. 1985. *The Self and Social Life.* New York: McGraw-Hill.

Sennett, Richard. 1977. *The Fall of Public Man.* New York: Knopf.

Shelley, Mary. 1965. *Frankenstein or, the Modern Prometheus.* New York: The New American Library.

Shelley, Percy Bysshe. 1979. "Alastor." In *The Norton Anthology of English Literature.* Vol. 2. Edited by M. H. Abrams et. al. New York: Norton.

Showalter, Elaine. 1990. *Sexual Anarchy: Gender and Culture at the Fin de Siecle.* New York: Penguin.

Simpson, David. 1982. *Wordsworth and the Figurings of the Real.* Atlantic Highlands, N.J.: Humanities Press.

Sinfield, Alan. 1986. *Alfred Tennyson.* New York: Basil Blackwell.

Smith, Paul. 1988. *Discerning the Subject.* Minneapolis: University of Minnesota Press.

Smith, Sidonie. 1987. *A Poetics of Women's Autobiography.* Bloomington: Indiana University Press.

Spengemann, William C. 1980. *The Forms of Autobiography: Episodes in the History of a Literary Genre*. New Haven, Conn.: Yale University Press.

Sprinker, Michael. 1980. "Fictions of the Self: The End of Autobiography." In *Autobiography: Essays Theoretical and Critical*. Edited by James Olney. Princeton, N.J.: Princeton University Press.

Sterrenburg, Lee. 1979. "Mary Shelley's Monster: Politics and Psyche in *Frankenstein*." In *The Endurance of Frankenstein*. Edited by George Levine and U. C. Knoepflmacher. Berkeley: University of California Press.

Stevenson, Robert Louis. 1981. *Dr. Jekyll and Mr. Hyde*. New York: Bantam.

Stillinger, Jack. 1991. *Multiple Authorship and the Myth of Solitary Genius* New York: Oxford University Press.

Tennyson, Alfred. 1973. *In Memoriam*. New York: Norton.

Tennyson, Hallam. 1899. *Alfred Tennyson: A Memoir by His Son*. London: Macmillan.

Todorov, Tzvetan. 1984. *Mikhail Bakhtin: The Dialogical Principle*. Minneapolis: University of Minnesota Press.

Tönnies, Ferdinand. 1963. *Gemeinschaft und Gesellschaft*. New York: Harper & Row.

Toulmin, Stephen. 1979. "The Inwardness of Mental Life." *Critical Inquiry* 6:1–16.

Veeder, William. 1986. *Mary Shelley and Frankenstein*. Chicago: University of Chicago Press.

Walker, Alice. 1983. *In Search of Our Mother's Gardens*. New York: Harcourt Brace Jovanovich.

Wasserman, Earl R. 1971. *Shelley: A Critical Reading*. Baltimore: Johns Hopkins University Press.

Williams, Raymond. 1973. *The Country and the City*. Oxford: Oxford University Press.

Wolfson, Susan J. 1988. "Individual in Community: Dorothy Wordsworth in Conversation with William." In *Romanticism and Feminism*. See Mellor 1988c.

Woolf, Virginia. 1929. *A Room of One's Own*. New York: Harcourt Brace Jovanovich.

———. 1966a. *Three Guineas*. New York: Harcourt Brace Jovanovich.

———. 1966b. *Collected Essays*. London: Hogarth Press.

———. 1985. *Moments of Being*. Edited by Jeanne Schulkind. New York: Harcourt Brace Jovanovich.

Wordsworth, William. 1974. *Prose Works*. Edited by W. J. B. Owen and J. W. Smyser. Oxford: Clarendon Press.

———. 1978. *Wordsworth: Poetical Works*. Edited by Thomas Hutchinson and Ernest De Selincourt. Oxford: Oxford University Press.

INDEX